DURCH STARTEN

ENGLISCH
AHS-ZENTRALMATURA

11 12

Verfasserinnen: Gabriela Sturm-Petritsch, Martina Spielauer

Diesem Buch ist ein Lösungsheft zu den Übungen beigelegt.

Entspricht der Rechtschreibreform 2006

Bibliografische Information der Deutschen Bibliothek:
Die Deutsche Bibliothek verzeichnet diese Publikation in der
Deutschen Nationalbibliografie; detaillierte bibliografische Daten
sind im Internet über http://dnb.ddb.de abrufbar.

VERITAS-VERLAG, Linz
www.durchstarten.at
Alle Rechte vorbehalten,
insbesondere das Recht der Verbreitung
(*auch durch Film, Fernsehen, Internet,
fotomechanische Wiedergabe, Bild-,
Ton- und Datenträger jeder Art*) oder
der auszugsweise Nachdruck
Lektorat: Klaus Kopinitsch

10. Auflage 2023

Grafische Gestaltung: Gottfried Moritz
Illustrationen: Helmut »Dino« Breneis
Satz: Anton Froschauer
Herstellung: Julia Bamberger
Bildredaktion: Alexandra Rittberger
Schulbuchvergütung/Bildrechte: © VBK/Wien
Alle Ausschnitte mit Zustimmung der VBK/Wien
Auf umweltfreundlichem Papier gedruckt bei: siehe
https://produkt.veritas.at/24400#additional

ISBN 978-3-7058-8611-7

VER1TAS
Gemeinsam besser lernen

INHALTSVERZEICHNIS

DURCH STARTEN

ENGLISCH
AHS-ZENTRALMATURA

11 – 12

7. – 8. Klasse AHS

INKL. 140 SEITEN ORIGINAL-MATURA-AUFGABEN

ÜBUNGSBUCH LÖSUNGSHEFT

VER1TAS

Gemeinsam besser lernen

RC 1 – MULTIPLE MATCHING: "20 TIPS TO LOSE 20 POUNDS"

Task 2

1 **A:** Check your attitude.
2 **S:** Weigh in.
3 **K:** Pick a plan.
4 **T:** Write down every bite.
5 **J:** Pay attention to portions.
6 **Q:** Play the numbers game.
7 **N:** Plan ahead.
8 **E:** Get help from your friends.
9 **B:** Dine out without pigging out.
10 **O:** Plan for a splurge.

11 **F:** Get some sleep.
12 **M:** Pile on the veggies.
13 **I:** Move it to lose it.
14 **L:** Pick up the pace.
15 **R:** Watch the liquid.
16 **D:** Get a B mentality.
17 **P:** Plan some 300-calorie meals.
18 **C:** Downsize your dishes.
19 **G:** Indulge your sweet tooth.
20 **H:** Keep it off.

Task 3

1. What kind of factors can trigger a person's desire to lose weight? ***They may be worried about health risks; special occasions; difficulty fitting into seats; clothing; breathlessness***
2. Why should you weigh yourself before going on a diet? ***To be able to compare before and after photos***
3. What is meant by "there's no shortage of ways to lose weight"? ***There are many different ways and you have to find the one that works for you.***
4. Why does it make sense to keep a daily food record and pay attention to portions? ***To keep track of how much you are eating because your caloric requirements are related to your size.***
5. How many calories do you have to burn in order to lose one pound? ***3,500 calories more than you consume***
6. In how far can friends and workmates be helpful when you are trying to lose weight? ***You may need someone to hold you accountable and offer support.***
7. How can you avoid eating too much when you are dining out? ***Choose the place with care, don't go famished, don't drink calories, eat low-calorie dishes, have dressings and sauces on the side.***
8. What is a *splurge* and how should a dieter handle situations in which it might come to splurging? ***Splurge = an act of spending a lot of money on something you do not really need; conserve calories without starving yourself.***
9. What is the correlation between sleep and hunger? ***Sleep deprivation increases a hunger hormone.***
10. What can you do in order to prevent feeling deprived when you are on a diet? ***Eat larger amount of fruits and vegetables because people tend to eat the same weight of food each day.***
11. How much exercise should you get when you are trying to lose weight? ***30 to 60 minutes a day***
12. Why can certain liquids have detrimental effects on a diet? ***They may contain hundreds of extra calories.***
13. What is the 80–20 rule? ***80% of what you eat should be lean protein, fruits, vegetables, low-fat dairy, high-fiber grain products and healthy fats.***
14. How can the size of your dishes influence the amount you eat? ***People tend to take less when they use smaller dishes.***
15. Are occasional treats harmful to the success of your diet? Why (not)? ***No, because you are less likely to feel deprived if you allow yourself occasional treats.***
16. Once you have lost weight, what do you need to do in order to keep it off? ***Limit your calories and get enough exercise.***

Task 4

1. a piece of advice — *pointer*
2. a thing that you do often and almost without thinking, especially sth that is hard to stop doing — *habit*
3. an increase in the amount of sth, especially in wealth or weight — *gain*
4. an instrument for measuring how far you have walked — *pedometer*
5. containing little or no fat — *lean*
6. having difficulty in breathing — *breathless*
7. meat from chickens, ducks and geese — *poultry*
8. person who is an expert on the relationship between food and health — *nutritionist*
9. person who is trying to lose weight on a diet — *dieter*
10. person whose job is to advise people on what kind of food they should eat to keep healthy — *dietitian*
11. served at the same time as the main part of the meal, but on a separate plate — *on the side*
12. something that you need or want; something that you must have in order to do sth else — *requirement(s)*
13. something that fits very tightly or closely — *tight-fitting*
14. the fact of not having sth that you need, like enough food, sleep, money or a home — *deprivation*
15. the food that you eat and drink regularly — *diet*
16. the part of food that helps to keep a person healthy by keeping the bowels working and moving other food quickly through the body — *fiber*
17. the state of no longer having sth or as much of sth — *loss*
18. to be different from each other in size, shape, etc.; to change or be different according to the situation — *vary*
19. to leave out sth that would normally be the next thing that you would do — *skip*
20. to make or adapt sth for a particular purpose, a particular person, etc. — *tailor*
21. to measure how heavy sb/sth is, usually by using scales — *weigh*
22. to suffer or die because you do not have enough food to eat — *starve*
23. to think or guess that the amount, cost or size of sth is smaller than it really is — *underestimate*
24. very hungry — *famished*
25. without enough food, education, and all the things that are necessary for people to live a happy and comfortable life — *deprived*

The Complete Text

Before you launch into any weight-loss plan, set a realistic goal, experts say. They suggest aiming for a loss of 10 to 20 pounds.

Begin by taking stock of your eating and exercise habits. Don't focus on everything at once, but pick a couple of weak areas and work on those. Here are 20 ways to help you lose 20 pounds:

Check your attitude.

Ask yourself whether this is a good time to start a plan or program. Are you really motivated? The people who are most successful at losing weight have a "wow" or "light bulb" moment, when something clicks and they decide they don't want to live this way anymore. Motivations vary. Some people are worried about diabetes or heart disease. Others are going to a class reunion, attending a wedding or approaching a hallmark birthday such as their 40th or 50th. Some people might have difficulty fitting into airline or movie-theater seats, are not able to wear most of their clothing or are breathless when they walk up a flight of stairs.

Weigh in.

Weigh yourself and have someone photograph you in tight-fitting clothes. This is so you can compare your before and after photos in a few months.

Pick a plan.

One diet doesn't fit all. There's no shortage of ways to lose weight, but you have to find something that works for you. Registered dietitians in private practice tailor programs to individuals. Weight Watchers provides practical advice and group support. There are many other commercial programs, Web sites and diet books that offer help. Shop around. Figure out what worked for friends who are similar to you.

Write down every bite.

Studies show that dieters who keep a daily food record usually lose more weight. So write down what you eat, how much and the calories, fat grams or carbs.

Pay attention to portions.

Some people underestimate the amount they are consuming. Keep in mind that your caloric requirements are related to your size.

Play the numbers game.

Count calories, carbs, fat grams or steps, but count something, nutritionists say. You have to burn 3,500 calories more than you consume to lose a pound. If you usually eat 2,200 calories a day to maintain your weight, you need to cut back by 500 calories or increase exercise by that much to create the 500-calorie deficit to lose 1 pound a week.

Plan ahead.

Set aside some time every day to decide what you will eat for meals and snacks, when you will prepare them, what you will eat if you go out and when you will exercise.

Get help from your friends.

Many dieters want someone to hold them accountable, making sure they stick with their program. Commercial weight-loss programs and health care professionals can help. Or simply check in with family, co-workers, neighbors and friends. They can offer support by taking walks with you at work or in the neighborhood. They might be willing to listen to you talk about what you're eating – or not eating. Or they can call you daily to see how you're doing.

Dine out without pigging out.

Some pointers: Choose your restaurant with care. Don't go famished or you'll overeat. Don't drink your calories. Order no-calorie or low-calorie drinks. Skip the bread basket. Start off with a low-calorie soup like minestrone or won-ton. And order salad dressings and sauces on the side. Try the "dip and stab" method. Dip a fork in a cup of dressing, then spear your salad.

Plan for a splurge.

If you are going to a big party or out to dinner, conserve calories for the big meal without starving yourself. At the other times during the day, eat more low-calorie foods such as simple soups, raw or cooked vegetables and light bread and popcorn.

Get some sleep.

New research indicates that sleep deprivation increases a hunger hormone and decreases a fullness hormone, which could lead to overeating and weight gain. So getting enough sleep might help you control your hunger.

Pile on the veggies.

Add vegetables, salads and low-calorie soups to your meal plans. Research shows that people eat the same weight of food each day, so experts believe that increasing fruits and vegetables so that meals are higher in fiber and water will help people lower their calories without feeling deprived.

Move it to lose it.

Ideally, people who are trying to lose weight should exercise for 30 to 60 minutes a day. A recent study showed that many types of exercise help with losing, and in fact, walking on your own can be as effective for weight loss as going to the gym.

Pick up the pace.

Start making small changes to your daily routine. Take a 10- to 15-minute walk before work in the morning, at lunch and then when you get home at night. Build from there. Or buy a pedometer and try to work up to 10,000 steps a day.

Watch the liquid.

Many people consume hundreds of extra calories a day with sodas, juices, alcohol and other high-calorie drinks.

Get a B mentality.

Consider yourself a B student when it comes to your diet and follow the 80-20 rule. About 80% of the foods you eat should be lean protein such as poultry, fish and beans; fruits and vegetables; low-fat dairy; high-fiber grain products; and healthier fats such as olive oil. The other 20% can be foods that are not as healthful.

Plan some 300-calorie meals.

Some examples: a BLT without mayo; one-half bagel with 1 ounce of cream cheese and a half-cup of orange juice; two poached eggs on an English muffin; a Wendy's junior cheeseburger. You can use meal replacement bars and shakes to help control calories.

Downsize your dishes.

People take less when they use smaller serving dishes and tall, narrow glasses instead of short wide ones, a study showed.

Indulge your sweet tooth.

If you allow yourself occasional treats, you're less likely to feel deprived, nutritionists say. Here are some ideas: a frozen chocolate kiss; cappuccino made with skim milk; individually wrapped mint; bite-size candy bar; gingersnaps.

Keep it off.

People who have lost weight and kept it off limit their daily calories to about 1,800 a day and walk about 4 miles a day, according to the latest study from the National Weight Control Registry, a group of 5,000 people who lost an average of 73 pounds and kept off at least 30 pounds for more than six years.

By Nanci Hellmich, USA TODAY, posted 1/4/2005 9:40 PM

RC 2 – TRUE/FALSE/JUSTIFICATION: "COUCH POTATOES, ARISE!"

Task 3

		T	F	Justification
0.	*People who lead a sedentary life are more likely to get a heart attack.*		X	*Among those at greatest ...*
1.	Walking for about 30 minutes a day is a good way of starting your workout program.	X		*Most national government guidelines*
2.	Ulla Schmidt stressed the importance of exercising exhaustively on a regular basis.		X	*Exercise can be integrated*
3.	Within a few months your physical health can be improved considerably if you stick to a good walking program.	X		*A good walking program*
4.	If you have been inactive for years you should start with a more modest workout load.	X		*Depending on how many*
5.	People who could easily jog 16 km when they were young need not necessarily begin with a very modest workout program.		X	*We're all 19 behind*
6.	Choosing an expensive activity can help you stick with your program.		X	*Also, don't choose activities*
7.	A personal trainer can give you any kind of support you might need in a given situation.	X		*If you can, try*
8.	Pain in the chest or lightheadedness must be taken as serious warning signals.	X		*Be alert for lightheadedness*

Task 4

1.	within easy reach	**not far away**	7.	to crunch numbers	**to calculate numbers**
2.	to have a thing nailed	**do something precisely or well: to catch, hit, seize, or execute something adroitly or precisely (slang)**	8.	creaky	**old and not in good condition; making creaks**
3.	a sedentary person	**someone spending a lot of time sitting down and not moving**	9.	solitary	**done alone; without other people**
4.	unaccustomed activity	**not usual, normal or familiar activity**	10.	to rein sb in	**to start to control sb more strictly**
5.	moderate	**staying within limits that are considered to be reasonable by most people**	11.	lightheadedness	**state of not being completely in control of your thoughts or movements; slightly faint**
6.	falloff	**a decrease in quantity or quality**	12.	winded	**out of breath**

RC 3 – MULTIPLE CHOICE: "SLICES OF LONDON – HORROR STORIES"

Task 3

1C When Peter Bryan was arrested, **he was about to eat one of his victims.**

2A Such public violence **is something that people in London were not really confronted with in real life.**

3D English murderers used to **avoid contact with other people.**

4B When the authoress of this text moved to Camden, she was **shocked when one of her neighbours turned out to be a murderer.**

5D What does the authoress mean when she says she got blasé? **She became accustomed to the violence around her and pretended that it was not really there.**

6A Why do you think the authoress came to the conclusion that she should start carrying an axe herself? **Because it seemed to be the logical reaction to all the violence.**

7C Which set of adjectives best describes how the attitude of the authoress changed due to the confrontation with violence and death? **naïve → ignorant → realistic**

Task 4

Adjective	Synonym	Antonym
culpable	*guilty*	*innocent*
diplomatic, thoughtful	*tactful*	*tactless*
experienced, clever	*streetwise*	*inexperienced*
humble	*modest, unassuming*	*immodest*
innocuous	*harmless*	*pernicious*
inspiring, stimulating	*exhilarating*	*depressing*
jaded, hardened	*blasé*	*excited*

Adjective	Synonym	Antonym
of poor quality, with no value	*trashy*	*valuable*
outgoing	*extrovert*	*introvert*
revolting, repulsive	*hideous*	*beautiful*
senseless	*pointless, meaningless*	*worthwhile*
strange, odd	*weird*	*ordinary*
tactful	*discreet*	*indiscreet*
wary	*cautious, careful*	*rash*

Task 5

Verb	Person	Action
assail	**assailant**	**assault**
attack	**attacker**	attack
blackmail	blackmailer **extortioner extortionist**	**blackmail extortion**
break into	housebreaker	break-in
bribe	**briber**	bribery
burgle	burglar	**burglary**
chase	**chaser**	**chasing**
counterfeit	**counterfeiter**	**counterfeit**
defraud	**fraud**	fraud
embezzle	embezzler	**embezzlement**
forge	forger	**forgery**
hijack	**hijacker**	**hijacking**
kidnap	kidnapper	**kidnapping abduction**
kill	**killer**	killing
molest	**molester**	**molesting**
mug	mugger	**mugging**

Verb	Person	Action
murder	**murderer murderess**	**murder manslaughter homicide**
perjure oneself	**perjurer**	perjury
pickpocket	pickpocket	**pickpocketing**
rape	**rapist**	rape
rob	**robber**	**robbery**
set a fire	**arsonist**	arson
shoot sb/at sb	**(sharp) shooter gunman**	**shooting shootout gunfight**
shoplift	shoplifter	**shoplifting**
smuggle	smuggler	**smuggling**
stab	**back stabber**	**stabbing**
stalk	stalker	**stalking**
steal	thief (pl: -ves)	**theft larceny**
strangle	**strangler**	**strangling**
swindle	**swindler**	swindle
take sb hostage	**hostage-taker**	**hostage-taking**
vandalise	vandal	**vandalism**

RC 4 – MULTIPLE MATCHING: "SURVIVING AGAINST ALL ODDS"

Task 2

Trauma		Who?	Clues
1.	*C*	Geoffrey Petkovich	weight of the water, water started coming in
2.	*G*	Ray Maynard	lifted, parallel to the ground, cord, people on the ground
3.	*F*	Max Dearing	hot, red flashing lights
4.	*B*	Ellen Hassman	looked at the ground as it reached up for us, sound of metal twisting and tearing
5.	*A*	Rodney Orr	big white things
6.	*D*	John L. Neldigch	howl, sheet of rain, trees snapping, debris shooting through the trailer, trailer lift off the ground and begin to rotate, been thrown 30 feet up into a tree
7.	*E*	Lester Morlang	rolled up in a ball doing somersaults, my mouth was packed with snow, didn't know which direction was up, started digging

Task 3

Who ...

... is reported to have been taken to the hospital?	*1. A*	*2. D*	
... had injuries in the head?	*3. A*	*4. F*	
... was enclosed by darkness?	*5. A*	*6. C*	*7. E*
... cried?	*8. B*	*9. E*	
... was not injured at all?	*10. B*		
... lost consciousness for a short time?	*11. D*		
... feared to faint?	*12. G*		
... was turned over and over again?	*13. E*	*14. G*	
... started the adventure on purpose?	*15. C*		

Task 4

Not afraid	Afraid	Very afraid	How do you react?
bold brave courageous fearless intrepid to show no fear unafraid	a fear of sth anxious apprehensive butterflies in your stomach (*infml*) fearful fright/frightening scare/scared scary (*infml*) to be frightened of to be scared of to fear sth (*fml*) to frighten sb/sth to scare sb/sth	a look of terror dread/to dread horror to feel panic to feel panicky (*infml*) panic-stricken terrified/terrifying terror to be scared stiff (of) (*infml*) to be scared to death to be terrified (of) to frighten the life out of sb to live in dread/fear of sth to make your blood run cold to make your hair stand on end to terrify sb to watch in horror very frightened	to freeze to have goose-flesh to have goose-pimples to have goose-bumps (AE) to jump to shake (with fear) to shiver to tremble

RC 5 – MULTIPLE MATCHING AND MULTIPLE CHOICE: "GLOBAL WARMING MAKING HURRICANES STRONGER"

Task 2

1 C	2 H	3 B	4 F	5 A	6 E

Task 3

a. **hurricane:** strong, ferocious, powerful

   storm: tropical, monsoon, dust, bad, big, devastating, disastrous, ferocious, fierce, great, heavy, raging, severe, terrible, tremendous, violent

b.

average duration average speed average temperature dissipated energy ocean surface release energy	storm duration storm intensity upward trend wind speed

c.

1.	to be contingent on	*to depend on something that may or may not happen in the future*
2.	to generate	*to produce, create something*
4.	to hold up	*to remain strong and working effectively*
5.	to predict	*to say that something will happen*
6.	to pummel	*to beat, to hit someone/something hard*
7.	to research	*to investigate, to study something intensively*
8.	to swirl	*to move around quickly in a circular movement*

Task 4

1.	Global warming is affecting storms	**C**	sooner now than in the future.				
2.	Global warming is producing	**C**	no effect on the number of gales.				
3.	Storms twirling in	**D**	the Atlantic and Pacific	have increased in	**A**	length and severity by half.	
4.	The severity and length of the storms	**D**	are directly related to	the growth in the temperatures of the ocean surface and global temperatures.			
5.	Emanuel	**C**	preferred examining facts collected from actual storms to using computer models.				
6.	Emanuel's results were appreciated by	**D**	a few scientists.				
7.	In the Atlantic and Caribbean	**A**	warm tropical oceans supply storms with energy.				
8.	Since the 1970s the energy set free in storms	**B**	has risen.				
9.	The temperatures of the Atlantic are	**A**	considerably increasing.				
10.	**C**	The energy of the storms and the surface temperatures of the sea	are closely connected.				
11.	These devastating hurricanes will	**B**	not stop in the next 20 years.				
12.	Saltiness and temperature differences in the ocean	**D**	change regularly.				
13.	In the future hurricanes will cause	**B**	considerable damage to property and loss of life.				

The whole text:

Study: Global Warming Making Hurricanes Stronger

Is global warming making hurricanes more ferocious? New research suggests the answer is yes. Scientists call the findings both surprising and "alarming" because they suggest global warming is influencing storms now – rather than in the distant future.

However, the research doesn't suggest global warming is generating more hurricanes and typhoons.

The analysis by climatologist Kerry Emanuel of the Massachusetts Institute of Technology shows for the first time that major storms spinning in both the Atlantic and the Pacific since the 1970s have increased in duration and intensity by about 50 percent.

These trends are closely linked to increases in the average temperatures of the ocean surface and also correspond to increases in global average atmospheric temperatures during the same period.

"When I look at these results at face value, they are rather alarming," said research meteorologist Tom Knutson. "These are very big changes." Knutson, who wasn't involved in the study, works in the National Oceanic and Atmospheric Administration's Geophysical Fluid Dynamics Laboratory in Princeton, N.J.

Emanuel reached his conclusions by analyzing data collected from actual storms rather than using computer models to predict future storm behavior. Before this study, most researchers believed global warming's contribution to powerful hurricanes was too slight to accurately measure. *Most forecasts don't have climate change making a real difference in tropical storms until 2050 or later.*

But some scientists questioned Emanuel's methods. For example, the MIT researcher did not consider wind speed information from some powerful storms in the 1950s and 1960s because the details of those storms are inconsistent.

Researchers are using new methods to analyze those storms and others going back as far as 1851. *If early storms turn out to be more powerful than originally thought, Emanuel's findings on global warming's influence on recent tropical storms might not hold up, they said.*

"I'm not convinced that it's happening," said Christopher W. Landsea, another research meteorologist with NOAA, who works at a different lab, the Atlantic Oceanographic & Meteorological Laboratory in Miami. Landsea is a director of the historical hurricane reanalysis.

"His conclusions are contingent on a very large bias removal that is large or larger than the global warming signal itself," Landsea said.

Details of Emanuel's study appear Sunday in the online version of the journal Nature.

Theories and computer simulation indicate that global warming should generate an increase in storm intensity, in part because warmer temperatures would heat up the surface of the oceans. *Especially in the Atlantic and Caribbean basins, pools of warming seawater provide energy for storms as they swirl and grow over the open oceans.*

Emanuel analyzed records of storm measurements made by aircraft and satellites since the 1950s. He found the amount of energy released in these storms in both the North Atlantic and the North Pacific oceans has increased, especially since the mid-1970s.

In the Atlantic, the sea surface temperatures show a pronounced upward trend. The same is true in the North Pacific, though the data there is more variable, he said.

"This is the first time I have been convinced we are seeing a signal in the actual hurricane data," Emanuel said in an e-mail exchange.

"The total energy dissipated by hurricanes turns out to be well correlated with tropical sea surface temperatures," he said. "The large upswing in the past decade is unprecedented and probably reflects the effects of global warming."

This year marked the first time on record that the Atlantic spawned four named storms by early July, as well as the earliest category 4 storm on record. *Hurricanes are ranked on an intensity scale 1 to 5.*

In the past decade, the southeastern United States and the Caribbean basin have been pummelled by the most active hurricane cycle on record. *Forecasters expect the stormy trend to continue for another 20 years or more.*

Even without global warming, hurricane cycles tend to be a consequence of natural salinity and temperature changes in the Atlantic's deep current circulation that shift back and forth every 40 to 60 years.

Since the 1970s, hurricanes have caused more property damage and casualties. Researchers disagree over whether this destructiveness is a consequence of the storms' growing intensity or the population boom along vulnerable coastlines.

"The damage and casualties produced by more intense storms could increase considerably in the future," Emanuel said.

Taken from: www.livescience.com By Associated Press (719 words)

RC 6 – MULTIPLE MATCHING AND NOTE FORM: "FACTSHEET: CHILD SOLDIERS"

Task 3

| 1 J | 2 B | 3 E | 4 G | 5 H | 6 C | 7 L | 8 A | 9 F | 10 D | 11 I |

Task 4

1. Give reasons why children become child soldiers.	force/poverty/abuse/discrimination/revenge/ separation from their families/displacement from home/ life in combat zones/poor education/food/survival
2. What do child soldiers not understand?	dangers/abuses
3. Why is the situation of girls a special one?	(higher) risk of sexual violence/abuse/exploitation
4. What does governmental breakdown make even more difficult?	identify who recruits children (as soldiers)
5. According to the new law, what is the minimum age to take part in conflicts?	18
6. To what extent does monitoring help the situation?	perpetrators can be sentenced/better understanding of (the) situation
7. What should families and communities avoid for children?	become involved in violence
8. What is understood by a "protective environment"?	a safe situation/re-recruitment is prevented
9. How can the children help themselves?	(to) give them a voice/let them have a say
10. What can be done for the victims?	protection of child soldiers/provide psychosocial support/ promote family reunification

Task 5

1. someone who is involved in fighting in a war: *combatant*
2. someone whose job is to carry people's bags or other loads or to look after a building by cleaning it: *porter*
3. to take someone away by force, to kidnap: *to abduct*
4. to persuade people to join the army, to conscript: *to recruit*
5. cruel, violent treatment of someone, misuse: *abuse*
6. to make a proposal into a law, to pass a law: *to enact*
7. fighting, a fight/battle: *combat*
8. to force a group of people to move away from the place where they normally live: *to displace*
9. to send home the members of an army, especially at the end of a war: *to demobilize*
10. without being forced, done willingly: *voluntary*
11. the activity of fighting in a war: *warfare*
12. to be forced to suffer or experience something very unpleasant: *to be subjected to*
13. a situation in which you treat someone unfairly in order to get an advantage for yourself: *exploitation*
14. when someone is kept in prison while waiting for trial: *custody*
15. to completely stop something by making it illegal: *to outlaw*
16. unfriendly, aggressive feelings or behaviour, full of anger: *hostility*
17. when people are ordered to serve in the army: *conscription*
18. an action that breaks a law: *violation*
19. to carefully watch and check a situation over a period of time to see how it develops: *to monitor*
20. someone who commits a crime or does something morally wrong: *perpetrator*
21. responsible for the effects of your actions: *accountable*
22. a court with the official authority to deal with a particular problem: *tribunal*
23. a situation in which two countries become friendly with each other again after quarrelling: *reconciliation*
24. the place where the enemies are facing each other in a war: *frontline*
25. to make a written agreement official by signing it: *to ratify*
26. to publicly support something that should be done: *to advocate*
27. advice and support given to someone with problems: *counselling*

Task 6

1. Complete the following collocations:
   - to **lay** the groundwork
   - to **have** a say
   - to **seek** revenge
2. Find synonyms for "war": *conflict, armed conflict, hostility, hostilities (pl), warfare, fighting, combat, battle*

Task 7

Noun (person)	Noun (abstract)	Verb	Adjective
combatant	combat	combat	combative
abductor	abduction	abduct	---
recruit, recruiter	recruitment	recruit	---
---	integration	integrate	---
---	reunification	reunify	---
---	ratification	ratify	---
advocate	advocacy	advocate	---
abuser	abuse	abuse	abusive
violator	violation	violate	---
perpetrator	perpetration	perpetrate	---

The Whole text

The facts

It is estimated that some 300.000 children – boys and girls under the age of 18 – are today involved in more than 30 conflicts worldwide. Children are used as combatants, messengers, porters and cooks and for forced sexual services. Some are abducted or forcibly recruited, others are driven to join by poverty, abuse and discrimination, or to seek revenge for violence enacted against them or their families.

Children are more likely to become child soldiers if they are separated from their families, displaced from their homes, living in combat zones or have limited access to education. Children may join armed groups as the only way to guarantee daily food and survival.

In some situations, the involvement of children in conflicts as soldiers may even be accepted or encouraged. Children may "voluntarily" take part in warfare, not realizing the dangers and abuses they will be subjected to. Most likely these children are responding to economic, cultural, social and political pressures.

The particular situation of girls in conflicts continues to require further attention. The potential risk of sexual violence, abuse and exploitation of children and women increase during armed conflicts, and specific measures must be taken to ensure their security and to strengthen their decision-making abilities. Still, in many instances, programmes to demobilize and reintegrate child soldiers fail to identify appropriate strategies for gaining access to these girls and young women. Ways must also be found to address the needs of girls abducted during war to serve as sexual slaves and who may have no alternative to remaining under the custody of their abductors.

Building a protective environment for children

Ending the use of child soldiers can be extremely challenging, particularly when children are enlisted for combat by armed, non-governmental groups. In addition, modern conflicts are characterized by governmental breakdown, making it difficult to identify and influence those recruiting and using children as soldiers.

Elements already in place

Legislation

In 2002 the Optional Protocol to the Convention on the Rights of the Child on the involvement of children in armed conflict entered into force. It outlaws the involvement of children under age 18 in hostilities, raising the previous standard of age (15 years) set by the Convention and the 1949 Geneva Conventions and their 1977 Additional Protocols. As well as requiring States to raise the age for compulsory recruitment and direct participation in conflict to 18, the Optional Protocol requires State parties to raise the minimum age for voluntary recruitment beyond the current minimum of 15. Another milestone was set in July 2002 when the Statute of the International Criminal Court entered into force, making the conscription, enlistment or use of children under 15 in hostilities by national armed forces or armed groups a war crime.

Monitoring

Violations of the laws of war that affect children need to be properly monitored and reported, so that perpetrators can be held accountable before tribunals or other truth and reconciliation mechanisms. This applies to the recruitment and use of children as soldiers, particularly in light of the provision in the Statute of the International Criminal Court. Adequate monitoring will also promote better understanding of and data on the numbers and situation of child soldiers.

Capacity

During conflict, the capacity of families and communities to protect and care for children is undermined. Nonetheless, their efforts to ensure that their children do not become involved in violence are important and must be supported. The protection of children by families and communities is the frontline in the war against recruiting children into armed groups. Capacity also involves focusing efforts and resources on the most underserved regions and population groups, including displaced populations, to guarantee equal access to quality services, in particular education.

UNICEF's response

Attitudes, customs and behaviours, and practices: A protective environment for demobilized child soldiers must include strategies to prevent their re-recruitment. It should also lay the groundwork for the eventual return to their families and communities.

Governmental and non-governmental commitment

This includes advocacy on behalf of children at the international, national and community level. This could include, for example, promoting ratification of the Optional Protocol on the involvement of children in armed conflict and advocating for national law reform and sensitization campaigns. It could also mean engaging in dialogue with non-governmental armed groups to uphold international standards for child protection and securing their commitment to end the recruitment and use of children in hostilities.

Children's life skills and participation

Giving children a voice – and listening to them – will allow children to have a say in their own protection and in the life of their community and country.

Services for victims of abuse

This includes providing protection to former child soldiers during demobilization and social reintegration programmes (education and vocational training) and providing psychosocial support (peer-to peer support, community-based support and psychosocial counselling). It also means promoting family reunification as a key factor for social reintegration and ensuring follow-up care for demobilized children, focusing on long-term social reintegration.

Taken from: UNICEF (823 words)

RC 7 – TRUE/FALSE/JUSTIFICATION: "MALALA YOUSAFZAI"

Task

		T	F	Justification
0.	Recently the adverse conditions in the Swat Valley have improved.		X	*Earlier, the situation was …*
1.	Malala's mastery of the language was unexpected for the reporter.	X		*She spoke an Urdu*
2.	A few students were very eager to talk to the reporter.	X		*Inside, the bureau chief*
3.	The head of the school belonged to the hidden top echelons of society in this area.		X	*The highly educated Yousafzai*
4.	What the reporter remembered best about Malala was her uncompromising look.	X		*Ashraf, who had been*
5.	The reporter was relentless because he had made Malala famous.		X	*Ashraf was savage regarding*
6.	According to the reporter, the influence of the media can damage the reputation of smart adolescents.		X	*He decried "the media's*
7.	When Malala was taken to a health center, she was always accompanied by a parent.		X	*She was mysteriously separated*
8.	People wondered why the General of the Army came to a local hospital to visit Malala.	X		*The question arose: Why / Why would the most*

RC 8 – NOTE FORM: "A VERY SHORT STORY"

Task

0	The others left the rooftop, when ___.	it got dark
1	When Luz made him ready for the operation, he was afraid of ___.	being too talky/blabby/talkative
2	It was impossible for him and Luz to register for marriage because they did ___.	not have birth certificates
3	He received Luz's messages only ___.	after the armistice / in a bunch
4	After the war Luz decided against ___.	coming home at once/going to America
5	Because he and Luz had a fight before they parted, he ___.	felt sick
6	After Luz returned to her job, she ___.	felt lonely
7	When Luz sent him a farewell letter, she already realized he ___.	would not understand
8	The story ends with Luz neither hearing from him nor ___.	marrying the major

RC 9 – NOTE FORM: "DEAD POETS SOCIETY"

Task 2

0.	Who did Neil expect when there was a knock at the door?	another of their buddies
1.	How did Neil feel in the presence of his father?	uncomfortable/nervous
2.	Which extracurricular activity did Mr Perry want his son to drop?	(the) school annual
3.	How did Mr Perry feel when Neil disputed him in public?	angry/furious/enraged
4.	What was Neil's reaction to his father's threats of guilt and punishment?	his resolve crumbled
5.	What did his friend Knox think Neil should do?	tell his father off
6.	What did Charlie's parents expect their son to become?	a banker
7.	What did Neil decide to do?	chuck the annual
8.	Who was Mr Nolan?	headmaster/(teacher)
9.	What – according to Meeks – did the people who worked on the annual really want to do?	impress Nolan
10.	How did all the boys feel at the end of this scene?	glum/frustrated/sad/disappointed

Task 3

1.	briskly	E	practically and confidently; showing a desire to get things done quickly
2.	to shuffle	I	to move from one foot to another; to move your feet in an awkward or embarrassed way
3.	an annual	L	a book that is published once a year, with the same title each time, but different contents
4.	resolve	F	strong determination to achieve sth
5.	to crumble	B	to begin to fail or get weaker or to come to an end
6.	to rip	A	to tear sth or to become torn, often suddenly or violently
7.	to hurl	M	to throw sth/sb violently in a particular direction
8.	to approve	K	to think that sb/sth is good, acceptable or suitable; to officially agree to a plan, request,
9.	to croak	J	to die (*very informal!*)
10.	to chuck	G	to give up or stop doing sth
11.	to slump	D	to sit or fall down heavily
12.	to slam	C	to put, push or throw sth into a particular place or position with a lot of force
13.	glumly	H	sadly, quietly and unhappily

LC 1 – NOTE FORM: "DIALECTS AND STANDARD ENGLISH"

0.	What is sometimes impossible to understand for speakers of Standard English?	*(the) New Englishes*
1.	What is "Singlish"?	*mixture English and Chinese* *mixture of two languages*
2.	What used to happen to dialects for many centuries?	*(were) degraded* *(were) stamped out* *disappeared*
3.	What is the English language doing at the moment?	*(it's) breeding dialects*
4.	Why do accents and dialects come into being?	*need for identity*
5.	Why do we need standard languages?	*(they) guarantee intelligibility*
6.	Why are people in Singapore increasingly adopting English as their first language?	*(carrier of) national identity*
7.	What might Singapore become in the long run?	*(an) English speaking country*

LC 1-TAPESCRIPT: "Dialects and Standard English"

Crystal:
At grass roots level some amazing things are happening, producing varieties of English that are quite unlike anything that we've heard of previously.

Presenter:
Professor David Crystal again.

Crystal:
If you go to places like Singapore and India and many of the countries in Africa, you will hear these 'New Englishes', as they are called. These English varieties where they are so different from Standard English that it is sometimes virtually impossible to understand what's going on, in fact, sometimes it is impossible to understand what's going on. If you listen to somebody speaking 'Singlish' in Singapore for instance, which is a mixture of English and Chinese, then because it is a mixture of the two languages, only if you know both are you likely to understand it. When I was last in Singapore I did not understand some of the 'English', in inverted commas, that people were speaking around me. They wouldn't speak it to me of course because it's a local dialect of identity. To me they would switch into Standard English. And that's the point, that as English develops in the 21st century we're going to see an increasing multi-dialectalization of it.

Presenter:
But that interests me very much for several reasons. You've used the word dialect, and I'm very pleased you did use the word dialect 'cause one of the things that has happened in our country or countries, whichever way you want to talk about it, is that the dialects were relentlessly over centuries degraded, often actively stamped out and they were fed into the more of standardization; standardization, centralization of English. Now then we also talked about the disappearance of thousands of tongues or languages in the next hundred years or so as a result of globalization of language and yet what seems to me to be happening, and what you've said confirms it, is that English itself is breeding dialects, which leaves us historically in this country in rather an odd position.

Crystal:
Extremely odd position. The minority dialect of English now is British English. Yes, it's only the same thing happening on the world scale, as it has always happened on a national scale: we're used to local accents and dialects; we're not used to international accents and dialects. It's the same process. The process that drives an accent or dialect into existence is the need for identity. Standard languages guarantee intelligibility; local accents and dialects give you identity, and at a world level this is exactly what's happening.

Presenter:
One of the most often quoted examples of this is the former British colony of Singapore. Professor Edgar Schneider of Regensburg University in Germany has been tracking what's happening to English here.

Schneider:

Singapore seems to be a very unique case because the local people are Chinese, Malay, Tamil and so on, but they are still adopting English as their first language as far as we can tell and increasingly so in conventional terms as their native language. There is an enormous percentage of the population where in the families English is used as the family language because the parents come from varying linguistic backgrounds and that has to do with questions of identity as well because apparently in Singapore it's English that is seen as a carrier of a new national identity. So I would dare to predict that in the long run Singapore might really be a more or less English-speaking country. I said in about 200 years, so I'm glad nobody can prove me wrong, but still.

Taken from: Heiko Benzin/Silvia Exer/Jutta Trinks; Advanced Listening Comprehension. Cornelsen Verlag 2007, page 85, CD 2, Track 11 (3 min. 17 sec.)

LC 2 – NOTE FORM: "SEXY ADS"

A recent study shows that the attitude that **(0.) 'sex sells'** may no longer apply to young women.

The models in the study had to be classified according to **(1.) seven/7 basic types.**

It turned out that just two categories of models remained, which were then referred to as **(2.) sexy-casual** and **(3.) classic beauty.**

The women's **(4.) emotional reaction/response** to the models was explored with the help of a technique called 'AdSAM'.

The women used **(5.) pictures** to communicate how they felt about the different models.

It turned out that most of the women in the study reacted with a feeling of **(6.) boredom** to very sexy models.

John Morris believes that women in general don't find sexy imagery very **(7.) appealing** and are consequently not willing **(8.) to buy** the brand associated with it.

It seemed that the women in the study labelled the models as sexy-sensual not so much because they really saw them that way but because they had been **(9.) programmed to think that.**

College women are an important target group for advertisers, because they have the **(10.) highest disposable income.**

LC 2-TAPESCRIPT: "Sexy Ads"

Apparently sex may not sell anymore, at least not for young women who, a new University of Florida study shows, are increasingly bored by sexy ads in magazines. Here is your UF advertising researcher John Morris.

Morris:

The study was really an attempt to measure how college women felt about models that are usually depicted in advertising that's directed towards them. And we began in the study by asking them to identify models by seven basic types. That went from wholesome kind of beauty, classic-beauty, to sexual, to sensual girl next door, those kind of categories that had been tested previously in advertising research, particularly with art directors and fashion designers. So, we had them classify the set of forty models in that fashion. First of all, what we found was that there really were only two types rather than seven types. Those were factored into two basic types that were: one, classic-beauty and second, sexy-sensual. So those were the categories that we call – that we labeled them: sexy-sensual and classic-beauty. We then asked the college students to give us their emotional response to these models and they did it on all forty models, but not everybody did every model so we had it all, all really mixed up so that they had a varying group of the models; everybody got at least some body in one of the categories. We used a technique called 'AdSAM', which essentially is a self-assessment manikin that uses a visual measure rather than a verbal measure. So we didn't ask them if they were happy about this or not. We let them use a manikin, a picture to tell us that. The findings were that the top model that showed the highest in the classic-beauty, was very positively received and that the kinds of feelings that people are having when they translate it into the database, it's part of the AdSAM process, you know, were things like appreciative, loved, joyful, but when we looked at the model that was considered the highest sexy-sensual the response was more like boredom. It wasn't they were antagonized by it, they weren't anxious about it, they weren't upset about it, they were just bored by the look of sexy-sensual.

Interviewer:

Does that seem to suggest to you that maybe young women are sort of exhausted with that sort of advertising? I mean that particularly it seems like in the late 90s and early oughts that's, you see so much of it now in magazines, television wherever, it's all about sort of sexy imagery. Are these women sort of turned off by that or tired of it or exhausted with how much they have seen?

Morris:

I think that they're not only – been exhausted by the exposure to this, but that they don't necessarily find this to be an appealing approach.

Interviewer:

And why is that? What does that sort of have to say to advertisers now? I mean, obviously you want – the old attitude has been that sexy sells. You know, is sexy not selling to this group? Do advertisers have to come up with a new approach then to reach this demograph?

Morris:

Well, we certainly don't know if it is selling or not selling. Through previous studies that we've done we know that positive emotional response that we have from this model are very predictive of intentions to buy and in interest in the brand, so if you translate that into this study then it says yes, that these women won't find that to be appealing enough to participate in the brand or buy. I think one other thing is very important here, is that these women seemed to be programmed to say this is sexy-sensual, so when we asked them to label these models they labeled them sexy-sensual, when I'm not sure whether they really think that or not. Clearly they think somebody thinks that or they have been somehow programmed to think that and therefore this is the label they put on it. But you would then think from that that these models' response emotionally would be something positive. You know, again, appreciative or interested or feeling lucky or something in that type of reaction, whereas they were just bored and uninterested. And that's really the – I think the most important part about it; the comparison between what they selected for this category. Now on the other hand they found those models that were selected in the classic-beauty sense to be very positive and have a strong engagement as part of our model and so therefore those were showing things like appreciative, joyful.

Interviewer:
How important are young women as a group for particularly – I me an, you know, a lot of these ads are for clothing, for perfume, for the kind of goods that young women would buy. How important is that demographic for retailers, for people who advertise to reach that or – how important are they as buyers?
Morris:
Well they are clearly very attractive to advertisers. 18 to 25, 18 to 34 even 18 to 49, particularly women, are the most sought after categories and have been for many many years. Not only that, but college women have the highest disposable income. So you combine with the fact that they are in the right age category, they are clearly in the right economic category, so this is a target that these advertisers certainly want to reach.

Taken from: Heiko Benzin/Silvia Exer/Jutta Trinks; Advanced Listening Comprehension. Cornelsen Verlag 2007, page 14, CD 1, Track 5 (5 min. 57 sec.)

LC 3 – MULTIPLE MATCHING: "YOUNG PEOPLE AND THE EU"

Speaker 1:	G	Young people in the EU have to face certain disadvantages.
Speaker 2:	C	Only the EU can guarantee a peaceful future.
Speaker 3:	A	Certain countries don't seem to be welcome in the EU.
Speaker 4:	E	The EU offers some wonderful opportunities for young people.
Speaker 5:	D	The EU has made life more expensive.

LC 3-TAPESCRIPT: "Young People and the EU"

Hello. I'm Monika Felbiger from Innsbruck and I think that although politicians are always telling us that the EU offers us a lot of advantages, I'm not so sure. I mean, look at me, for example. I'm 18 and got my Matura last year. I wanted to study medicine in Innsbruck, but although I had good grades my application was refused. They said there were simply too many applicants for the places available and I was so disappointed. But do you know what made me angry about it? I wasn't turned down because the other Austrian students were better than me, but because of all the German students who had come to Austria after not getting a university place at home. Now, I think that's really unfair.

Hi. My name's Bastiaan De Vries from Gouda in the Netherlands. I like the idea of the European Union because it brings people closer together. In these times of international friction, I think it's really important to have an organization like the EU and to persuade as many European countries as possible to join it. You know, I just can't understand people who are against enlargement. Yes, l admit that taking in countries with undeveloped economies costs money, but we need to help each other if we all want to live a peaceful and decent life.

My name's Alara Serif and I'm very much in favour of Turkey becoming a member of the EU. I was born in Turkey and spent my early childhood there. Then my father got a good job in Linz, and we moved here nine years ago, when I was ten. We've lived here ever since and although I like visiting my family in Turkey I now feel much more at home in Austria, which is why I just can't understand all the fuss about Turkey joining the EU. You know, years of talks and negotiations with 'you must do this' and 'you mustn't do that: Is that really necessary, or is it just an excuse to keep Turkey out? The people of Turkey want to enjoy the advantages of being in the EU, too. Is that so strange? And why punish the ordinary people because of the Turkish government's human rights record? Is that fair?

Hello. I'm Pierre Bernard from Lyon in France and I think the EU's great for young people. I'm now in my final year at school and we have a teacher who always encourages us to take part in EU projects. For the last three years we've taken part in a Comenius project called 'Working and living in Europe' and we've learnt so much! We've also been on study trips within the EU and I've got to know so many interesting people and places. You just wouldn't believe what a wonderful place Europe is. Now I even have friends in Finland and Estonia. We phone and send text messages all the time. Without the Comenius project this would certainly not have been possible for me. So I think that people should stop moaning about the bureaucrats in Brussels and realise how lucky we are!

Hi, my name's Kevin Doyle and I'm from Cork in Ireland. So, you want to know whether I've got used to the euro? Well, no, not really, and sometimes I think I never will. You see I still always tend to convert euros back into Irish pounds, which is silly, I know, because you can't really compare the two currencies any longer, can you? But it's not the getting used to the euro that's my main argument against the EU. What gets me is how expensive life has become back home in Ireland. Before the euro was introduced, for example, a hundred pounds was real money, money that you could do a lot with, shopping and so on. But today? The equivalent of around 120 euros may sound a lot, but I can't buy nearly as much with it because of terrible price increases. As far as I can see, the introduction of the euro was just an excuse for retailers to print their own money!

Taken from: David Clarke/Claudia Zekl; Focus on Modern Business 4/5. Veritas Verlag 2007, page 44, Serviceteil page 72, CD Track 7 (5 min. 03 sec.)

LC 4 – MULTIPLE CHOICE: "THE UN CLIMATE CONFERENCE IN NAIROBI"

		Nairobi was chosen as the location of the conference because of	
		A	its wish to promote Kenya internationally.
0.	✗	B	the increasing needs of the Third World.
		C	sending too many greenhouse gases out into the air.
		D	its climate.

		Sarah Higgins	
		A	lives four hours away by car from Nairobi.
1.		B	lives in a beautiful, mountainous region close to Nairobi.
		C	moved from Sweden to Kenya 30 years ago.
	✗	D	has been living in Kenya for more than three decades.

		Sarah Higgins and her husband have succeeded in	
	✗	A	planting a lot of trees.
2.		B	buying a flower farm.
		C	installing sprinkler systems.
		D	helping all the other farmers around them.

		According to Sarah,	
		A	the protection of environment is given careful attention.
3.		B	the government does its best.
	✗	C	the educational process is slow.
		D	there are a lot of resources for underdeveloped countries.

		Achim Steiner of the UN Environment Program supports solutions that	
		A	are fast.
4.		B	use high tech products.
		C	are expensive, but effective.
	✗	D	people take responsibility for themselves.

		The local farmers face difficulty because	
		A	their own actions have failed.
5.	✗	B	they do not have enough means to adjust.
		C	they have no information on climate change.
		D	they have no access to credit.

		The public has come to see that	
		A	the governments will decide on new emission standards.
6.		B	they will not get money for new projects.
	✗	C	the governments need to take action.
		D	the Adaptation Fund will be administered by the First World.

		Kofi Annan delivered one important message:	
	✗	A	Decision makers on a global level urgently need to combat climate change.
7.		B	Investing in Africa's infrastructure would create jobs.
		C	We must seek solutions to stop the global CO_2 emissions.
		D	Ignoring the needs of the developing world is unfair and short-sighted.

LC 4-TAPESCRIPT: "The UN Climate Conference in Nairobi"

But first on "Living Planet" this week, the United Nations Climate Change Conference taking place at the moment is being held in Kenya's capital Nairobi. The choice of location is in part to focus the world's attention on the growing needs of developing countries in the face of climate change. Kenya is a perfect example. It bears no responsibility for emitting the greenhouse gases that are causing global warming, yet its population is already suffering as a result of erratic rainfall and rising temperatures. Kenya doesn't have the money it needs to adapt to climate change, so, with little hope of any concrete decisions emerging from this conference, some Kenyans are taking the situation into their own hands and adapting to climate change on a local scale. Anja Kuepers is in Nairobi and has this report.

At the end of a bumpy two-hour car journey from Nairobi through the stunning Aberdare Mountains and past beautiful Lake Naivasha lies Sarah Higgins' farm. A British woman with short spiky hair and a beaming smile, she's lived in Kenya for more than thirty years and greets her visitors with a warm welcome. "Right, well what I'm going to say to you is you probably all need a comfort stop and there's tea and coffee, so follow me." Sarah Higgins and her husband grow wheat; they own cattle and they also have an interest in one of the many flower farms dotted around the area. She says that human interference and the changing climate have made it harder for all farmers in the area to grow their crops successfully. But rather than sitting back and accepting an uncertain future, the Higgins decided to do something about it. So they planted trees, thousands of trees on land where crops can't grow and the results have been surprisingly successful. "Now we're finding the clouds whizzing along and sort of stopping, "Hey, there's some trees, guys". And we get the rain back again, so it actually paid us to plant those trees. It's brought some of the rain back to us." (...)
Sarah is passionate about spreading environmental awareness and is involved in education projects for children in particular. But the issue still isn't taken seriously enough, she says, "The educational movement is too slow. There is not enough effort put behind it unfortunately, really don't think." And we as a small association are doing our best, but where's the government coming from? Why is environment not out there?
Sarah's farm is a world away from the lush, well-manicured gardens surrounding the United Nations conference centre in Nairobi. Almost 6,000 delegates have been here for two weeks debating the fight against climate change. One of their main aims is to increase the resources available to developing nations, to help them adapt to the effects of global warming.
Achim Steiner is executive director of the United Nations Environment Program. He sings the praises of simple and cheap ways of coping with today's changing weather patterns, "The world needs to look more carefully at some of the low tech solutions that people can take charge of themselves because they can act while otherwise the world would have to wait for ten, twenty years until societies are ready."
And no matter how successful small-scale initiatives like Sarah's are, they're not enough to combat the effects of climate change. Hans Verolme is the director of WWF's Global Climate Change Program, based in Washington D.C., "I think it is particular difficult for African farmers to respond to this challenge. They bear no responsibility and they have very few tools to adapt."
Deciding on new emission reduction targets won't happen at this conference, but it is hoped a decision will be made about the Adaptation Fund and who it should be managed by. This provides money for projects that reduce greenhouse gas emissions in developing countries. People are starting to realize how urgently the world's governments need to take action. But, Hans Verolme says, the main problem lies in the decision-making system. (...)
The fact that Kofi Annan, Secretary General of the United Nations, came to address the politicians and policy makers here in Nairobi, shows how seriously climate change is being taken. It's the first time he's made an appearance at any UN climate change event. "The Nairobi conference must send a clear signal, a clear message, credible signal that the world's political leaders take climate change seriously. The question is not whether climate change is happening or not. But whether in the face of this emergency we ourselves can change fast enough."

Taken from: Heiko Benzin/Silvia Exer/Jutta Trinks; Advanced Listening Comprehension. Cornelsen Verlag 2007, page 28, CD 1, Track 9 (4 min. 52 sec.)

LC 5: NOTE FORM: "AN INTERVIEW WITH SOMEONE WHO FOUNDED A MAGZINE"

0.	What does *Time Out* feature?	what's going on
1.	In 1968, where could you find the information where events happened?	a) (a) magazine called *What's On*
		b) evening paper / music press
2.	Whom did he create the magazine for?	himself / people wanting / who wanted the same
3.	Where did they sell the new magazine at first?	a) hand to hand / in the street
		b) (at) newsagents
4.	When Tony took control of the magazine at university what did he transform it into?	(a) (contemporary) arts magazine
5.	What was Tony believed to do during the summer holidays?	(to) teach in France / go to France
6.	What did he do instead?	started (doing) the magazine
7.	How often are most magazines published?	fortnightly / every two weeks
8.	What led to the magazine becoming a weekly?	(the) threat of competition
9.	What was the attitude of publishers as well as advertisers to Tony's readership like?	dismissive, not significant
10.	Who is primarily the readership of *Time Out*?	intelligent young people

LC 5-TAPESCRIPT: "An Interview With Someone Who Founded A Magazine"

Interviewer: ... OK, welcome back to the programme. Well, for the hundred thousand or more people in London who buy every issue, *Time Out* is an invaluable guide to what's going on in the city. In its lists they can find everything from films, plays, concerts and night clubs to exhibitions, sports, opera, dance and special events. And I'm talking now to Tony Elliott, the man who started it all, back in 1968. Tony, what gave you the idea?

Tony Elliott: Well, back then it was very hard to find out about those things. There were magazines, there was a magazine called *What's On*, which was a weekly, which is still around, rather, kind of, conventional in its approach, and you could look in the evening paper or you could look in the music press, um, to get information, but nothing covered everything all in one place. Um, so I perceived there was a gap and I suppose to some extent I just produced a magazine for myself, and it turned out a lot of other people wanted the same thing.

Interviewer: At first, the magazine was just a sheet sold hand to hand in the street, wasn't it?

Tony Elliott: Well, I started with a few like-minded people and we did actually put it into newsagents – people do seem to think we started as a bunch of idealistic amateurs, but I have to say that I think we were actually pretty professional from day one. It was coming out every three weeks so I'd spend three or four days actually going round something like 300 newsagents. The selling in the street was partly to do with getting copies sold so that we actually had some cash but it also had this kind of in-built market research thing where you'd show people what you were doing and they'd go "Oh really" and a lot of people said, "Oh, that's a modern *What's On*, that's what we've been looking for."

Interviewer: So, did you have any publishing experience before this?

Tony Elliott: Mmm, I did a regular column for a magazine at university which was quite serious. It used to do single themes per issue, like provincial theatre or education or racialism, and then when I took it over I promptly changed it into being a kind of contemporary arts magazine. We did interviews with artists, rock stars, writers, people like that.

Interviewer: Were you still at university when you started *Time Out*?

Tony Elliott: Yeah, technically I was actually on holiday for the summer vacation, and as far as the university was concerned I was supposed to be going to France to teach. I think I'd told them I would do, because, you know, you go away for a term or a year if you're studying French, and um, then I just started doing the magazine.

Interviewer: And, er, didn't go back.

Tony Elliott: Yes, well there was a point when I suddenly realised that I was doing what I wanted to do.

Interviewer: So it soon took off, didn't it? I mean it was monthly first and then it went weekly, didn't it, in a very short time?

Tony Elliott: Well, it started monthly and then we went three-weekly – for some reason that was the highest frequency we could do. Then we went fortnightly, which is quite a valid frequency for publication, and then inevitably we went weekly – stimulated, I have to say, by the threat of some competition from some people who were starting a similar publication.

Interviewer: Oh, yes, I was going to say, someone else must have spotted the gap, I mean you identified it, but there must have been big publishing houses who thought, "Hang on, we can have some of this too".

Tony Elliott: I think the truth is nobody really realised what the significance of the magazine was, 'cos in a sense it started very tiny, very small, and then built up and built up and a lot of publishers and a lot of advertisers also were very, um, dismissive of our readers. I mean, still, even today, you get occasional accusations like "It's not a particularly significant readership" and "A lot of students read it, don't they?" and things like that. People just didn't realise that, um, that we were creating a readership that was very significant.

Interviewer: The readership's grown up with you as well, hasn't it? A lot of people I imagine who were buying it as students in the Sixties are now buying it as parents of teenage children these days.

Tony Elliott: That would imply our readership's now older, which isn't the case. And although the numbers have expanded, well it's true that there are more people over 35 buying it than there were when it started, the readership hasn't really changed, it's still basically intelligent young people who do things.

Interviewer: OK, well, we'll take a quick break now and then I'll be back to talk to Tony some more ...

Taken from: Cambridge Certificate in Advanced English 5. Cambridge University Press 2003, Test 1, Paper 4, Part 3 (4 min. 40 sec.)

LC 6 – NOTE FORM: "THE EUROPEAN DREAM – A MODEL FOR THE WORLD?"

0.	Why has the American Dream lost its importance?	*Americans are overworked / underpaid*
1.	Why would Jim Hill from Nevada like to return to Europe?	*Current American mindset / current American political situation / quality of life (in Europe)*
2.	How would an American now define the American Dream?	*Get ahead in (the) world*
3.	In contrast to the individuality in the American Dream, what does the European Dream emphasize?	*It's communal / no one falls behind*
4.	Why do the Americans have a better life?	*(Americans/they) are richer*
5.	In what respect have the Europeans surpassed the Americans? Give one example.	*Quality education / good health care / time off from work / safe communities and environment*
6.	In what subjects at lower levels of education do European children outdo the Americans?	*Math and science*
7.	When would you prefer to go to a clinic in the US?	*You are seriously ill / you can afford it*
8.	Name one advantage of the European health care.	*National insurance / more doctors per population / lower infant mortality*
9.	Why is America placed 27th in infant mortality?	*have more childhood (adult) poverty*
10.	How do Europeans contribute to sustain the environment?	*Use 1/3 (a third) less energy / gasoline is taxed*

LC 6-TAPESCRIPT: "The European Dream – A model for the World?"

Clark:

Is the American Dream dying and is the new expanded European Union, with its European Dream, now the model for the world? Best-selling US author and leading social thinker Jeremy Rifkin says the American Dream, once coveted around the world, is becoming an object of derision. Americans are increasingly overworked, underpaid, squeezed for time and unsure about their prospects for a better life. The American Dream is losing its shine and is being eclipsed by a new vision from the European Union, which is capturing the imagination of the world. Jeremy Rifkin outlines this theory in his new book The European Dream. Is he right, is Europe now the model for the future? Well, Mr Rifkin joins us for this edition of Amsterdam Forum. [...]

This is an email from Jim Hill. He's in Reno, in Nevada. Jim says, 'I think Europe is certainly becoming the new model for the world to follow. I was privileged to live in the Netherlands for four years in the late 1980s and early 1990s. I find myself now wishing I could leave America and go back to Europe, especially with the current American mindset and political situation, but also because of the quality of life enjoyed by Europeans as opposed to Americans.' Do you think that's correct, that the quality of life in much of Europe now surpasses that of the US?

Rifkin:

If you ask an American what is the American Dream, they'll say, 'That I can get ahead in the world.' If you ask a European what the European Dream is, they'll say, 'to have a good quality of life for my family.' And that's the real demarcation between America and Europe. Our dream is very individualistic, the European Dream is much more communal. To have a quality of life the whole community has to tax itself and make sure that no one falls too far behind. If you take a look at the reality of that central core of the European Dream – quality of life – certainly you'd have to say that the EU 15, the most advanced industrial countries, have passed up America in many ways. Let me give you some examples. If the good life is the pay check, we Americans are 28 % richer than Europeans. But if the good life is quality education, good health care, time off from work, safe communities and environment, Europe's begun to pass us up.

Education – at the university level America's still unbeatable. We have the best university graduate schools. But at the primary and secondary school level, many of the EU 15 now, their children outperform our kids in both math and science literacy.

Health care – If you're seriously ill and you can afford the best health care, you'll come to America, to the Mayoh Clinic or John Hopkins – unsurpassable. On the other hand, garden variety health care – the EU 15's passed us up. We have 40 million people in America without health care insurance. In Europe, everyone's covered by national insurance. In Europe, you have more doctors per population. You live a year longer than we do in the EU 15, which is rather interesting since you smoke so much, and you have much lower infant mortality. The US ranks 27th among industrial countries in infant death. That's disgraceful. Every EU country has low infant mortality. The reason – we have more childhood and adult poverty than Europe. And so, while Europe has poverty, you do not allow single mothers or their children to be totally abandoned by society.

Take a look at the workplace. We get two weeks off a year – discretionary to the employer. It's not mandated by law. The average European gets four weeks off a year. Europeans really do work to live and we Americans live to work.

Then there's the question of environment, sustainable development. Here's an area where Europeans walk the walk. While you have 455 million human beings, and we only have 280 million in our country, you use a third less energy, you're better on conservation, you're willing to tax gasoline and tax the population for conservation, you signed the global warming accords, the biodiversity treaty. We've not done very well when it comes to environment and sustainable development.

Taken from: Heiko Benzin/Silvia Exer/Jutta Trinks; Advanced Listening Comprehension. Cornelsen Verlag 2007, page 35, CD 1, Track 11 (3 min. 58 sec.)

LC 7– MULTIPLE MATCHING: "CHOOSING THE RIGHT HOLIDAY"

Anita	C	The English Lake District is a natural adventure park and offers new activities every day.
Kirti	A	You will never feel bored in Vienna, the city of music, art and unforgettable architecture.
Claire	G	*Earthwatch Expedition* supports a project which protects the cheetah in Namibia.
Kirk	F	Northern England offers you both adventure activities and comfortable holiday accommodations.
Oliver	B	Deep-Ocean Travel is planning two unique journeys to the ocean floor.

LC 7-TAPESCRIPT: "Choosing the right holidays"

Anita

Although we've got two small children, we would still like to have an active holiday with lots to do. My husband Jack loves all kinds of water sports, while I like walking and hiking. The kids also enjoy the great outdoors.

Kirk

We spent two weeks camping in Connemara last August, but it rained a lot of the time. So this year we want to go somewhere where there's plenty to do even if the weather's bad. We can't take a long holiday this year, but we're hoping to get away for a short break – a long weekend perhaps.

Claire

WeIl, I want to go somewhere completely different, somewhere I can really switch off. But I don't want a lazy holiday – oh no – I'm a very active person who always needs something interesting to do. I love nature and am very interested in conservation, so perhaps I can find something in that area.

Kirk

I like a mix of comfort combined with the great outdoors. Unfortunately, I can't have a foreign holiday this year, but I'm sure I'll find something suitable nearer to home – Scotland or northern England, perhaps. I've never been there before so maybe I'll give it a try.

Oliver

Have you heard about this new kind of tourism, ecotourism? You know, space flights and trips to the bottom of the sea? I mean, yes, they do cost a lot, but I think they're actually tremendous value for money. After all, you're quite literally having the experience of a lifetime.

Taken from: David Clarke/Claudia Zekl; Focus on Modern Business 4/5, Veritas Verlag 2007, page 83, CD Track 12 (1 min. 45 sec.)

LIU 1 – MULTIPLE CHOICE: "RULE NUMBER 1: FOLLOW ALL RULES"

0.	1.	2.	3.	4.	5.	6.	7.	8.	9.	10.	11.
B	A	D	B	C	A	C	D	A	D	C	B

The complete text

I did a foolish thing the other evening. I went into one of our local bars and seated myself without permission. You just don't do this in America, but I had an important recurring thought that I wanted to scribble down before it left my head (...), and anyway the place was practically empty, so I just took a table near the door.

After a couple of minutes the hostess – the Customer Seating Manager – came up to me and said in a level tone, "I see you've seated yourself."

"Yup," I replied proudly. "Dressed myself too."

"Didn't you see the sign?" She tilted her head at a bog sign that said "Please Wait to be seated."

I have been in this bar about 150 times. I have seen the sign from every angle but supine.

"Is there a sign?" I said innocently. "Gosh, I didn't notice it."

She sighed. "Well, the server in this section is very busy, so you may have to wait some time for her to get to you."

There was no other customer within 50 feet, but that wasn't the point. The point was that I had disregarded a posted notice and would have to serve a small sentence in purgatory in consequence.

It would be entirely wrong to say that Americans love rules, but they have a certain regard for them. They behave towards rules in much the way the British behave towards queues – as something that is fundamental to the maintenance of a civilized and orderly society. I had, in effect, queue-jumped the "Wait to Be Seated" sign.

Source: Bill Bryson, Notes from a Big Country, p. 56 f.

LIU 2 – WORD FORMATION: "WE THE PEOPLES OF EUROPE"

0.	*holding*
1.	dishonest
2.	threaten
3.	courageous
4.	regulations
5.	freedom
6.	acceptable

7.	variations
8.	consisting
9.	truly
10.	elections
11.	processes
12.	achieved

The complete text

The European Union now stands at a crossroads – The Irish "no" to the referendum on the Treaty has seen to that – and must rethink how it is to proceed. Are the bureaucrats of Brussels going to be allowed to fudge the treaty yet again and blackmail Ireland into holding another referendum and ensuring that the next time round the Irish people vote "yes"? Or will the EU leaders accept that the Treaty is dishonest and undemocratic, and examine the fundamental problems that threaten the future of what is perhaps the most important and courageous political experiment of the last century? The Treaty represents an attempt to combine a Constitution and a set of working regulations and is, in consequence, a mess. The Constitution of the EU should be as short as possible and should set out the principles by which the EU will operate: democracy, free movement of people, observance of human rights, freedom of speech and the press and so on. This must be acceptable to all EU members. Second, there must be a set of regulatory laws of rules that govern the ways in which 27 countries work together and these must be flexible to accommodate the variations that are inevitable in a community consisting of 27 countries and 475 million people.

Above all, if the EU is to work to the advantage of all its members it must be truly democratic. Democracy is not just about periodic elections; it is about people taking part in decision-making processes and feeling that their voices are both heard and taken into account. For this state of affairs to be achieved, the EU must rethink itself from the grassroots up.

Source: North-South Publication, October 2008, p. 62 f., slightly adapted

LIU 3 – BANKED GAP-FILLING: "RUNNER HOBBLES HOME AFTER 5 YEARS AND 20,000 MILES"

0.	1.	2.	3.	4.	5.	6.	7.	8.	9.	10.	11.	12.	13.
E	C	G	A	O	N	H	L	K	P	D	F	I	M

The complete text

Having clocked up 20,000 miles on a five-year-journey run around the globe with nothing but her cart for company, Rosie Swale-Pope is entitled to put her feet up.

Crutches held aloft, the 61-year-old grandmother of two returned to an enthusiastic welcome in Tenby yesterday, as her mission to run solo across the northern hemisphere came to a triumphant end. Hundreds of well-wishers turned out to cheer their heroine as she crossed the pink ribbon.

It was in her Welsh hometown in 2003 that Mrs Swale-Pope had begun her journey to highlight awareness of prostate cancer after her husband, Clive, died of the disease.

Yesterday, nearing the line, she modestly described her feat as "just a fun run that's got out of hand". The adventure had taken her across Europe and into Russia, where she survived two Siberian winters, the US and Canada.

She camped in blizzards and suffered frostbite, broken ribs and double pneumonia. She was hit by a bus, was almost swept to her death in a swollen river and had to outpace bears, wolves and robbers.

As she returned across less fearsome Welsh terrain, pains in her legs caused by stress fractures compelled a stay in a Haverfordwest hospital that she insisted be kept brief, and she hobbled the last stretch on crutches. She nevertheless looked fit and well yesterday as she arrived in the seaside town.

"I'm pleased I fractured my hip because it's made it more exciting and I got here just fine," she said. "I thank the head consultant of Withybush Hospital for letting me go. I looked in his eyes and said, 'I've got to do it'."

She was joined at the last stage by Tenby Aces Cycling Club and the Trots Running Club, and the throngs greeting her included new friends that she had made on her way and who had arrived from Alaska and Chicago.

Clutching a glass of champagne, she said: "I can't believe you've all turned out for me. I'm overwhelmed. It's a journey that came out of sorrow and pain and heartache, but it's a journey that has turned to joy."

Source: THE TIMES, August 26, 2008, p. 13, slightly adapted

LIU 4 – EDITING: "ABOUT A BOY"

Once or twice Will decided he couldn't face it and went shopping or to the cinema; but most of the time he was in ~~home~~ at four-fifteen, waiting for the buzzer – sometimes because he couldn't be bothered to go out, sometimes because he felt he owed ~~to~~ Marcus something. What and why he owed him he didn't know ~~of~~, but he could see he was serving some purpose in the kid's life at the moment, and as he served no ~~second~~ purpose in anybody else's he was hardly going to die of compassion fatigue. It was still a bit of a drag, though, having some kid inflict himself on you every afternoon. Will ~~who~~ would be relieved when Marcus found a purpose to ~~the~~ life somewhere else. On the third or fourth visit he ~~has~~ asked Marcus about Fiona, and ended up wishing he hadn't, because it was quite clear that the boy was messed up about it. Will couldn't blame him ~~on~~, but couldn't think of anything to say that would be of even the smallest consolation or value, so he ended up simply swearing sympathetically and, given Marcus's age, ~~down~~ inappropriately. Will wouldn't make that mistake again. If Marcus wanted to talk about his suicidal mother, ~~when~~ he could do it with Suzie, or a counsellor, or someone like that, someone capable of something more than an obscenity.	✔ home to of second ✔ who the has ✔ on ✔ down when ✔	0. 00. 1. 2. 3. 4. 5. 6. 7. 8. 9. 10. 11. 12. 13.

Source: Nick Hornby, about a boy, p. 103 f.

LIU 5 – OPEN GAP-FILLING: "I'M A STRANGER HERE MYSELF"

0.	*us*		
1.	who	7.	from
2.	Our	8.	without
3.	go	9.	since
4.	for	10.	has
5.	if	11.	late
6.	around	12.	both

The complete text

When we moved to this little town in New Hampshire, people received us as if the one thing that had kept them from total happiness to this point was the absence of us in their lives. They brought *us* cakes and pies and bottles of wine. Not one of them said, "So you're the people *who* paid a fortune for the Smith place," which I believe is the traditional greeting in England. *Our* next-door neighbors, upon learning that we were intending to *go* out to eat, protested that it was too, too dreary to dine in a restaurant on one's first night in a new town and insisted we come to them *for* dinner there and then, as *if* feeding six extra mouths was the most trifling of burdens.

When word got **around** that our furniture was on a containership making its way **from** Liverpool to Boston, evidently by the way of Port Said, Mombasa, and the Galapagos Islands, and that we were temporarily **without** anything to sleep on, sit on, or eat from, a stream of friendly strangers (some of whom I have not seen **since**) began traipsing up the walk with chairs, lamps, tables, even a microwave oven.

It was dazzling, and it **has** remained so. At Christmas this year we went to England for ten days and returned home **late** at night and hungry to find that a neighbor had stocked the fridge with **both** essentials and goodies and filled vases with fresh flowers. This sort of thing happens all the time.

Source: Bill Bryson, I'm a Stranger Here Myself

LIU 6 – MULTIPLE CHOICE: "THE 'DIRT' ON CLEAN"

0.	1.	2.	3.	4.	5.	6.	7.	8.	9.	10.
B	D	C	B	A	A	D	C	C	D	B

"When people hear that I've written a history of cleanliness, they often **assume** that I'm a clean-freak," says Canadian writer Katherine Ashenburg, author of *Clean: An Unsanitised History of Washing*. "I'm **definitely** not. My interest in writing the book didn't stem from cleanliness so much as from my **curiosity** about the everyday lives of people in past ages."

But in her new book, Ashenburg certainly dishes the dirt on clean. **While** our ancestors' bathing habits might disgust us, our bathing habits would also disgust them. "The thought of a daily hot shower would have filled the 17th century Frenchman with fear," she says. That's because after the Black Plague in the 14th century, the French thought that hot baths made **one** ill – and for 200 years Europeans avoided hot baths just like the plague. And while some cultures consider body odour **offensive**, others find it sexy. Before a return to Paris, for instance, Napoleon ordered his wife Josephine to 'stop washing'! Ready for more dirt on clean? Read on.

For the modern, middle-class North American, 'clean' means that you shower and apply deodorant **each and every** day without fail. For the aristocratic seventeenth-century Frenchman, it meant that he changed his linen shirt daily and dabbled his hands in water but never touched the rest of his body with water or soap. For the Roman in the first century, it involved two or more hours of splashing, soaking and steaming the body in water of various temperatures, raking off sweat and oil with a metal scraper, and giving himself a final oiling – all done daily, in **company** and without soap.

Even more than in the eye or in the nose, cleanliness exists in the **mind** of the beholder. Every culture defines it for itself, choosing what it sees as the perfect point between squalid and over-fastidious. The modern North American, the seventeenth-century Frenchman and the Roman were each **convinced** that cleanliness was an important matter of civility and that his way was the royal road to a **properly** groomed body.

Taken from: Current, Mary Glasgow Magazines, Sept./Oct. 2008, pages 24 and 25

LIU 7 – WORD FORMATION: "DO CELEBRITIES INFLUENCE YOU TO TAKE DRUGS? – A UN REPORT THINKS SO"

0.	*abuse*		
1.	addiction	6.	offenders
2.	singling	7.	refusal
3.	glamorise	8.	suspected
4.	impressionable	9.	possession
5.	particularly	10.	voluntarily

"They're trying to make me go to rehab/I said no, no, no," sings Amy Winehouse in her award-winning song *Rehab*. ... Everyone seems to know about the British star's non-stop battles with alcohol and drug **abuse**. News writers and paparazzi record each mishap on a daily basis – one journalist calls Winehouse a 'tattooed train wreck'.

And now even the United Nations has got in on her act: "Amy Winehouse may adopt a defiant pose and slur her way through *Rehab*, but does she realise the message she sends to others who are vulnerable to **addiction** and who cannot afford expensive treatment?" asks Antonio Maria Costa, executive director or the UN's Office on Drugs and Crime.

His words reflect the 2008 annual report from the UN International Narcotics Control Board (INCB). Without **singling** out any celebrities by name, for the first time ever the report claims that drug-abusing singers, actors and sport stars **glamorise** drug use – especially cocaine. And they encourage **impressionable** teens to use drugs: "Celebrity drug offenders can profoundly influence attitudes, values and behaviour towards drug abuse, **particularly** among young people," the report states.

What's more, it claims, the criminal justice system treats celebs far more leniently than ordinary **offenders**, who often face stiff penalties and even jail time: "Celebrities should not be treated any more leniently than any other non-celebrity," says the report's author Hamid Ghodse.

While the song *Rehab* describes Winehouse's **refusal** to enter a rehabilitation centre, she has in fact checked herself into rehab several times without success. And while she's been arrested more than once for **suspected** drug possession, Winehouse has so far escaped with little more than a fine.

Amy is not alone: in 2005, British tabloids splashed front-page photos of supermodel Kate Moss using cocaine – yet she was never charged with **possession** of an illegal drug. Instead, she **voluntarily** entered rehab, and her career has thrived since the publicity.

Taken from: Current, Mary Glasgow Magazines, Sept./Oct. 2008, pages 11 and 12

LIU 8 – BANKED GAP-FILLING: "UP CLOSE AND PERSONAL"

0.	1.	2.	3.	4.	5.	6.	7.	8.	9.	10.	11.	12.	13.
J	F	O	L	E	I	B	D	A	G	K	N	M	C

The words 'donuts' and 'cutting edge' are rarely seen in the same sentence, but in Buffalo, New York, the ring-shaped snacks are at the center of an **experiment** that could influence shopping **experiences** in the future. Two Dunkin' Donuts stores will soon be testing a system that can **scan** your face and play an ad on a digital screen that is **targeted** to your age, gender, and demographic group.

This is the first time such a system has been used by a mainstream **advertiser** in the U.S. It works in the same way as systems used by police and immigration **agencies** to identify criminals in crowds. A camera above a screen **captures** an image and analyzes facial features such as the eyes, nose, and bone structure. The information is then used to **select** ads to be played on the screen as you look at products or at the cash register.

"It's in the region of 85 percent **accurate**, which is a very high level of precision for advertisers and marketers," says Barry Salzmann, head of YCD Multimedia, which **invented** the display platform. "What we're doing basically is creating the shopping environment of the future. Imagine you walk in, and instead of seeing **printed** materials, it's all digital screens." Those who have seen the movie Minority Report, in which Tom Cruise is followed by ads wherever he **goes**, won't find this hard to imagine.

So are we now facing a future – some say it could be the norm in 20 years – in which we are **bombarded** with personalized messages about deodorant and other things and in which we can't hide anywhere?

When asked about these **high-tech** displays in real life, John Underkoffler, the science and technology expert who worked on the Steven Spielberg film, said there's really no going back.

Taken from: Spotlight, Das Magazin für Ihr Englisch, Dez. 2008, page 24; AE

LIU 9 – EDITING: "WHEN GIRLS GET VIOLENT"

0.	With her bright smile and clear, perfect skin, it's *both* difficult to believe	*both*
00.	that Amy, 18, was once a gang member in the poor London	✔
1.	neighbourhood *in* where she grew up. It's even harder to imagine	in
2.	that she was well known for her violence. But *when* at an early age,	when
3.	Amy's life was already *be* set on a troubled course. From the age	be
4.	of four, she was beaten and raped by her stepfather, someone	✔
5.	who was seen as an important man in the community. "I *did* felt	did
6.	nobody would believe me if I told how every day he came *for* and	for
7.	forced me to have sex," she says. She thinks her mother may	✔
8.	have been aware but 'chose not to *have* see'.	have
9.	Alone and unhappy at home, she turned *around* to drugs at a very	around
10.	early age. "I was six when I tried weed and skunk," Amy says,	✔
11.	"and the wonderful thing was that they ha*ve* sedated me so that	have
12.	I could block out what was *being* going on with my stepfather.	being
13.	I was coming up for ten when someone gave me charlie (cocaine),	✔
14.	and then *when* I began smoking crack. That was extraordinary because	when
15.	we were all filled *as* with this uncontrolled sense of power. I felt as if	as
16.	no one *who* would ever break me again.	who

Taken from: Spotlight, Das Magazin für Ihr Englisch, Okt. 2008, pages 24 and 25

LIU 10 – OPEN GAP-FILLING: „DO WE HAVE A ROYAL TRADITION?"

Do we have a royal tradition?
by Amy Argetsinger

We were supposed to be the land without kings, but from the **very** start, we've cultivated a number of dynasties. John Adams, for example, was our second president, and his son, John Quincy Adams, became our sixth. Franklin Roosevelt, the 32nd president, was a distant cousin of Teddy Roosevelt, the 26th.

It was the Kennedys, **however**, who first brought us the sense that politics could be a family business. And **while** some voters were suspicious about handing so much power to one family, others loved the idea, especially after the death of President John F. Kennedy. It was **as** if they believed the leadership qualities they missed so much might also be found **in** men with his same teeth and hair and confident style.

With the Bush family, though, the men who **rose** to the top offices – George Bush and his sons George W. Bush and former Florida Governor Jeb Bush – were very different from each other. The only things they had in **common**, really, were their basic conservative politics and their last name. But maybe that was all voters needed: to them, Bush was a brand. They knew what they were getting when they voted for that name.

When Hillary Clinton **ran** for Senate, and later for president, it was the first time in this country that a woman had followed so successfully in her husband's political **footsteps**. Hillary Clinton is as different from her husband as the Bushes are from each other, yet she had been **such** an important part of Bill's White House that voters understood that she, too, could offer more **of** whatever they had liked previously.

Spotlight, Jänner 2012

0.	*very*		
1.	however	6.	common
2.	while	7.	ran
3.	as	8.	footsteps
4.	in	9.	such
5.	rose	10.	of

VOCABULARY

BEZIEHUNGEN UND SOZIALE NETZWERKE

Task 1

Part 1: 1 – B, 2 – I, 3 – J, 4 – A, 5 – F, 6 – H, 7 – E, 8 – D, 9 – K, 10 – C, 11 – G

Part 2: 1 – B, 2 – J, 3 – G, 4 – E, 5 – C, 6 – H, 7 – F, 8 – A, 9 – I, 10 – D, 11 – K

Task 2

to accept sb
to apologize **to** sb
to be happy
to be married **to** sb
to count **on** sb
to divorce sb
to get engaged **to** sb
to go out **with** sb
to have/go on a date **with** sb
to make peace **with** sb
to propose **to** sb
to accuse sb **of** doing sth

to be divorced
to be honest **with** sb
to be selfish
to criticize sb
to forgive sb
to get married **to** sb
to gossip **about** sb
to ignore sb
to obey sb
to separate
to trust sb
to agree **with** sb

to understand sb
to be jealous **of** sb
to be wrong **about** sb
to date sb
to get a divorce
to get **over** sb
to have sth in common **with** sb
to keep a secret
to pay attention **to** sb
to support sb

Task 3

1. blog
2. chat
3. comments
4. crowdsourcing
5. crowdfunding
6. Digg
7. emoticon
8. engage
9. Facebook
10. forum
11. flash mob
12. invite (evite)
13. lifecasting
14. live streaming
15. lurker
16. MoBlogging
17. MisTweet
18. MySpace
19. profile page
20. smartphone
21. social networking
22. subscribe
23. tag
24. transparency
25. troll
26. tweet
27. unfriend
28. viral

Task 4

1. band   2. purge   3. request   4. status   5. embarrassing   6. discreet   7. provides   8. predators   9. facilitates

WOHNEN UND UMGEBUNG

Task 1

beauty spot
blocks of flats
building site
business parks
Central Business District (CBD)
cycle lanes
department store
green belt
home town

inner city
land/property prices
litter (bins)
low-cost houses
low-rise tower blocks
main road/street
multi-storey car park
no-go/unsafe areas
open space

pillar box
public conveniences
red-light districts
shanty town
shopping mall
tower block
urban redevelopment
urban sprawl

Task 2

positive		neutral	negative		
atmospheric	picturesque	cosmopolitan	bustling	hectic	remote
clean	quiet	elegant	crowded	noisy	run-down
lively	relaxing	historic	deserted	packed	shabby
magnificent	safe	rural	dirty	polluted	stressful
off the beaten track	spacious	urban	filthy	quaint	
peaceful					

MODE UND TRENDS

Task 1

1 – H, 2 – B, 3 – A, 4 – E, 5 – F, 6 – J, 7 – C, 8 – D, 9 – I, 10 – G

Task 2

1 – candle, 2 – rage, 3 – glove, 4 – day, 5 – statement, 6 – tune, 7 – each, 8 – kill, 9 – smart, 10 – fill, 11 – man, 12 – eye

Task 3

1. stylish/chic/fashionable – latest
   (most recent, newest)
2. timeless
3. vintage
4. must-have
5. hand-me-downs
6. works wonders for
7. casual
8. blast from the past
9. faux pas
10. dress for the occasion
11. dressed to the nines

Task 4

1. a slave to fashion – sb who always feels the need to wear the latest fashions
2. fashion victim – sb who wears fashionable clothes even when they do not look good on him
3. fashionista – sb who is obsessed with fashion
4. fashion icon – a person who is famous for their sense of fashion
5. trailblazer – sb wo is a leader or revolutionary in a certain field
6. knockoffs – copies of haute couture fashions
7. accessories – additional articles that complete or enhance outfits

Task 5

1. Ready-to-wear clothing is clothing that you can buy right off the rack in a store.
   Haute couture clothing is expensive, custom-made, one-of-a-kind clothing. You can't walk into a store and buy a couture dress.
2. You put on nice clothes to go out somewhere special.
3. You wear different styles or items of clothing that aren't part of a set outfit.
4. You use or do too much of something.
5. the catwalk or runway
6. It's something that everyone already knows or no one is interested in anymore.
7. it fits you = it's the right size
   it suits you = it looks good on you
8. to go out of fashion

ERNÄHRUNG, GESUNDHEIT UND SOZIALE ABSICHERUNG

Task 1

1 – L, 2 – I, 3 – D, 4 – J, 5 – H, 6 – N, 7 – G, 8 – M, 9 – E, 10 – C, 11 – F, 12 – K, 13 – A, 14 – B

Task 2

(1) maintained
(2) improve
(3) limiting
(4) prevent
(5) cutting
(6) accepting
(7) linked
(8) develop
(9) volunteering
(10) have

Task 3

Related verbs			
to be allergic **to** pollen	to check **into** a hospital	to give birth **to** a baby	to operate **on** sb
to be examined **by** a doctor	to come **down** with pneumonia	to give **up** smoking	to recover **from** an illness
to be **in** bad shape	to cope **with** stress	to go **on** a diet	to suffer **from** asthma
to be **in** good health		to inject sb **with** sth	to take **out** a prescription

Task 4

1. nutrients – substances in food that provide energy or help form tissues
2. carbohydrates – a class of energy-giving nutrients that include sugar, starch, and fiber
3. fats – a class of energy-giving nutrients
4. proteins – a class of nutrients made up of amino acids
5. vitamins – a class of nutrients that contain carbon and are needed in small amounts to maintain health and allow growth
6. minerals – a class of nutrients that are chemical elements needed for certain processes
7. nutrient deficiency – the state of not having enough of a nutrient to maintain good health
8. food guide pyramid – a visual tool for planning your diet that divides foods into six food groups
9. vegetarian – a diet in which few or no animal products are eaten
10. overweight – heavy for one's size
11. obesity – the state of having excess body fat
12. body image – how you feel about your appearance
13. food allergy – an abnormal response to a food that is triggered by the body's immune system
14. lactose intolerance – a reduced ability to digest the milk sugar lactose
15. lifestyle disease – an illness caused by unhealthy behaviors
16. risk factor – anything that increases the likelihood of injury, disease, or other health problems
17. sedentary – not taking part in physical activity on a regular basis
18. wellness – a person's overall health
19. life skills – tools for building a healthy life
20. coping – dealing with troubles or problems in an effective way.
21. symptom – a change that a person notices in his or her body or mind
22. depression – sadness and hopelessness that keeps a person from carrying out every day activities
23. eustress – positive stress

24. resiliency – the ability to recover form an illness or hardship
25. physical fitness – the ability of the body to carry out daily physical activities without getting out of breath, sore, or overly tired
26. chronic disease – a disease that develops gradually and continues over a long period of time
27. dehydration – a state in which the body has lost more water than has been taken in
28. sleep deprivation – lack of sleep
29. insomnia – the inability to sleep even if one is physically exhausted
30. intoxication – the physical and mental changes produced by drinking alcohol
31. drug – any substance that causes a change in a person's physical or psychological state
32. side effect – any effect that is caused by drugs and that is different from the intentional effect
33. carcinogens – chemicals or agents that cause cancer
34. side stream smoke – the smoke that escapes from the tip of a cigarette, cigar, or pipe
35. mainstream smoke – smoke that is inhaled through a tobacco product and exhaled by a tobacco smoker

Task 5

1. ONCOLOGY	**4.** PEDIATRICS	**7.** PATHOLOGY	**10.** PSYCHIATRY
2. GERIATRICS	**5.** DERMATOLOGY	**8.** INTERNAL MEDICINE	**11.** ANESTHESIOLOGY
3. ORTHOPEDICS	**6.** SURGERY	**9.** RADIOLOGY	

Task 6

1. supervise	**5.** outpatient	**9.** boost	**13.** incurable
2. rehabilitation	**6.** discharged	**10.** infectious	**14.** immunize
3. dress	**7.** administer	**11.** routine	**15.** increase
4. scope	**8.** preventive	**12.** intravenously	**16.** monitor

SPORT

Task 1

Sports	barriers	walks	tool	confidence	challenges
	levels	gaps	behaviours	awareness	work

Task 2

When participating in sport you can	fitness	patience
	endurance	fulfilment
	anxiety and depression	failures
	persistence	losses
	determination and competitiveness	abilities

Task 3

1 – L, 2 – G, 3 – A, 4 – E, 5 – O, 6 – C, 7 – F, 8 – D, 9 – J, 10 – B, 11 – M, 12 – H, 13 – N, 14 – K, 15 – I

SCHULE UND BILDUNG

Task 1

1.	2.	3.	4.	5.	6.	7.	8.	9.	10.	11.	12.	13.	14.	15.	16.	17.	18.	19.	20.
G	L	H	M	R	S	D	K	B	O	N	P	T	C	A	I	F	Q	J	E

Task 2

☐	attend		✔	prepare for
✔	cram for		✔	re-sit
✔	fail		✔	retake
✔	flunk	**an exam**	✔	revise for **an exam**
☐	make		✔	sit
☐	participate in		✔	take
✔	pass		✔	do well/badly in

Task 3

pupils	visit/attend a school/course/classes take/make a course/lessons	do/make progress	drop out/from of school are kept in for/after school
	pay/give attention	keep up on/with with their studies fall after/behind with their studies	are expelled of/from school
	learn from/by heart make/do their homework submit/admit an assignment	cheat in/by an exam	get thorough/through
		chat with/up their classmates make/do mistakes	get a place in/at a university do/make their doctorate

Task 4

teachers assign/set homework, admonish, downgrade, educate, examine, give lessons/feedback, instruct, motivate, praise, supervise, teach, test, upgrade …

ARBEITSWELT

Task 1

apply for, **do**, **find**, **get**, **have**, **look for**, **take** a job
do, **find**, **get**, **have**, **look for** work
work for a company
be on, **take** maternity leave/sick leave
work nine-to-five / **have** a nine-to-five job
do a job-share
take time off
do shift-work / **work** (in) shifts / to **be** a shift worker / to **be** on day shift/night shift

offer sb a job
He's only **doing** his job.
work in marketing
meet, **miss** a deadline
be on, **work** flexi-time
work regular/irregular/unsociable hours
work full-time, overtime, part-time

1. do – make	**3.** get – be	**5.** have – are – work	**7.** be	**9.** was – make
2. talk	**4.** have	**6.** be – do	**8.** go	**10.** work

Task 2

5. a person whose job it is to look after the documents in an office
8. a person who pays somebody to work for him
7. a person who is paid regularly to work for an organization
12. a person in an office who arranges meetings, makes phone calls, prepares letters
14. a person who works at home and uses a computer, the internet
11. a person whose job it is to help customers and sell things in a shop
10. a person whose job it is to organize and control the work
16. a person who spends most of his time working
13. a person who is in charge of an activity or a group of people
9. a senior manager in a business
2. a person whose work involves physical strength or skill with their hands
15. a person who works in an office rather than doing physical work.
6. a person whose job it is to manage all or part of a company
3. the person that other people have to obey.

Task 3

1. D – professions	**2.** B – vocation	**3.** A – career	**4.** C – benefits	**5.** D – wage

Task 4

1. apply for	**6.** flexible – core	**11.** downsizing	**16.** pension/retirement
2. employer	**7.** freelance – Freelance – socialise	**12.** sacked/sack	**17.** retire
3. interview – applicant – interviewer – employees	**8.** living – pursue	**13.** resign – fired – resign – dismisses – dismissal	**18.** retirement
4. interviewee	**9.** hierarchical	**14.** laid off	**19.** sick pay
5. pecking	**10.** culture	**15.** redundant	**20.** dead-end

Task 6

Being under stress **–**
benefits and compensation **+**
bonuses **+**
challenging work **+**
flexible work schedules, flexible hours **+**
generous incentive scheme **+**
high employee turnover **–**
high levels of stress **–**
job satisfaction, find work satisfying **+**
job security **+**
lack of hierarchy **–**
lack of training/development **–**

lack of transparency **–**
monotonous, repetitive work **–**
no room for advancement **–**
pressure **–**
promotion politics: if fair **+**
receive a promotion **+**
steady job **+**
think non-traditionally **+**
too much red tape **–**
unfair pay **–**
work longer hours **–**
work-life balance **+**

FREIZEITVERHALTEN

Task 1

1. What	**3.** What	**5.** What	**7.** What	**9.** What	**11.** Do	**13.** What	**15.** Are
2. Do	**4.** What	**6.** What	**8.** Which	**10.** What	**12.** Do	**14.** What	**16.** Do

Task 2

1. on playing	**5.** to playing	**9.** jogging	**13.** up – parachuting.	**16.** plucking
2. about collecting	**6.** fix	**10.** practising	**14.** by watching	**17.** staying in – doing
3. into exploring	**7.** travelling	**11.** organising	**15.** in arranging	**18.** Going to
4. for riding	**8.** in designing	**12.** creating – playing		

Task 3

1.	2.	3.	4.	5.	6.	7.	8.	9.	10.	11.	12.	13.	14.
B	L	K	G	C	M	I/A	N	H	J	A/I	E	F	D

KONSUMGESELLSCHAFT

Task 1

1.	experiences	5.	paradise	9.	reasonably-priced	14.	promotion
2.	memorabilia	6.	beaten path	10.	costly	15.	brand
3.	Impulse / impulse	7.	upmarket	11.	seductive	16.	talks
4.	second-hand	8.	1. retailer / 2. wholesaler	12.	Product placement	17.	prominently
				13.	discounts		

Task 2

1. J   2. H   3. E   4. A   5. I   6. K   7. B   8. L   9. G   10. C   11. F   12. D

Task 3

a life of luxury + affluent + afford + bankrupt – be loaded + broke – enough to get by – hard up – have money to burn +	haven't got a penny to her name – in the red – live from hand to mouth – live in poverty – live in the lap of luxury + make ends meet – make a good living + money is tight – on the breadline –	peanuts – prosperous + rolling in money + short of money – spend money like water + tighten our belts – wealthy + well-off + worth a fortune +

Task 4

1. I   2. F   3. B   4. H   5. J   6. A   7. D   8. G   9. E   10. C

Task 5

1. Money is extremely important, everything in the world would stop without money.
2. She has a lot of money and she wastes it by spending it foolishly.
3. A phrase used to refer to sb who has got a lot of money and power.
4. Money is neither plentiful nor easily obtained.
5. Babysitting is a very easy way of earning money.
6. It didn't cost any money.
7. You have to pay too much for parking.
8. Repairing a car is very expensive and costly.
9. They are extremely expensive.
10. The car is well worth the money spent on it.
11. She rose from a state of extreme poverty to one of great wealth.
12. They're always trying to *keep up with the Joneses*. They try to match the lifestyle of your neighbours.
13. to buy sth that costs much less than usual
14. The kids shop until they cannot physically do it anymore.

TRADITION UND WANDEL

Task 1

	traditional/tribal society	modern/complex society
life	living in small groups, hunting, gathering and simple farming, herding, tribal warfare, short life spans	populous societies, centralized state governments
strangers	no strong political leaders, no strangers, encountering strangers is frightening and dangerous, everybody knows everybody else	encounter strangers every day
production	small-scale, derived from indigenous and ancient cultural practices	industrial production, development of large-scale societies
subsistence, economy	production for use/subsistence, simple division of labor, cooperation; family, clan, village	production for profit, growth complex division of labor (specialization, differentiation) individualized, mechanized
consumption	satisfy basic needs, rituals	consumption needs, competitive consumerism
materials	accumulation for redistribution, collective ownership	cult of wealth, private ownership
pay	no work for pay, no contracts	pay for goods and services, contracts
possessions	few possessions, similar standard of living	many possessions, inequitable distribution of wealth and resources
ecology	subsistence, sacred land	exploitation of nature
transport	transport by humans or animals	machine transportation
diet	limited but nutritious	varied but questionable diet
community, communication	community cohesion; family important; face-to-face relations	social separation, little sense of community, family pulled apart, impersonal communication
lifestyle	more leisure, more time, time means lived life; spiritual focus, conversation	less leisure, no time, time is money; consumption replaces conversation

Task 2

1. D   **2.** H   **3.** K   **4.** F   **5.** I   **6.** C   **7.** A   **8.** J   **9.** E   **10.** G   **11.** B

TRANSPORT UND TOURISMUS

Task 1

On land		On water	Air transport
2 wheels	**4 wheels**		
bicycle/bike	ambulance	barge	airship
moped	school/shuttle/double-decker bus	cabin cruiser	(hot-air) balloon
motorbike	estate/family/saloon/sports car	canoe	helicopter
mountain bike	coach	(car) ferry	jet
racing bike	convertible	catamaran	light aircraft
scooter	fire engine	container ship	plane
	four-by-fours/four-wheel drive/	cruise ship	
	all-terrain vehicle (ATV)	dinghy	
	hatchback	fishing/rowing boat (rowboat)	
	horse and cart	hovercraft	
	juggernaut	hydrofoil	
	limousine	kayak	
	lorry (BE)/truck (AE)	lifeboat	
	minibus	liner	
	off-road car/vehicle	motor boat/speedboat	
	pick-up truck	oil tanker	
	slow/express/freight	punt	
	train	raft	
	tram	submarine	
	van	trawler	
		tug/tugboat	
		yacht	

Task 2

railway	buses	planes	
a return/round-trip ticket	(bus) lane	aisle	gate
a single ticket	(bus) line	board/boarding (pass/card)	go through customs
arrive at platform 1	(bus) ride/trip/journey	bumpy flight	hand luggage/baggage
buffet/restaurant car	(bus) route	business class	immigration officer
catch	(bus) service	cabin crew	landing
change at	catch	check-in desk	runway
change trains	miss a bus	conveyor belt	security check
compartment	It is full up.	departure lounge	stopover
to depart/leave from	run/come every 10 minutes	direct flight	take-off, to take off
late arrival	The children are bussed to school.	disembark	taxi
luggage rack		economy class	terminal
passengers		first class flight	window seat
platform		flight attendant	
through train			
ticket office			
weekly/monthly/annual season ticket			
window seat			

Task 3

	bus	train	plane	taxi	bicycle	car
person	driver	driver	pilot	driver	cyclist	driver
verb	drive	drive	fly	drive	ride	drive
noun	fare	fare	air fare	fare	—	—
verb	catch/take/ride AE	catch/take	take	take/get	go on (my)	go by
verb	get on/off	get on/off	get on/off	get in/out	get on/off	get in/out
using	go by bus	by train, by rail	by air, by plane	go by taxi	by bike	by car
place	bus station/coach station/bus stop	railway station	airport	taxi rank / AE cab stand	—	—

Task 4

1. after a long, difficult, hard time there is the promise of better things
2. can only think about a single subject
3. away from the common routes
4. to get rid of your energy by doing or saying something

5. one last drink before you start a journey
6. do something correctly/well
7. lost energy, interest or enthusiasm, so you did it less well
8. to go somewhere by his own efforts, without help

Task 5

1 – B, 2 – H, 3 – A, 4 – D, 5 – I, 6 – J, 7 – F, 8 – C, 9 – E, 10 – G

Task 6

1. Sustainable tourism
2. Adventure tourism
3. Ecotourism
4. Alternative tourism
5. safari –safari
6. globetrotter
7. Mass tourism
8. All-inclusive holidays
9. package tour
10. culture shock
11. half-board – full-board – self-catering
12. code of conduct

Task 7

1. a person who watches travel films on TV, reads books on travelling from the comfort of his armchair.
2. without taking many possessions.
3. have a holiday from work.
4. a place/situation where one feels completely happy and at ease.
5. to get back his strength and energy.
6. enjoy yourself very much.
7. not well known and far away from the places that people usually visit.
8. what you will do if everything else fails.
9. have a splendid time, have the best time ever.
10. when you travel, you learn a lot about the people, the places, the culture …

LANDESKUNDLICHE ASPEKTE

Task 1

1. comprises
2. capital
3. metropolitan
4. municipality
5. area
6. lies
7. borders
8. separates
9. populous
10. occupies
11. islands

Task 2

1. known
2. immigrated
3. derived
4. influenced
5. denotes – refers

Task 3

1. densely
2. residence
3. diverse
4. racial
5. ethnic

Task 4

1 – F, 2 – I, 3 – A, 4 – C, 5 – D, 6 – G, 7 – J, 8 – H, 9 – B, 10 – E

Task 5

1. Old English – Latin – Old Norse
2. English
3. English
4. Spanish
5. English – French
6. English

Task 6

1. predominantly – widely
2. frequently
3. broadly
4. commonly
5. authentically
6. heavily

Task 7

1. financial
2. significant
3. mechanised
4. capitalist
5. producer
6. recognised
7. wealthiest
8. service

Task 8

Like any **other** country, Britain is known to be full of customs and traditions that have existed **for** hundreds of years and are famous **all** over the world. But there's **more** to British customs than drinking tea or eating fish ‚n' chips. By the way, **it** is claimed that English people drink 165 million cups of tea every day. A typical English breakfast is said **to** consist of eggs, bacon, mushrooms, fried bread **and** baked beans. But **in** fact, English people are more **likely** to have some cereal, a slice of toast, a cup of coffee and a glass of orange juice for breakfast. When English people are waiting for a bus or to **be** served in a shop, they always **form** a nice queue and they can become very rude if you "**jump**" the queue. The British are not only said to **be** reserved in manners, dress and speech, they are also famous for their politeness, self-discipline and special sense **of** humour.

Task 9

1. practised
2. adults
3. agnostic, atheist
4. pluralism

KUNST UND KULTUR

Task 1

1. B – intervals
2. D – dress rehearsal
3. A – props
4. C – stalls
5. A – box office
6. D – aisle
7. C – usherette
8. D – prompter
9. B – conductor

Task 2

a. horror film
b. science fiction
c. weepy
d. animated cartoon
e. romantic comedy
f. fantasy film
g. documentary
h. thriller
i. epic
j. western
k. historical film
l. travelogue

Task 3

1. F   2. H   3. C   4. E   5. –   6. A   7. G   8. –   9. D   10. B

Task 4

1. C – stars
2. A – shot on location
3. C – based on
4. B – low-angle shot
5. A – dolly shot
6. C – cross-cutting
7. A – flashback
8. B – climax
9. C – special effects
10. B – gaffer
11. A – boom operator
12. B – art director

Task 5

noun	person	verb
edition	editor	edit
novel	novelist	—
play	playwright	write
poem/poetry	poet	—
art	artist	—
criticism	critic	criticize

noun	person	verb
acting	actor/actress	act
cast	cast	cast
composition	composer	compose
—	conductor	conduct
dance	dancer	dance
drama	dramatist	dramatize
—	prompter	prompt

Task 6

1. B   2. D   3. E   4. H   5. G   6. A   7. C   8. F

MEDIEN

Task 1

1. D   2. F   3. A   4. I   5. H   6. C   7. J   8. E

Task 2

1. scandal
2. advertisement
3. editorial
4. crossword
5. caption
6. headline
7. obituary
8. edition
9. feature
10. paparazzi

Task 3

1. –   2. B   3. D   4. F   5. E   6. C   7. A   8. –

1. –   2. E   3. C   4. A   5. F   6. D   7. –   8. B

Task 4

1. sitcoms
2. soap opera
3. documentaries
4. Telethons
5. chat show, talk show
6. news bulletin, newsflash
7. commercial
8. broadcast
9. announcer, newsreader/newscaster
10. presenter
11. live coverage
12. footage
13. makeover
14. break the news to
15. catch up on news

KOMMUNIKATION

Task 1

verb	abstract noun	noun (person)	adjective
challenge	challenge	challenger	challenged/challenging
chat, chatter	chat, chatter	chatterbox	chatty
communicate	communication	communicator	communicative
contact	contact	contact (C)	—
converse	conversation	conversationalist	conversational MIND: converse (=opposite)
express	expression	—	expressive, expressionless
gossip	gossip	gossiper	gossipy, gossiping
impress	impression	—	impressed, impressionable, impressive
inform	information (U)	informer, informant	informative, informal (=relaxed, friendly)
interact	interaction	—	interactive
message	message	messenger	—
perceive	perception	—	perceptive, perceptible
receive	reception	recipient, receiver	receptive, receiving
transmit	transmission, transmitter	—	—
verbalize	verbalization, verb	—	verbal

Task 2

| 1. I | 2. D | 3. F | 4. H | 5. L | 6. A | 7. G | 8. C | 9. K | 10. E | 11. J | 12. B |

Task 3

| 1. K | 2. F | 3. H | 4. D | 5. A | 6. L | 7. I | 8. C | 9. J | 10. E | 11. G | 12. B |

Task 4

| 1. J | 2. D | 3. B | 4. E | 5. H | 6. L | 7. K | 8. A | 9. G | 10. F | 11. C | 12. I |

Task 5

1. spending a long time getting to the main point.
2. tell me what has been worrying you.
3. talk about the most important thing, cut out all the small talk.
4. understand what someone is trying to tell you even if they are not expressing themselves directly, understand what sb wants you to do by their actions.
5. speak to you quickly.
6. heard news from sb who heard the news from sb else, often used when people are gossiping.
7. Just without telling anyone else, only you and I talk about this, nobody else.
8. having similar views, feelings or thoughts; thinking and acting in harmony.
9. say sth (to sb) in support of her.
10. hear sth from the person who has direct personal knowledge of it, who is involved.
11. the mother is extremely talkative, she talks without stopping.
12. talking fast without stopping.
13. not having any effect on her.
14. says sth directly and clearly, without trying to be diplomatic.

NATUR UND UMWELT

Task 1

coniferous forest
conservation area
deciduous forest
densely (heavily) populated

equatorial region
forest fire
hot desert
mountain range

national park
paddy field
polar region
sparsely (thinly) populated

tea plantation
thermal springs
tidal wave
volcanic eruption

Task 2

Verb	Noun (abstract)	Noun (person)	Adjective	Synonyms
consume	consumption, consumerism	consumer	consumable	eat, drink, use (up)
contaminate	contamination, contaminant	—	contaminated	pollute, poison
contribute	contribution	contributor	contributory	give, supply
destroy	destruction	destroyer	destructive	damage
dispose of	disposal of	—	disposable	throw away
emit	emission	emitter	—	give off
—	environment	environmentalist	environmental	surroundings, habitat
—	extinction	—	extinct	die out, no longer exist
influence	influence	—	influential	affect
pollute	pollution, pollutant	polluter	—	make sth dirty
recycle	recycling	—	recyclable	use sth again
reduce	reduction	reductionist	reducible	make sth smaller, lessen, diminish
sustain	sustainability	—	sustainable	support, maintain
threaten	threat	—	threatening	endanger, warn

Task 3

1. pollution – contaminants – pollution – harmful – smog
2. Nuclear waste
3. global warming – climatic/climate changes – sea-levels – ice caps – floods
4. ozone layer – radiation
5. Acid rain
6. "greenhouse effect" – carbon dioxide – atmosphere – carbon dioxide – fossil fuels – fossil fuels – deforestation – rainforests
7. toxic wastes – wastes
8. biodiversity – Deforestation
9. extinct – extinction – endangered
10. exhaust fumes
11. preserve – biodiversity
12. genetically modified – genetically modified – factory farmed

Task 4

tidal energy	preservation	bottle bank	sustainable	natural habitat
recycle	unleaded petrol	renewable energy	environmentalist	solar power

Task 5

An earthquake **shakes sth, hits sth, destroys sth, devastates sth, strikes sth.**
An avalanche **strikes sth, engulfes sb/sth.**
A blizzard **hits (sth), strikes (sth), blows, rages.**
A drought **affects sth.**
An epidemic **spreads rapidly, sweeps (sth), breaks out, strikes (sth).**
A famine **strikes.**
A fire **breaks out, starts, blazes, burns, rages, spreads, sweeps through sth, damages sth, destroys sth, guts sth, goes out, smoulders.**
A flood **hits sth, strikes sth, inundates sth, causes sth, subsides.**
A hurricane **hits sth, strikes (sth), damages sth, destroys sth, devastates sth, blows.**
A storm/a thunderstorm **hits sth, strikes sth, rages, is brewing, is coming, blows up, breaks, bursts, abates, blows itself out, subsides, batters sth, buffets sth, lashes sth, ravages sth, sweeps sth.**
A tornado/a typhoon/a cyclone **sweeps through sth, hits sth, strikes sth, damages sth, destroys sth, devastates sth.**
A volcano **erupts.**

MODERNE TECHNOLOGIE

Task 1

to **go** online	to **back** up your files	to **cut** and paste something
to **put** something on the Web	to **download** podcasts	to **enter** a web address
	to **sign** off a computer	to **surf** the Net

Task 2

1B, 2B, 3B, 4A, 5A, 6A

Task 3

1. technophile	**3.** automated	**5.** state-of-the-art
2. computer literate	**4.** outdated	**6.** high-tech

Task 4

1. firewall	**4.** IT	**7.** uploaded	**10.** satnav	**12.** WiFi hotspot
2. server	**5.** search engine	**8.** computer buff	**11.** digital natives	**13.** screensavers
3. applications	**6.** download	**9.** broadband		

PERSÖNLICHE ZUKUNFT, PLÄNE

Task 1

start leave go to enter	**school/college/ university**	take fail pass revise for	**an exam**	get	a certificate a degree a job a qualification a diploma married rich
make earn	**a lot of money**	have	children a family	start provide for	**a family**

Task 2

1 – C, 2 – I, 3 – B, 4 – J, 5 – D, 6 – A, 7 – E, 8 – G, 9 – H, 10 – K, 11 – F, 12 – L, 13 – N, 14 – M

Task 6

Things I want to have	Things I want to be	Things I want to feel	Things I want to do	Things I don't want to be
well paid job	healthy	love	work with my hands	stuck in a rut
estate car	wise	contentment	voluntary work	stuck behind a desk
power	content	joy	manual labour	dissatisfied
loving family	famous	job satisfaction	run my own business	stressed
good working conditions	successful	happiness	work full-time	
part-time job	independent		realize my dreams	
money	confident		start a family	
	my own boss			
	self employed			
	a good team player			
	knowledgeable			

INTERKULTURELLE ASPEKTE

Task 1

minority
multiculturalism
minority

melting pot (n.)
multiculturalism (n.)
melting pot (n.)

minority
melting pot (n.)
multiculturalism (n.)

Task 2

multicultural (adj.) people or ideas from many different countries, races, religions, languages and traditions
multiracial (adj.) made up of different races
multiethnic (adj.) people of several ethnic groups
marginalized (adj.) put in a powerless, unimportant position within a society/group

Task 3

1. D **2.** E **3.** C **4.** – **5.** A **6.** F **7.** – **8.** B

Task 4

1. Outback
2. Oz
3. Aussie
4. the Aboriginals/ Aborigines
5. tribe
6. civilisation
7. the Stolen Generations
8. walkabout
9. rite of passage
10. trial

Task 5

1. D **2.** F **3.** A **4.** I **5.** B **6.** H **7.** C **8.** E **9.** G

Task 6

1. G **2.** F **3.** A **4.** C **5.** H **6.** E **7.** D **8.** B

Task 7

verb/adjective	noun
to be prejudiced against/in favour of sb/sth, to have a prejudice	prejudice against/in favour of
to prejudge sb/sth	—
to be disadvantaged, to be at a disadvantage, sth puts sb at a disadvantage	disadvantage (of, to)
to be discriminated against, to discriminate against sb/sth	discrimination
to segregate sb from sth	segregation (U), segregationist
to desegregate	desegregation
to marginalize/marginal	marginalization
tolerant/intolerant	tolerance (U)/intolerance (U):
to oppress	oppression
to be inferior or superior to others	inferiority (U)/superiority (U) in sth
inequitable/equitable	inequality - equality
to deny sb sth	denial
—	civil rights movement, struggle for equal rights
—	non-violent protests

Task 8

1. D **2.** F **3.** – **4.** A **5.** E **6.** B **7.** – **8.** C

Task 9

Let's have a look at human rights violations. It should be everybody's duty to prevent majority-minority tensions from developing into conflict. There **is** no **security** without **human** rights, **and that, of** course, **includes** minority **rights**, too. **Integration** involves **responsibilities** and **rights** on **both** sides. **Education** should **provide** children **with the necessary** skills **to** live **in** a multi-**ethnic** society. **Prejudices** create **stereotypes** which **are** built **on** distorted **images** of **people**. At **last** I'll **explain** to **you** the Jim Crow **law**, which **enforced** racial **segregation** by **preventing** black **people** from **drinking** water **from the same** water **fountains** as **a** white **person** could. **Therefore**, blacks **were** denied **the** same **rights** as **the** whites.

ERWACHSENWERDEN UND IDENTITÄTSFINDUNG

Task 1

1. close-knit family.
2. sibling rivalry
3. Family gatherings – bond with
4. striking resemblance
5. stable home environment
6. lot in common

Task 2

1 – J, 2 – A, 3 – H, 4 – F, 5 – K, 6 – O, 7 – M, 8 – E, 9 – G, 10 – C, 11 – B, 12 – D, 13 – L, 14 – N, 15 – P, 16 – Q, 17 – I

Task 3

1. OBEDIENT	4. GIFTED	7. NAUGHTY	10. SICKLY	13. NEGLECTED
2. WELL-BEHAVED	5. DISOBEDIENT	8. SULKY	11. ABANDONED	14. ILLEGITIMATE
3. BRIGHT	6. MISCHIEVOUS	9. WILFUL	12. ABUSED	

Task 4

ROLE MODELS

A role model is someone who demonstrates a particular behaviour, skill, or social	✔
role for another person to emulate. Role models might **have** emerge because of character	have
and conduct or because of particular skills and talents. **Unlike** pop stars, actors, sportsmen –	unlike
they are all role models who can have a positive or a negative effect on children. Young	✔
people not only look up to them and hold them **up** in high esteem, they also copy their	up
actions, mannerisms and behaviours. Positive role models are **not** important because they	not
set examples for people to observe and follow **on**. When people increase positive	on
behaviours, they also increase their feelings of self-worth. Patterning **to** behaviours from	of
positive role models can also help people build positive values. Positive role models	✔
provide **for** a sense of hope and show that dreams and goals can be fulfilled. They feel a	for
sense of **a** duty to work for the common good of the community. Not only are they	a
compassionate, peaceful, and trustworthy, they also possess **in** high standards and	in
values. They are committed to what they do and can work through challenges.	✔
Although they are **be** admired for their courage and strength, they remain humble and	be
modest. However, **if** there are also negative role models. Every day newspapers feature	if
reports about instances of **much** questionable behaviour from celebrities: from betting	much
scandals to doping, from racist remarks to violent outbursts. Children also **try** copy the	try
language and fashion of their role models and – in the case of negative idols – might	✔
end up **with** speaking or dressing inappropriately for their age.	with

POLITIK UND INSTITUTIONEN DES ÖFFENTLICHEN LEBENS

Task 1

1. politics	4. politics	7. policy	10. politics	13. policies
2. politicians	5. politics	8. apolitical	11. policy	14. politics
3. apolitical	6. politics	9. unpolitical	12. policy	15. political

Task 2

to appoint sb **to** a post	to be elected **to** a committee	to be eligible **to** vote
to buy **off** a politician	to be **on** shaky ground	to bring sth **under** control
to run **for** office/president	to campaign **for** sb	to have a say **in** sth
to take advantage **of** sb	to draw **up** a bill	to stay **in** office
	to go **to** the polls	to throw support **behind** sth
	to have the backing **of** one's party	
	to lose sight **of** sth	

Task 3

1. oligarchy	3. candidate	5. autocratic	7. opposed	9. executive
2. republic	4. eligible	6. voting	8. election	

Task 4

1 – B, 2 – D, 3 – A, 4 – C

Task 5

Act of Parliament	verabschiedetes **Gesetz**
administration	Verwaltung, Organisierung
administrative **staff**	Verwaltungspersonal
adult **citizen**	volljährige(r) Bürger(in)
ballot box	**Wahlurne**
ballot paper	**Stimmzettel**
civil servant	Staatsbeamter/-beamtin
constituency	**Wahlkreis**
decision-making	Entscheidungsfindung
domestic policy	Innenpolitik
first-past-the-post system	**Mehrheitswahlrecht**
foreign **policy**	Außenpolitik
polling **station**	Wahllokal
proportional representation	Verhältniswahlrecht
taxation	Besteuerung
universal **suffrage**	allgemeines Wahlrecht

Task 6

1 – D, 2 – J, 3 – F, 4 – C, 5 – G, 6 – B, 7 – H, 8 – E, 9 – I, 10 – A

1 – F, 2 – C, 3 – D, 4 – E, 5 – B, 6 – A

Task 7

1. ballot   **2.** policies   **3.** ran for   **4.** bill   **5.** turnout   **6.** vote

Task 8

1. polling station   **2.** register   **3.** votes   **4.** hung   **5.** swing   **6.** Floating   **7.** ratings

Task 9

parliament – a national representative body having supreme legislative powers within the state
coalition – a form of government in which several parties cooperate
majority – the political party, group, or faction having the most power by virtue of its larger representation or electoral strength
minority – a group or party having fewer than a controlling number of votes
constitution – a system of fundamental laws and principles that prescribes the nature, functions, and limits of a government
electorate – all the people who are eligible to vote in an election
separation of powers – a model of governance under which the state is divided into branches, each with separate and independent powers and
areas of responsibility so that no one branch has more power than the other branches
  • the executive branch has sole responsibility for the daily administration of the state bureaucracy
  • the legislative branch has the power to pass, amend, and repeal laws
  • the judicial branch is the system of courts that interprets and applies the law in the name of the state
checks and balances – the system of dividing power among the three branches of government (executive, legislative, and judicial) to prevent any
one from having too much power
fishing expedition – an investigation by one party seeking damaging information about another
ideology – an integrated system of ideas about politics, values, and culture
left-wing – liberal
lobby – a group seeking to influence an elected official
nomination – when a political party chooses its official candidate for a particular office
political suicide – an action that is likely to be so unpopular with voters as to cause a politician's probable loss in the next election
poll – a survey used to gauge public opinion concerning issues or to forecast an election
primary – a state election in which party members vote for a candidate from within their party
red tape – government paperwork and procedures that are slow and difficult
spin – a politician's attempt to shape the way the public looks at an issue, much the way a tennis player uses spin to direct the ball (political
advisers who spin are known as „spin doctors")

DIE GLOBALISIERTE WELT

Task 1

type of globalisation	economic	technological	cultural	criminal
technological	environmental	criminal	economic	economic
cultural	political	environmental	political	

Task 2

1. G   **2.** E   **3.** D   **4.** A   **5.** F   **6.** C   **7.** H   **8.** B

Task 3

	+/-		+/-
People can improve their standard of living	+	Loss of individuality	–
Instant communication	+	Global spread of information	+
Respect for cultural identities	+	Migration to richer countries has increased	–
Gap between rich and poor countries grow	–	More efficient, less polluting technologies	+
Creativity and innovation are encouraged	+	Brain drain of skilled workers	–
Indigenous and national culture and languages can disappear	–	Freedom of trade, barriers between countries are removed	+
Greater chance of spreading diseases worldwide, e.g. AIDS, bird flu, Ebola	–	Factories are built because environmental laws are not as strict as they are at home	–
Interests of the richest countries dominate world trade at the expense of developing countries	–	TNCs bring wealth and foreign currency to local economies when they buy local resources, products, services	+
labour intensive industries take advantage of cheaper labour costs	+	Profits of TNCs are sent back to mother countries	–
People and goods can travel more quickly, costs have decreased	+	LEDCs provide the North with cheap labour and raw materials	–

AI – Amnesty International	NGO – Non Governmental Organization
IMF – International Monetary Fund	TNC – Transnational Company
LEDC – Less Economically Developed Countries	WTO – World Trade Organization

Task 4

1. Sweatshops
2. human rights
3. brands
4. cash crop
5. child labour
6. free trade
7. fair trade
8. shrinking world
9. headquarters
10. wages
11. increases

MENSCHENRECHTE

Task 1

The Universal Declaration of **Human** Rights is the general statement of human **rights** principles and sets **out** a list of basic rights for everybody whatever their **race**, sex, colour, religion, language, opinion, property, **origin** and birth. It was **adopted** in 1948 and from then on the UN **drafted** a lot of **treaties** and declarations. It is important that all **people** are careful about the **violations** of human rights. Human rights need to be **protected** by every **individual**. We must **assert** our right to **speak** and to be heard.

Task 2

1. E
2. C
3. A
4. –
5. –
6. F
7. B
8. D

Task 3

verb	noun (abstract)	noun (person)
to migrate	migration	migrants
to immigrate	immigration	immigrant
to emigrate	emigration	emigrant
to alienate	alienation, alienage, alienism	alien
—	foreignness	foreigner
—	asylum	asylum seeker
—	citizenship	citizen
—	refuge	refugee
to deport	deportation	deportee
to expel	expulsion	—
to persecute	persecution	persecutor
to flee	—	fugitive
to escape	escape	escapee

Task 4

1. B
2. C
3. F
4. –
5. A
6. –
7. D
8. E

1. D
2. F
3. B
4. A
5. –
6. C
7. E
8. –

Task 5

push factors affecting forced migration:		pull factors:
years of hardship	natural disasters	to stream into the promised land
racial discrimination	lack of food, famine	hope for a better life
persecution	harshness of their lives	opportunity for working
war	extreme poverty	better-paid jobs
forced labour, slavery	being pushed out of a country	
overpopulation		

GESELLSCHAFTLICHE GRUPPIERUNGEN

Task 1

1. D
2. F
3. A
4. H
5. C
6. B
7. E
8. G

REGELN, VORSCHRIFTEN, GESETZE

Task 1

Crime	Criminal	What does he do?
abduction	**abductor**	abducts people
arson	arsonist	puts sth on fire
assault	**assailant**	assaults people
bribery	**briber**	bribes people
burglary	burglar	**burgles** houses
drug dealing drug **trafficking**	drug dealer drug trafficker	deals with drugs traffics in drugs
forgery	forger	forges sth
fraud	**fraudster**	deceives people
hooliganism	hooligan	
human trafficking	human **trafficker**	illegally moves people
manslaughter	manslayer	kills people

money laundering	money **launderer**	launders money
mugging	mugger	**mugs** people
murder/homicide	**murderer**	murders people
perjury	perjurer	perjures himself
pimping	**pimp**	pimps sb to sb
rape	**rapist**	rapes people
robbery	robber	**robs** people/places
speeding	**speeder**	speeds
tax dodging	tax **dodger**	dodges taxes
theft	thief	steals things
torture	**torturer**	tortures people
vandalism	vandal	**vandalizes** sth

Task 2

1. charge
2. fine
3. broken the law

4. guilty.
5. life sentences
6. statement

7. innocent
8. evidence
9. sentenced

10. parole
11. acquitted

12. verdict
13. jury

Task 3

1. trial
2. victim
3. testified
4. plaintiff

5. witnesses
6. investigating
7. prosecution
8. hearsay

9. convicted
10. bail
11. cross-examination

12. alibi
13. custody
14. Capital

15. offence
16. evidence
17. verdict

Task 4

Criminals	Law courts	Sentences & Punishments	
accused	appeal	community service	license suspension
arsonist	defence	corporal punishment	life in prison
burglar	evidence	death penalty	prison sentence
defendant	inquiry	find sb innocent/guilty	put sb on probation
forger	judge	fine	release on bail
juvenile offender	jury	house arrest	suspended sentence
	lawyer	imprisonment	verdict
	offence	jail time	
	prosecution		
	testimony		
	trial		

Task 5

1 – Q, 2 – G, 3 – T, 4 – M, 5 – C, 6 – N, 7 – A, 8 – H, 9 – K, 10 – L, 11 – R, 12 – D, 13 – P, 14 – O, 15 – I, 16 – U, 17 – F, 18 – B, 19 – J, 20 – E, 21 – S

Task 6

1 – G, 2 – O, 3 – L, 4 – A, 5 – J, 6 – B, 7 – N, 8 – D, 9 – P, 10 – F, 11 – M, 12 – E, 13 – K, 14 – C, 15 – Q, 16 – I, 17 – H

GRAMMAR

Adjective – Adverb

1. Tom acted **unbelievably stupidly** at Muriel's wedding. (*unbelievably* – vor Adjektiven oder anderen Adverben; *stupidly* – bezieht sich auf das Verb *act* – wie hat er etwas gemacht)
2. ✓ The weather was **excellent** while we were on holiday. (nach *to be* folgt immer das Adjektiv)
3. ✓ He laughed **loud/loudly** at the joke. (beide Formen sind richtig, *loudly* wird in formellem Kontext bevorzugt)
4. Sophie stared **directly** back at him. (*directly* = straight; *direct* = without stopping)
5. ✓ She has never felt so **confident**. (nach *feel* folgt das Adjektiv)
6. Wearing this black dress, she thought she looked really **good**. (*well* bedeutet gesund; *look* = aussehen)
7. The hotels in LA are **extremely expensive** but ours was **reasonably cheap**. (*extremely, reasonably* beziehen sich auf die folgenden Adjektive; *expensive, cheap* beziehen sich auf *to be*)
8. ✓ The customer became **violent** when the manager asked him to leave. (nach *become* folgt das Adjektiv)
9. Sue waved her hands around **in a lively manner/way/fashion**. (Adjektive, die auf -ly enden, bilden das Adverb nicht mit -ly, sondern werden in eine präpositionale Phrase umgewandelt)
10. Have you seen John **lately**? (*lately* = recently)

Articles, Determiners, Pronouns

1. **Each** of the children has a wonderful souvenir for their parents. (*every*, *each* + singular noun; *each of* + plural noun)
2. Sadly, there were **few** people at the funeral. (*a few* = ein paar, genügend; *few* = wenige, nicht genug)

3. Many people are afraid of **death**. (kein Artikel bei abstrakten Begriffen ohne nähere Bestimmung)
4. **Both** players were warned, but **neither** of them took it seriously. (*either* = einer von zweien; das Verb danach steht im Singular; *both* = beide; das Verb danach steht im Plural; *neither* = keiner von beiden; *none* = keiner aus einer Gruppe)
5. **None of us wanted** to play. (*none of* = keiner aus einer Gruppe von drei oder mehr)
6. **Most people** believe that **marriage** and **family life** are the cornerstones of **society**. (*the most* nur beim Superlativ; *most* = die meisten; kein Artikel bei abstrakten Begriffen ohne nähere Bestimmung)
7. **Unemployment** is a serious problem nowadays. (kein Artikel bei abstrakten Begriffen ohne nähere Bestimmung)
8. Don't hesitate to call me **anytime** you like. (*anytime* = wann immer du willst)
9. They were talking for *a long time,* but the problem was that they were not really listening to **each other**. (*listening to each other* = einander zuhören; *listening to themselves* = sich selbst zuhören)
10. This friend of **ours** has got **his own** yacht. (*ours* = Possessivpronomen; *us* = Objektpronomen; *own* + Possessivpronomen, nicht mit Artikel)

Comparative Adjectives and Adverbs

1. If you can't swim **faster than** that, you're going to lose.
2. ... but I found them much **friendlier/more friendly than** I had expected.
3. Nowadays everybody dresses **more informally**.
4. **The earliest** I can come is nine o'clock.
5. His **latest** film was his **least** successful – a total flop!
6. If Mary had **as few** meals **as** Pam, she would be **thinner**.
7. His **elder** sister keeps getting **fatter** and **fatter**. And **the more** she eats **the more depressed** she becomes.
8. ... **the furthest/farthest** he has ever been is Italy.
9. Tim did badly but his friend did even **worse**.
10. ... could you speak **more slowly**, please!

Conditionals and Wish-Sentences

1. **B would have been** (*third conditional* – die Situation ist bereits vorbei und nicht mehr zu ändern)
2. **D passes** (*first conditional* – mögliche Handlung in der Zukunft)
3. **A had** (*wish + past tense* um Missfallen, Bedauern bezüglich einer gegenwärtigen Situation auszudrücken)
4. **C melts** (*zero conditional* mit *present tense* im Hauptsatz – allgemeine Gültigkeit, Naturgesetz)
5. **A wouldn't be** (*mixed conditional* – eine vergangene Handlung hat Auswirkung auf die Gegenwart)
6. **B had** (*second conditional* – unwahrscheinliche Handlung in der Gegenwart oder Zukunft)
7. **C had known** (*wish + past perfect tense* um Bedauern bezüglich einer vergangenen Situation auszudrücken)
8. **D would stop** (*wish + would* um auszudrücken, welches Verhalten man sich von anderen erwarten/wünschen würde)
9. **D leave** (*unless* statt *if ... not + present tense* um Konsequenzen gegenwärtiger Handlungen auszudrücken)
10. **B might have come** (*third conditional*, die Situation ist bereits vorbei und nicht mehr zu ändern; *might* oder *could* können statt *would* verwendet werden)

Gerund – Infinitive

1. Do **you regret not finishing** your studies?
2. Susan does **not mind Mary coming** as well.
3. Tom **suggests taking the bus**. (*suggest* nie mit Infinitiv!)
4. I **look/am looking forward to seeing** him again.
5. Mum **remembers posting the letter** I wrote. (*to remember doing sth* = sich daran erinnern, etwas getan zu haben; *to remember to do sth* = daran denken, dass man etwas tun muss)
6. Jack **insisted on catching** the next train.
7. The singer **was worth waiting for**.
8. This door **appears to be locked**.
9. I **stopped to speak to** my brother. (*to stop to do sth* = stehenbleiben, innehalten, um etwas (anderes) zu tun; *to stop doing sth* = aufhören etwas zu tun)
10. The noise **prevented Phil (from) hearing** what they said.

Modals

1. **Do you really have to/Must you really make** so much noise? (*Musst* du so viel Lärm *machen*!)
2. I **must/have to/need to/should know** more about the problem. (Ich *muss/sollte* mehr darüber *wissen*.)
3. In Austria, school children **don't have to/don't need to/needn't/haven't got to wear** uniforms. (Sie *brauchen/müssen keine* Uniformen *tragen*.)
4. You **needn't have brought** your umbrella. (Du *hättest* ihn *nicht mitbringen müssen*.)
5. **Did you have to shout** at her like that? (*Musstest* du sie so *anschreien*?)
6. Don't worry, he **can't have seen** you. (Er *kann* dich *nicht gesehen haben*.)
7. ... the journey **may/might/could take** hours. (Sie *könnte* Stunden *dauern*.)
8. We really **should/ought to/must/have to spend** more time with her. (Wir *sollten/müssen* mehr Zeit mit ihr *verbringen*.)
9. All my friends **are allowed to/may/can be** there until ten. – You **are not allowed to/may not/must not stay** out after dark! (Sie *dürfen/können* dort *bleiben*. – Du *darfst nicht ausbleiben*.)
10. I **might/may have misheard** the name. (Ich *könnte/kann* mich *verhört haben*.)

Nouns – Countable and Uncountable

1. Five **beers** and two **coffees**, please. (zählbar)
2. Nowadays it is not easy to find a **job**. (*a job* = zählbar; *work* = unzählbar)
3. The lady at the tourist information desk was very helpful. She gave us some very useful **advice**. (unzählbar)
4. The team **are** not going to win again. **They are** useless. (Das Verb wird im Plural verwendet, wenn das Team als Sammlung von Einzelnen gesehen wird.)

5. The team *is* at the bottom of the second division. (Das Verb wird im Singular verwendet, wenn das Team als Einheit gesehen wird.)
6. Have you got a copy of the complete *works* of Shakespeare? (= a work of art)
7. Would you like some *fruit* after dinner? (= Obst, Einheit)
8. Fish and chips *is* not a very healthy meal. (ein Gericht, eine Einheit)
9. The United States *has* a very violent history. (Ländername, Einheit)
10. For further *information* apply to the manager. (unzählbar)

Passive

1. A lot of new roads *are now being built* (by the government).
2. Another terrorist *has just been arrested* (by the police).
3. *Will this article be published* in the (their) next issue?
4. The new bridge *will have been constructed* by the end of the month.
5. The attic *hadn't been cleaned* in years.
6. Our car *couldn't be used* because it *was being seviced*.
7. He *was told* to finish his experiments by Monday.
8. A new (company) branch *is going to be opened* in Rome.
9. He *should have been asked* first.
10. Every effort *was being made* to come to an agreement.

Phrasal Verbs

1. I've *run out of* eggs and cheese. I'm going to the supermarket for some.
2. When Karen was rummaging through the attic, she *came across* her old school books.
3. Jane and Julian were already *looking forward to* their wedding, but then they had to *put it off* because the bride's father was in the hospital.
4. Thieves *got away with* Munch's *The Scream* and were never found.
5. Tommy doesn't *get along* with his brother; they have little in common.
6. They don't want to *put up with* their neighbour's dirt any longer. They're going bananas.
7. While we were in New York, we *called on* the Raymonds.
8. Nobody should *look down on* mentally handicapped people just because they are different.
9. He bought her a Porsche to try to *make up for* his infidelity.
10. Nowadays it's hard to *keep up with* all the latest breakthroughs in medicine, but as far as I know scientists have failed so far to *come up with* an explanation for cancer.

Prepositions

1. *in* time; *on* time (*in time* = early enough; *on time* = nicht zu spät, zu dem erwarteten Zeitpunkt)
2. *in* the end; *at* the end of (*in the end* = schließlich; *at the end of* = am Ende des/der …)
3. *in* the city centre; *on* the outskirts; *in* the open air; *in* the sky
4. *at* eight o'clock; *in* the morning; *on* a fine sunny morning; *on* a trip; *to* the country
5. *into* Baker Street; *towards* her; *at* the next crossroads
6. *by* public transport; *in* a taxi; *on* the bus
7. *until* Monday; *by* Saturday (*he'll be away until Monday* = er wird am Montag zurück sein; *she'll be back by Saturday* = sie wird bis spätestens Samstag zurückkommen, vielleicht aber auch schon früher)
8. *while* we were; *in* Paris; *at* a wonderful hotel; *during* our stay; *on* a tiny Greek Island; *on* the beach (*while* leitet einen Nebensatz ein, daher folgt darauf ein Verb; *during* ist eine Präposition, daher steht danach ein Substantiv)
9. *of* my family; *in* the picture; *to* America; *at* the age of 14; *in* the corner
10. *by* credit card; *at* home; *in* cash

Questions, Negations, Tag Questions

1. *How* is your sister today? Is she better? Let's go for a walk, shall we?
2. *What does* your younger sister look like? She resembles Kate Hudson, doesn't she?
3. *What size* shoes do you wear? Have you tried the shoes one size bigger?
4. *Didn't you study* at New York University? You didn't fly to Hawaii, did you?
5. *Who do* you want to speak *to*? Have you talked to the personnel manager yet?
6. *Who offered* you a job?
7. *Didn't* you catch her in the gym this morning?
8. I am late, *aren't I*?
9. You want to look good, *don't you*?
10. He has never been to Australia, *has he*? When do you recommend is the best time to go there?

Relative Clauses

1. Harry, *whose* parents had died and *who* then lived with the Dursleys, was brought up in a cupboard under the stairs, *where* he did not feel very comfortable. (*non-defining relative clause*, zusätzliche Information, die aber nicht notwendig ist, um das Nomen eindeutig abzugrenzen, deswegen Kommas; *who* – weil Harry eine Person ist; *whose* ist besitzanzeigend, Genitiv; *where* bezieht sich auf den Ort)
2. Matilda is the most extraordinary girl *(that)* I have (ever) read about. (nach Superlativen *that*; kann weggelassen werden)
3. The Orient Express is a famous train *which/that* runs between Vienna and Paris. (*which* und *that* beziehen sich auf ein Ding, kein Komma bei *defining relative clauses*: Zusatzinformation ist notwendig zur eindeutigen Unterscheidung)
4. Rosemary, *whose* blond hair was all over her face, wore a canary yellow cardigan, *which* Tommy had bought on their honeymoon in California. (*whose* – besitzanzeigend; *which* – bezieht sich auf ein Ding, darf nicht weggelassen werden, da *non-defining relative clause*, deswegen Kommas und deswegen darf man auch *that* nicht einsetzen!)
5. The window was at the back of the house *behind which* there was a golden field of wheat.
6. The only thing *that* made him sad was saying goodbye to his children. (*that* – wegen *only*)

7. Ellie, *who* Richie has always dreamt of, works in a shop *which/that* sells handicrafts and self-made jewellery. (= *informal*); Ellie, *of whom* Richie has always dreamt, works in a shop *which/that* sells handicrafts and self-made jewellery. (= *formal*) (*who/of whom* beziehen sich auf eine Person; Komma, weil es ein *non-defining relative clause* ist, und deswegen kann *who* auch nicht weggelassen werden; *which* und *that* beziehen sich auf ein Ding; kein Komma bei *defining relative clauses*)

8. Ned turned and walked away, *which* made her very angry. (*which* bezieht sich auf den ganzen Satz vorher)

9. The gift shop sells these gorgeous notebooks, *two of which* I have already bought. (*non-defining*, deswegen Kommas; *which* bezieht sich auf ein Ding; vergleiche auch: *most of whom*)

10. The old man *(who/that)* Maggie looked after for a year died last Sunday, *when* big fireworks took place. (= *informal*); The old man *after whom* Maggie looked for a year died last Sunday, *when* big fireworks took place. (= *formal*) (*who/that* kann bei *defining relative clauses* weggelassen werden, nicht aber, wenn die Präposition vor dem *relative pronoun* steht; *when* bezieht sich auf Zeitangabe; Komma weil *non-defining relative clause*)

Reported Speech

1. Jude **complained** that she was so depressed because first of all, Cliff had still given her no hint as to what was going on between them.

2. I **advised** her to ask him and to talk to him. I **encouraged** her not to sit around brooding.

3. Jude **promised/agreed** (that) she would (or: Jude promised/agreed to try). When Cliff/he came back from his business trip, she would clarify everything. Secondly, Jude/she had put on weight since Christmas and she couldn't fasten the buttons of her Levi's jeans any more.

4. I **persuaded** her to write down everything she had eaten and check if she had stuck to the diet.

5. Jude **replied** that I should know that she liked picking and mixing different diets. And thirdly, on New Year's Eve she had intended to stop smoking. Now she is/was smoking 20 cigarettes a day (der Sprecher redet über eine gegenwärtige Situation, die in der jetzigen Sprechsituation noch immer gilt. Die Zeit muss nicht unbedingt geändert werden). She **asked** (me)/**wanted to know** what she should do.

6. I **admitted** that she couldn't go on like that. I **suggested** that she should stop thinking about all that. Finally, I **invited** her to go out with you and me tonight.

7. She **murmured** that it was a good idea. She **asked/wanted to know** what time we were meeting.

8. I **told** her seven thirty at Café Paris and advised her not to worry.

9. Then Jude **asked/wanted to know** how the candlelight dinner with George had been the day before and if/whether we had enjoyed ourselves.

10. I **answered** that it had been fantastic and I had been on cloud nine.

Tenses

Present Tense:

1. I can't talk now. I **am driving** (*present progressive*: Handlung findet gerade im Moment des Sprechens statt)

2. Charles **is living** with some friends (*present progressive*: temporäre, vorübergehende Situation), until he **finds** a flat (*present simple* nach *when, as soon as, until*)

3. My parents **live** in Manchester. (*present simple*: permanente Situation)

4. Rainfall **results** from warm air, which **contains** water vapour. (*present simple*: Tatsachen, Fakten)

5. It **is costing** the Millers a fortune at the moment to … (*present progressive*: temporär, eine bestimmte Zeit lang)

6. It **costs** a fortune to fly first-class to Sydney. (*present simple*: Zustand)

7. Our neighbour's son **is constantly having** parties until five in the morning. (*present progressive + always*: wiederholte Handlung, über die wir unseren Unmut äußern)

8. Campbell **passes** to Almunia who **shoots** … (*present simple*: Sportberichte). Arsenal **are attacking** much more in the second half. (*present progressive*: Hintergrundereignisse)

9. Robert **is thinking** of moving to California. (*present progressive*: Handlung findet im Moment statt; *think* bedeutet hier: *nachdenken über*, daher kann es in die ing-Form gesetzt werden)

10. Up to a million people **gather** in Times Square every New Year's Eve. (*present simple*: regelmäßige, gewohnheitsmäßige Handlung – jedes Jahr)

The Future:

1. Peter and Mary **are coming**. (*present progressive*: definitive, fixierte Abmachung)

2. Wait here and I **will ('ll) get** you a plaster. (*will-future*: erst zum Zeitpunkt des Sprechens entschieden, nicht vorher)

3. The game **is starting** at 7.05 pm. (*present progressive*: genaue, fixe Abmachung)

4. I **will be having** my gym lesson then. (*future progressive*: zu einem bestimmten Zeitpunkt in der Zukunft wird man gerade dabei sein, das zu machen)

5. The plane **leaves** at … and **arrives** … (*present simple*: genaue Abflugs- und Ankunftszeit laut Fahrplan)

6. I've decided that we **are going** to recycle. (*going-to-future*: Absicht, Plan, man hat bereits entschieden)

7. I **will phone** him later. (*will-future*: spontane Entscheidung zum Zeitpunkt des Sprechens)

8. Don't worry! Before they get here, I **will have finished** painting the windows. (*future perfect*: zu einem bestimmten Zeitpunkt in der Zukunft wird das beendet sein)

9. The lion **will become** extinct in 20 years. (*will-future*: Voraussage, die auf Erfahrung oder eigener Meinung beruht; eine Zeitangabe ist auch notwendig)

10. What **are you going to buy** with the money you won? (*going-to-future*: Frage nach der Absicht, den Plänen)

Past Tense and Present Perfect Tense:

1. I am writing in reply to the advertisement **which appeared on 2 November.** (*past simple*: bestimmter Zeitpunkt)

2. Your bike looks very clean. – **Have you washed it?** (*present perfect simple*: Ergebnis wird betont)

3. Paul lives in Edinburgh. I think **he has lived there all his life.** (*present perfect simple*: er lebt noch immer dort)

4. I'm not really sure but **I think I first met him nine years ago.** (*past simple*: bestimmter Zeitpunkt)

5. When Frank came home last night, **his wife was waiting for him.** (*past progressive*: lange Handlung, die unterbrochen wird)

6. Now look at you! You're all covered in dirt! **Of course I am! I have been cleaning the cellar!** (*present perfect progressive*: die Handlung, nicht das Ergebnis wird betont)

7. How is your brother? – I have no idea **I haven't heard from him for ages.** (*present perfect simple*: Handlung dauert bis jetzt an)

8. I am starving because **I havent' eaten anything today.** (*present perfect simple*: Ergebnis)

9. When and where **were you born?** (*past simple*: abgeschlossene Handlung zu einem bestimmten Zeitpunkt)

10. You really should smoke less, **you have been smoking too much recently.** (*present perfect progressive*: Handlung dauert noch an)

Past Tense and Past Perfect Tense:

1. It *was* about half past eight on a rainy November night and Mr and Mrs Brown *had gone* to bed early.
2. They *had put out* all the lights and *were just going* to sleep when Mrs Brown *heard* a strange noise coming from downstairs.
3. Mr Brown *got up* to investigate.
4. When he *reached* the bottom of the stairs, he *noticed* that the noise *was coming* from the living room, and it *sounded* as if somebody *was trying* to open the window that *led* into the garden.
5. Mr Brown *was* really scared, but he *gathered up* his courage, *picked up* an old walking stick and *tiptoed* into the living room.
6. When he *got* to the window, he *peered* cautiously round the edge of the curtain. He *was* relieved to see that the noise *was* nothing more than a branch of a bush scraping against the window.
7. Meanwhile, however, the Brown's dog, who *had been sleeping* in the kitchen, *had also woken up* and *had silently followed* Mr Brown into the living room.
8. While Mr Brown *was looking out* the window, the dog *crept up* behind him and *rubbed* his nose against his master's ankle.
9. This *gave* Mr Brown such a surprise that he *lost* his balance and *fell* against the window, breaking the glass and cutting his hand.
10. He *swore* at the dog and *kicked* it out of the room.

Word Order

1. *He could regularly hear* his father's deep voice reading to them on winter evenings.
2. The *frightened* people hid in the cellars until the attack was over.
3. ✓ On the one hand he can become absolutely furious and on the other hand he is under the immensely strong influence of his wife.
4. He gave her a *beautiful big round red wooden jewellery box* for her birthday.
   Opening the present, she stammered she had never seen such a gorgeous box before.
5. When *they finally parted* she drove *the 30 kilometres back to her parents*.
6. ✓ Jenny was never any good at hiding her true feelings.
   ✓ What is more, she hates being laughed at.
7. They waited *silently in the station for an hour*.
   But the people outside where freezing to death.
8. We flew to New York in August. Austrian Airlines fly there *daily*.
   New York is an exciting place to live in.
9. ✓ She wanted to move abroad, but her parents tried to talk her out of it.
10. Not only did Jack win a million dollars, but he *also met* his future wife.

10. Auflage

ISBN 978-3-7058-8611-7

VORWORT

Der Titel dieses Buches „Durchstarten zur AHS-Matura" spricht eigentlich für sich selbst: Es soll dir helfen, dich auf die bevorstehende Englischmatura vorzubereiten. Da die Matura sehr angelehnt ist·an internationale Zertifikate wie das *Cambridge First Certificate*, haben wir auch eine Aufstellung der wichtigsten dieser Prüfungen für dich zusammengestellt – vielleicht möchtest du ja die eine oder andere davon ablegen. Diese Prüfungen sind zwar mit Kosten verbunden, aber der Vorteil ist, dass sie weltweit standardisiert und anerkannt sind und dir eine Fülle von Arbeits- und Studienmöglichkeiten im Ausland eröffnen.

Doch zurück zur Englischmatura!

Die Schwerpunkte liegen im Bereich der Leseverständnis-übungen (*Reading Comprehensions*), Hörübungen (*Listening Comprehensions*), *Language in Use*-Aufgaben und der Textsorten (*Writing*). Deshalb findest du in diesem Buch vier sehr ausführliche Kapitel zu diesen Punkten mit vielen wertvollen Hinweisen und Aufgabenstellungen, um dein Können zu verbessern und Sicherheit zu gewinnen. Die Hörübungen sind von *native speakers* mit verschiedenen Akzenten gesprochen.

Bei der Matura wird natürlich erwartet, dass du dich zu einer Fülle von Themen schriftlich und mündlich äußern kannst. Es ist nicht möglich, in einem Buch wie diesem alle Bereiche des englischen Wortschatzes abzudecken. So haben wir einige wichtige Grundthemen sehr ausführlich für dich aufbereitet, und du kannst dir aus den Kapiteln *Vocabulary* und *Functions* die Gebiete heraussuchen, die für dich wichtig sind. Die dazugehörigen Übungen im Kapitel **Wortschatz** (*Vocabulary*) sollen ein Anreiz sein, dich mit den Vokabeln auseinanderzusetzen, können aber leider nicht die eigentliche Lernarbeit ersetzen. Um deinen aktiven und passiven Wortschatz zu erweitern, musst du schon regelmäßig Vokabel lernen und auch immer wieder wiederholen – da führt leider kein Weg daran vorbei! Kenntnisse der englischen **Grundgrammatik** werden in der Oberstufe meist vorausgesetzt, aber es wird wahrscheinlich ein paar Bereiche geben, in denen du noch nicht so sattelfest bist. Um deine persönlichen Schwachstellen zu identifizieren, solltest du das Kapitel *Grammar* durcharbeiten. Die Ergebnisse der Mini-Tests sagen dir, was du noch üben musst.

Im **Anhang** (*Appendix*) des Buches findest du Übersichtabellen zu *Link Words and Phrases*. Dort kannst du in Zweifelsfällen nachschlagen oder auch für dich unbekannte Wörter in deine Lernlisten oder Lernkartei aufnehmen.

Das **Stichwortverzeichnis** (*Index*) am Ende des Buches führt alle wichtigen Stichwörter in alphabetischer Reihenfolge an, damit du schnell das findest, was du suchst.

Im **Lösungsheft** sind alle Lösungen zu sämtlichen Übungen und auch die *Tapescripts* zu den Hörübungen enthalten.

Folgende Symbole sollen dir helfen, dich in diesem Übungsbuch besser zurechtzufinden:

Querverweis auf Grammatikkapitel	Querverweis auf Wortschatz- oder Textsortenkapitel	Lerntipp
Skills Training	Merkkästchen	Infokästchen

Wie sollst du mit diesem Buch üben? Natürlich kannst du an einer beliebigen Stelle anfangen und zuerst das üben, was dir am schwersten fällt, zB die Hörübungen. Andererseits aber empfiehlt es sich auch abzuwechseln. Du könntest dir etwa einen Monatsplan erstellen und dir vornehmen, in diesem Zeitrahmen aus jedem Teilbereich eine gewisse Anzahl von Themen und Übungen zu machen. Mehr Tipps zum Thema „*Lernen lernen*" findest zu übrigens auf den Seiten 7 und 8.

Wenn du **original Zentralmaturaaufgaben trainieren** möchtest, kannst du gratis das **w** downloaden. Nähere Informationen dazu findest du auf der inneren Umschlagseite 2.

Nun bleibt uns nur noch, dir viel Erfolg bei der Arbeit mit diesem Buch und natürlich vor allem bei der Englischmatura zu wünschen!

Gabriela Sturm-Petritsch und *Martina Spielauer*

Lade dir gratis die **VERITAS Mediathek-App** herunter. Suche in der App dieses Buch und höre die Hörübungen!

App Store (Apple)

Play Store (Android)

DIE AHS-MATURA IN ENGLISCH

DIE SCHRIFTLICHE REIFEPRÜFUNG

Die Prüfungsaufgaben der vier Teile werden zentral vom Bundesministerium für Bildung, Wissenschaft und Forschung (BMBWF) erstellt. Die Gesamtarbeitszeit beträgt 270 Minuten. Es ist bei **keinem** Teil das Wörterbuch erlaubt. Die Reihenfolge der einzelnen Teile ist wie folgt:

Rezeptiver Teil:	
Reading Comprehension (Leseverstehen) 60 Minuten	Vier verschiedene Lesetexte werden mit je einer der folgenden Aufgabenstellungen abgetestet: ■ *multiple matching* ■ *multiple choice* ■ *note form* (die Lücken werden mit 1–4 Wörter vervollständigt) ■ *true/false/justification*
Listening Comprehension (Hörverstehen) max. 45 Minuten	Vier verschiedene Hörtexte (je ca. 1–5 Minuten Länge) werden zweimal vorgespielt. Es gibt pro Hörtext eine Aufgabenstellung: ■ *multiple matching* ■ *multiple choice* ■ *note form* (die Lücken werden mit 1–4 Wörtern vervollständigt) Die sprachliche Produktion soll auf ein Minimum reduziert sein.
Produktiver Teil:	
Language in Use (Sprachverwendung im Kontext) 45 Minuten	In 4 Teilen werden grammatikalische Strukturen und Wortschatz mit folgenden Aufgabenstellungen abgetestet: ■ *multiple choice* ■ *word formation* ■ *banked gap filling* ■ *open gap filling* ■ *editing*
Writing tasks (Schreiben) 120 Minuten	Es sind zwei Texte zu schreiben, wobei es keine Wahlmöglichkeit gibt. ■ A. Entweder ein *essay, report, article* oder *blog* – 400 Wörter ■ B. Entweder ein *report, article, blog* oder *e-mail* – 250 Wörter Die Aufgaben unterscheiden sich bezüglich Textsorte, Perspektive, Register ... voneinander. Die Themen beziehen sich auf alltägliche Lebenssituationen, auf Familie, Freundeskreis, Freizeit, Schule, Unterhaltung, Reisen, Arbeitswelt ...

Die einzelnen Teile werden durch kurze Pausen getrennt. Jeder der vier Teile wird mit 25% gleich gewichtet. Für eine positive Beurteilung muss sowohl der rezeptive als auch der produktive Teil positiv sein (50%). Insgesamt müssen für eine positive Note bei der schriftlichen Matura 60% erreicht werden.

DIE MÜNDLICHE REIFEPRÜFUNG

Aus einem Themenpool von 18 Themen (12 Themen bei Wahlpflichtfach) wählst du ein Thema. Du bekommst dann eine Aufgabenstellung, die aus 2 Teilen besteht: einem monologischen *(individual long turn)* und einem dialogischen *(paired activity)* Teil. Nach 15 Minuten Vorbereitungszeit beginnt der monologische Teil, bei dem du zwei Bilder miteinander vergleichst. Gleich darauf findet der dialogische Teil statt, bei dem du mit einem Partner über ein Thema diskutierst und ihr euch auf eine Lösung einigen sollt. Die Gesamtdauer beträgt ca. 15 Minuten.

INTERNATIONALE ZERTIFIKATE

Es gibt mehrere international anerkannte Sprachprüfungen, die man zusätzlich im 11. oder 12. Schuljahr ablegen kann, um im englischsprachigen Ausland zu arbeiten oder zu studieren, um sein Englisch zu verbessern bzw. als Selbstbestätigung, um einen qualifizierten Nachweis über die eigene Sprachkompetenz zu erhalten oder um einen besseren Job oder einen Platz an einer Universität zu bekommen. Hier findest du eine Übersicht über die gängigsten Prüfungen in Österreich. Die wohl bekanntesten sind die Cambridge-ESOL-Prüfungen, die in mehreren Schwierigkeitsstufen angeboten werden:

The First Certificate in English FCE	Council of Europe's Level B2	ALTE Niveau 3
The Certificate in Advanced English CAE	Council of Europe's Level C1	ALTE Niveau 4
Certificate of Proficiency in English CPE	Council of Europe's Level C2	ALTE Niveau 5
Business English Certificates BEC: BEC Preliminary, BEC Vantage, BEC Higher		

Die Reifeprüfung in Österreich entspricht dem Niveau B2 des Europarats (in manchen Bereichen auch schon C1). In anderen Worten bietet sich die FCE-Prüfung am Ende der 7. Klasse AHS oder am Beginn der 8. Klasse AHS, auch im Hinblick auf die Matura, gut an. Wer sich dann noch weiterbilden möchte, könnte nach der Matura die CAE-Prüfung ablegen.

Die Cambridge-Prüfungen FCE und CAE bestehen aus folgenden Teilen:

Paper	FCE	CAE
Reading and Use of English	75 Minuten, 7 Texte, 52 Fragen (*multiple-choice cloze, open cloze, word formation, key word transformation, multiple choice, cross-text multiple matching, gapped text, multiple matching*)	90 Minuten, 8 Texte, davon 5 Grammatik- und Vokabelübungen und 3 Leseübungen, 56 Fragen (*multiple-choice cloze, open cloze, word formation, key word transformation, multiple choice, cross-text multiple matching, gapped text, multiple matching*)
Writing	80 Minuten, 2 Schreibaufgaben (mindestens ein Brief oder E-Mail) zu je 120–180 Wörtern	90 Minuten, 2 Schreibaufgaben bis zu 260 Wörtern
Listening	40 Minuten, 4 Aufgaben, 30 Fragen (*multiple choice, sentence completion, multiple matching*)	40 Minuten, 4 Aufgaben, 30 Fragen (*multiple choice, sentence completion, multiple matching*)
Speaking	14 Minuten, 4 Teile, bestehend aus einem individuellen Gespräch mit dem *interlocutor*, einem einminütigen *long-turn* jedes Kandidaten, einer *two-way conversation* zwischen den beiden Kandidaten und einer Diskussion zu vorgegebenen Themen	15 Minuten, 4 Teile, bestehend aus einem individuellen Gespräch mit dem *interlocutor*, einem einminütigen *long-turn* jedes Kandidaten, einer *two-way conversation* zwischen den beiden Kandidaten und einer Diskussion zu vorgegebenen Themen
Gesamtdauer	3 Stunden 30 Minuten	4 Stunden

Die BEC-Prüfungen bestehen aus 3 Levels und prüfen die englische Sprache in wirtschaftlichen und geschäftlichen Zusammenhängen ab. Diese Prüfungen bestehen aus vier verschiedenen Teilen, nur der *Use of English*-Teil fehlt.

Für das amerikanische Englisch gibt es eigene Prüfungen, zB *TOEFL* (*Test Of English As A Foreign Language*).

Genauere Details, wo, wann und wie man sich zu Prüfungen anmelden kann, findest du auf den folgenden Internetseiten:

www.cambridgeesol.at	www.ets.org
www.britishcouncil.org/de/austria.htm	www.amerika-institut.at
	www.ets.org

LERNEN LERNEN

 Eine umfangreiche Anleitung zum Thema „Lernen lernen" würde den Rahmen dieses Buches sprengen, daher wollen wir hier für dich nur einige wichtige Punkte und Tipps kurz zusammenfassen.

Eine positive Einstellung

Wenn du nicht lernen willst, wirst du dir beim Lernen sehr schwer tun. Tritt also deinen Lernaufgaben mit einer positiven Grundeinstellung gegenüber. Freude und Lust steigern die Lernfähigkeit, während Angst und Unlust sie vermindern. Lernen wird umso leichter, je mehr Spaß du daran hast!

Motivation

Definiere dein Ziel, das du erreichen möchtest: die Matura, ein Berufswunsch, etc. Das Lernen ist das Hilfsmittel, das dich an dein Ziel bringt. Wann immer dir das Lernen schwer fällt, mache dir dein Ziel wieder bewusst.

Belohnung

Lernerfolge sollten belohnt werden – gönne dir etwas, denn das erhöht wiederum die Motivation.

Entspannung

Unter Druck wirst du nicht besonders gute Lernerfolge erzielen. Auch zu hohe Erwartungen und zu viel Ehrgeiz können Lernblockaden auslösen. Gehe spazieren, höre Musik, mache autogenes Training, etc., um zu entspannen.

Eine angenehme Lernumgebung

Nur wenn du dich auch körperlich wohl fühlst, wirst du dein ganzes Potential ausschöpfen können.
- Achte auf die richtige Körperhaltung (Oberfläche des Sitzplatzes etwa 20 cm unterhalb des Schreibtisches).
- Eine neigbare Schreibtischplatte entlastet die Augen.
- Alles Wichtige sollte in Griffweite sein, unwichtige oder ablenkende Dinge lege zur Seite.

Außerdem brauchst du
- gutes Licht – vor allem Tageslicht – und Ruhe;
- viel frische Luft, denn ohne Sauerstoff kann dein Gehirn nicht so gut arbeiten;
- eine angenehme Raumtemperatur (nicht zu warm!).

Manche Menschen umgeben sich beim Lernen auch gerne mit
- bestimmten lernstimulierenden Düften, zB Lemongrass;
- Musik, die entspannt oder anspornt.

Ortswechsel

Lerne nicht immer am selben Ort. Wechsle den Raum, die Position, lerne auch einmal im Gehen. Dein Gehirn wird die Lerninhalte auch mit der anderen Bewegung und dem neuen Ort verbinden.

Lerntechniken kennen lernen und ausprobieren

Richtig Lernen lernen zahlt sich aus, denn du wirst effizienter lernen und dir dadurch Zeit und Mühe sparen.

Lerntypen und Lernmethoden

Versuche herauszufinden, welcher Lerntyp du bist, und richte dein Lernverhalten danach aus:
- Der visuelle Typ möchte die Lerninhalte sehen und schreiben, um sie zu behalten.
- Der auditive Typ merkt sich diejenigen Lerninhalte am besten, die er hört und laut wiederholt.
- Der kinästhetische Typ will die Lerninhalte er*fassen* und be*greifen*.

Noch bessere Lernerfolge wirst du erzielen, wenn du es schaffst, dir auch die Lernweisen anzueignen, die nicht deinem Typ entsprechen. Flexibilität bedeutet Freiheit, und je mehr Lernmethoden du beherrschst, desto besser und schneller wirst du dein Ziel erreichen. Es gibt Lernsituationen, die dir die Lernmethode vorgeben, die du anwenden musst. Oder manche Lehrer werden dir Aufgaben stellen, die ihrem eigenen Lerntyp am nächsten kommen. Je mehr Sinnesorgane an deinem Lernprozess beteiligt sind, desto effektiver lernst du. Erweitere also deine Kapazitäten und trainiere deine Anpassungsfähigkeit – auch wenn es am Anfang schwerfällt.

Beide Gehirnhälften nutzen

Um optimal zu lernen, musst du beide Gehirnhälften aktivieren und nutzen. Normalerweise bleibt die rechte Gehirnhälfte eher auf der Strecke, weil Lernen bei uns sehr „linkslastig" ist, d.h., wir lernen über die Schrift, die Sprache und logische Gedankengänge. Lernen durch Bilder, Vergleiche, Beispiele und Zusammenhänge läuft hingegen über die rechte Gehirnhälfte ab. Wirkliche Lernerfolge wirst du erzielen, wenn du zum Beispiel:

- *Mind maps* beim Lernen einsetzt;
- komplizierte Lerninhalte in Geschichten verpackst;
- bildhafte Darstellungen des zu erlernenden Stoffes anfertigst.

Lernen heißt verknüpfen

Wenn du etwas Neues lernst, so wird diese neue Information an bereits vorhandenes Wissen angeknüpft. Dein Gehirn stellt Beziehungen zwischen Informationen her und je mehr du über ein Thema weißt, desto leichter bleiben neue Fakten hängen, weil du schon über viele Anknüpfungspunkte verfügst.

Trainiere dein Gehirn

Ein Muskel, den du nicht bewegst, wird verkümmern. Genauso ist es mit deinem Gehirn und deshalb solltest du es regelmäßig und abwechslungsreich trainieren. Je öfter du die bestehenden Verbindungen in deinem Gehirn aktivierst, desto stabiler werden sie. Du kennst das sicher: Wenn du etwas zum ersten Mal ausprobierst, fällt es oft noch schwer und erfordert deine ganze Konzentration (zB neue Tanzschritte); aber je öfter du es machst, umso automatischer geht es vor sich, scheinbar ohne dass du dich konkret darauf konzentrieren musst.

Völlig ungenützte Verbindungen in deinem Gehirn werden mit der Zeit deaktiviert, lassen sich aber sehr leicht wieder zum Leben erwecken. Was man einmal wirklich gut gelernt und geübt hat, verlernt man selten für immer.

Zeitplan und Lernprogramm

Um Lerninhalte dauerhaft zu verarbeiten, musst du sie öfter wiederholen, das bedeutet, du solltest rechtzeitig vor einer Prüfung zu lernen beginnen. Ein schriftlicher Zeitplan, auf dem du die täglichen Lernportionen einträgst und im Lauf der Zeit abhakst, ist dabei nicht nur hilfreich, sondern auch motivierend, weil du siehst, wie viel du bereits geschafft hast. Allerdings muss dein Lernplan realistisch sein, denn wenn du ihn nicht einhalten kannst, wirst du frustriert sein. Dein Lernplan sollte auch fixe Zeiten für Pausen und Wiederholungen vorsehen.

Beginne dein Lernprogramm immer mit eher leichten Aufgaben, denn auch dein Gehirn muss sich erst aufwärmen. Lies dir vor dem Schlafengehen wichtige Lerninhalte noch einmal durch, um sie zu festigen. Und ganz wichtig: Gönne dir ab und zu einen völlig freien Tag, damit dein Gehirn wieder Kraft tanken kann.

Pausen

Oft wird beim Lernen die Bedeutung der Pausen unterschätzt. Wenn du deinem Gehirn keine Lernpausen gönnst, wird es die neuen Informationen nicht richtig verarbeiten können. Wie oft und wie lange du beim Lernen am besten Pausen einlegst, musst du für dich selbst herausfinden; für den Anfang probiere es vielleicht mit 15 Minuten Pause nach 45 Minuten lernen. In den Pausen solltest du dich bewegen, frische Luft schnappen oder dich stärken mit einem Stück Obst oder auch einer kleinen (!) Süßigkeit. Und natürlich Wasser trinken nicht vergessen! Wenn du am Computer arbeitest, musst du deinen Augen zwischendurch unbedingt Gelegenheit geben auszuruhen, indem du aus dem Fenster schaust oder im Zimmer umherblickst.

 Negativeinflüsse auf deinen Lernerfolg:

■ Zu wenig Schlaf	■ Vor dem Lernen sehr viel essen
■ Mangel an Bewegung	■ Zu viel und zu lange an einem Tag lernen
■ Voller Bauch	■ Ganz kurz vor Prüfungen lernen
■ Einseitige Ernährung (zu viel Süßes!)	■ Dich zu lange mit demselben Stoff beschäftigen
■ Zu geringe Aufnahme von Flüssigkeit	■ Ähnliche Stoffgebiete unmittelbar hintereinander lernen
■ Konsum von Suchtmitteln	■ Die Lerninhalte immer in der gleichen Reihenfolge lernen

---

READING COMPREHENSION

INTRODUCTION

Ein Teilbereich der neuen **Standardisierten Reifeprüfung in Englisch** ist die Überprüfung des Leseverständnisses, **Reading Comprehension (RC).** Die Art der Aufgabenstellungen sind mit der *Cambridge First Certificate*-Prüfung vergleichbar. Das bedeutet, dass du innerhalb von **60 Minuten** verschiedene Aufgaben zu vier unabhängigen Texten zu lösen hast. Es darf bei der **RC** kein Wörterbuch verwendet werden.

	Mögliche Aufgabenstellungen
Multiple Matching	Passende Überschriften für bestimmte Textpassagen finden, gezielt Informationen im Text finden und den richtigen Fragen zuordnen
Multiple Choice	Verständnisfragen zum Inhalt des Textes mit jeweils vier Antwortmöglichkeiten
Note form	Sätze vervollständigen, Fragen beantworten mit bis zu maximal vier Wörtern
True/false/justification	Erkennen, ob eine Aussage richtig oder falsch ist und im Text die Stelle finden, in der der Beweis steht

In diesem Übungsbuch gehen den eigentlichen Leseverständnisaufgaben immer sogenannte **„Pre-Reading Tasks"** voraus. Diese sollen auf das Thema des Textes hinführen und eine gewisse Erwartungshaltung schaffen.
Im Anschluss an die eigentliche Aufgabe sollen dir verschiedene **„Comprehension Tasks"** und **„Vocabulary Tasks"** helfen, deine Lesefähigkeit und deinen Wortschatz noch zu verbessern.

10 GOLDEN RULES FOR READING COMPREHENSIONS

Hier findest du eine Reihe von allgemeinen Richtlinien, die dir helfen sollen, **RCs** richtig anzupacken.

1. Predicting The Content
Bevor du überhaupt zu lesen beginnst, solltest du versuchen, Vermutungen über den Inhalt des zu bearbeitenden Textes anzustellen. Dabei helfen dir neben dem Titel auch eventuell vorhandene Untertitel oder Fotos.

2. Understanding The Task
Lies dir die Aufgabenstellung genau durch und versichere dich, dass dir völlig klar ist, was du zu tun hast.

3. Reading The Text – ❶
Nun lies dir den Text ein erstes Mal durch, um zu erfahren, worum es geht, jedoch ohne irgendetwas auszufüllen. Am besten legst du deinen Stift zur Seite, damit du nicht in Versuchung kommst, voreilige Schlüsse zu ziehen. Allfällige Lücken im Text (fehlende Wörter, Überschriften, Sätze oder gar Absätze) ignoriere, so gut es geht. Etwaige *Multiple Choice*-Fragen oder Zuordnungsaufgaben beachte zunächst noch nicht.

Skimming
"To skim something" means to read something quickly in order to find a particular point or the main points.
Zu diesem Zeitpunkt solltest du vor allem bestrebt sein, den Grundgedanken und die Hauptpunkte des Textes zu erfassen. Bleibe daher nicht an Details hängen, auch nicht an einzelnen unbekannten Wörtern!

4. Reading The Text – ❷
Nun, da du weißt, worum es in dem Text geht, lies ihn noch einmal und versuche, die vorhandenen Lücken gedanklich zu füllen. **Make sensible guesses!** Stelle dabei folgende oder ähnliche Überlegungen an:
■ Welche Information fehlt hier?
■ Was ist die Kernaussage eines Absatzes und welche Überschrift könnte daher den Inhalt dieser Passage gut zusammenfassen?
■ Welche Wortart muss ergänzt werden, damit ein Satz vollständig wird?

5. Reading The Missing Bits/Multiple Choice Questions/Multiple Matching Instructions

Behalte jetzt unbedingt deine Überlegungen aus Schritt 4 im Hinterkopf!

Lies dir die fehlenden Textteile sorgfältig durch und überlege, welche Lücken sie füllen. Beginne mit den Lösungen, die dir eindeutig erscheinen. Je vollständiger dein Lückentext wird, desto kleiner wird die Anzahl der noch offenen Lösungsmöglichkeiten. Und umso einfacher wird es dann auch, die schwierigen Stellen richtig zu beantworten.

Wenn es gilt, *Multiple Choice*-Fragen zu lösen, so studiere diese genau durch. Meist beziehen sich die ersten Fragen auf bestimmte Textstellen, während die letzten den gesamten Text umfassen, sodass du Informationen aus verschiedenen Abschnitten zusammenfügen musst, um die richtigen Antworten zu finden.

Bei *Multiple Matching Tasks* unterstreiche die Schlüsselwörter in den Fragen, die dir bei der Suche nach den richtigen Antworten helfen werden. Überlege dir genau, nach welchen Informationen du suchen musst.

Scanning

"To scan" means to look at every part of a text carefully, especially because you are looking for a particular piece of information.

Nun heißt es auf Detailsuche gehen, um auch wirklich die richtigen Antworten zu finden.

Doch auch jetzt sollten dich einzelne unbekannte Wörter nicht zu sehr stören, denn sehr oft wird die Bedeutung aus dem Zusammenhang klar.

6. Choosing The Correct Answer

Entscheide dich für die richtigen Antworten, indem du nach genauen Hinweisen und Schlüsselwörtern im Text suchst. Stelle dir immer wieder folgende Fragen:

- Passt der gewählte Satz inhaltlich auch wirklich zu dem gesamten Absatz?
- Gibt es vielleicht im Satz vor oder nach der Lücke einen eindeutigen inhaltlichen Bezug zu meinem Lösungsvorschlag?
- Welche Wörter finde ich in den einzelnen Absätzen, die zu den einzusetzenden Überschriften passen?
- Bringen die von mir eingefügten Absätze auch nicht die chronologische Reihenfolge oder die Argumentationslinie des Gesamttextes durcheinander?
- Habe ich alle sprachlichen Hinweise (übereinstimmende Zeitformen, Pronomen, die auf bereits erwähnte Substantive verweisen, etc.) in den benachbarten Textstellen beachtet?
- Ist die von mir gewählte Wortart für diese Stelle im Text auch die richtige?

7. Eliminating The Wrong Answer

Wenn Lücken zu füllen sind, so wird dir normalerweise eine Antwortmöglichkeit mehr angeboten, als du brauchst. Überprüfe unbedingt, ob die übrig gebliebene Variante auch wirklich an keiner Stelle passt. Auch bei *Multiple Choice*-Fragen solltest du immer die Gegenprobe machen. Frage dich also nicht nur, warum die von dir gewählte Antwort richtig ist, sondern auch, warum die übrigen drei falsch sein müssen.

8. Reading The Text – ❸

Zum Abschluss lies dir noch einmal dein vollständiges Werk komplett durch, um festzustellen, ob der Text nun so auch wirklich inhaltlich sinnvoll und sprachlich korrekt ist.

9. Guessing The Answer

Bevor du eine Frage unbeantwortet oder eine Lücke ungefüllt lässt, weil du die richtige Lösung einfach nicht herausfinden kannst, ist es immer noch besser zu raten! Du kannst dadurch nur gewinnen!

10. Checking Completeness

Wirf noch einen letzten Blick zurück, ob du auch wirklich alle Fragen beantwortet und alle Aufgaben gelöst hast.

RC 1 – MULTIPLE MATCHING: "20 TIPS TO LOSE 20 POUNDS"

Task 1 **Pre-Reading**

Before you start reading try to **come up with a list of tips of your own**. What should you do in order to lose weight and what should you avoid?

Task 2 **Reading**

In the text below the sub-headings of all the paragraphs have been removed. Skim the text quickly for its general meaning and then read the list of possible sub-headings A–T. Choose the best one for each paragraph. Ignore the words in **bold print** until you get to Task 4.

Before you launch into any weight-loss plan, set a realistic goal, experts say. They suggest aiming for a **loss** of 10 to 20 pounds.

Begin by taking stock of your eating and exercise **habits**. Don't focus on everything at once, but pick a couple of weak areas and work on those. Here are 20 ways to help you lose 20 pounds:

1

Ask yourself whether this is a good time to start a plan or program. Are you really motivated? The people who are most successful at losing weight have a "wow" or "light bulb" moment, when something clicks and they decide they don't want to live this way anymore. Motivations **vary**. Some people are worried about diabetes or heart disease. Others are going to a class reunion, attending a wedding or approaching a hallmark birthday such as their 40th or 50th. Some people might have difficulty fitting into airline or movie-theatre seats, are not able to wear most of their clothing or are **breathless** when they walk up a flight of stairs.

2

Weigh yourself and have someone photograph you in **tight-fitting** clothes. This is so you can compare your before and after photos in a few months.

3

One **diet** doesn't fit all. There's no shortage of ways to lose weight, but you have to find something that works for you. Registered **dietitians** in private practice **tailor** programs to individuals. Weight Watchers provides practical advice and group support. There are many other commercial programs, Web sites and diet books that offer help. Shop around. Figure out what worked for friends who are similar to you.

4

Studies show that **dieters** who keep a daily food record usually lose more weight. So write down what you eat, how much and the calories, fat grams or carbs.

5

Some people **underestimate** the amount they are consuming. Keep in mind that your caloric **requirements** are related to your size.

6

Count calories, carbs, fat grams or steps, but count something, **nutritionists** say. You have to burn 3,500 calories more than you consume to lose a pound. If you usually eat 2,200 calories a day to maintain your weight, you need to cut back by 500 calories or increase exercise by that much to create the 500-calorie deficit to lose 1 pound a week.

7

Set aside some time every day to decide what you will eat for meals and snacks, when you will prepare them, what you will eat if you go out and when you will exercise.

8

Many dieters want someone to hold them accountable, making sure they stick with their program. Commercial weight-loss programs and health care professionals can help. Or simply check in with family, co-workers, neighbors and friends. They can offer support by taking walks with you at work or in the neighborhood. They might be willing to listen to you talk about what you're eating — or not eating. Or they can call you daily to see how you're doing.

9

Some **pointers**: Choose your restaurant with care. Don't go **famished** or you'll overeat. Don't drink your calories. Order no-calorie or low-calorie drinks. **Skip** the bread basket. Start off with a low-calorie soup like minestrone or won-ton. And order salad dressings and sauces **on the side**. Try the "dip and stab" method. Dip a fork in a cup of dressing, then spear your salad.

10

If you are going to a big party or out to dinner, conserve calories for the big meal without **starving** yourself. At the other times during the day, eat more low-calorie foods such as simple soups, raw or cooked vegetables and light bread and popcorn.

11

New research indicates that sleep **deprivation** increases a hunger hormone and decreases a fullness hormone, which could lead to overeating and weight **gain**. So getting enough sleep might help you control your hunger.

12

Add vegetables, salads and low-calorie soups to your meal plans. Research shows that people eat the same weight of food each day, so experts believe that increasing fruits and vegetables so that meals are higher in **fiber** and water will help people lower their calories without feeling **deprived**.

13

Ideally, people who are trying to lose weight should exercise for 30 to 60 minutes a day. A recent study showed that many types of exercise help with losing, and in fact, walking on your own can be as effective for weight loss as going to the gym.

14

Start making small changes to your daily routine. Take a 10- to 15-minute walk before work in the morning, at lunch and then when you get home at night. Build from there. Or buy a **pedometer** and try to work up to 10,000 steps a day.

15

Many people consume hundreds of extra calories a day with sodas, juices, alcohol and other high-calorie drinks.

16

Consider yourself a B student when it comes to your diet and follow the 80-20 rule. About 80% of the foods you eat

should be **lean** protein such as **poultry**, fish and beans; fruits and vegetables; low-fat dairy; high-fiber grain products; and healthier fats such as olive oil. The other 20% can be foods that are not as healthful.

17

Some examples: a BLT without mayo; one-half bagel with 1 ounce of cream cheese and a half-cup of orange juice; two poached eggs on an English muffin; a Wendy's junior cheeseburger. You can use meal replacement bars and shakes to help control calories.

18

People take less when they use smaller serving dishes and tall, narrow glasses instead of short wide ones, a study showed.

19

If you allow yourself occasional treats, you're less likely to feel deprived, nutritionists say. Here are some ideas: a frozen chocolate kiss; cappuccino made with skim milk; individually wrapped mint; bite-size candy bar; gingersnaps.

20

People who have lost weight and kept it off limit their daily calories to about 1,800 a day and walk about 4 miles a day, according to the latest study from the National Weight Control Registry, a group of 5,000 people who lost an average of 73 pounds and kept off at least 30 pounds for more than six years.

Nanci Hellmich, USA TODAY

Missing Sub-Headings:

A   Check your attitude.
B   Dine out without pigging out.
C   Downsize your dishes.
D   Get a B mentality.
E   Get help from your friends.
F   Get some sleep.
G   Indulge your sweet tooth.
H   Keep it off.
I   Move it to lose it.
J   Pay attention to portions.
K   Pick a plan.
L   Pick up the pace.
M   Pile on the veggies.
N   Plan ahead.
O   Plan for a splurge.
P   Plan some 300-calorie meals.
Q   Play the numbers game.
R   Watch the liquid.
S   Weigh in.
T   Write down every bite.

Task 3   Comprehension

Answer the following questions.

1. What kind of factors can trigger a person's desire to lose weight?
2. Why should you weigh yourself before going on a diet?
3. What is meant by *"there's no shortage of ways to lose weight"*?
4. Why does it make sense to keep a daily food record and pay attention to portions?
5. How many calories do you have to burn in order to lose one pound?
6. In how far can friends and workmates be helpful when you are trying to lose weight?
7. How can you avoid eating too much when you are dining out?
8. What is a *splurge* and how should a dieter handle situations in which it might come to splurging?
9. What is the correlation between sleep and hunger?
10. What can you do in order to prevent feeling deprived when you are on a diet?
11. How much exercise should you get when you are trying to lose weight?
12. Why can certain liquids have detrimental effects on a diet?
13. What is the 80-20 rule?
14. How can the size of your dishes influence the amount you eat?
15. Are occasional treats harmful to the success of your diet? Why (not)?
16. Once you have lost weight, what do you need to do in order to keep it off?

Task 4   Vocabulary

Look at the words/phrases in bold print in the text and match them with the following meanings.

1. a piece of advice
2. a thing that you do often and almost without thinking, especially sth that is hard to stop doing
3. an increase in the amount of sth, especially in wealth or weight
4. an instrument for measuring how far you have walked
5. containing little or no fat
6. having difficulty in breathing
7. meat from chickens, ducks and geese
8. person who is an expert on the relationship between food and health
9. person who is trying to lose weight on a diet
10. person whose job is to advise people on what kind of food they should eat to keep healthy
11. served at the same time as the main part of the meal, but on a separate plate
12. something that you need or want; something that you must have in order to do sth else
13. something that fits very tightly or closely
14. the fact of not having sth that you need, like enough food, sleep, money or a home
15. the food that you eat and drink regularly
16. the part of food that helps to keep a person healthy by keeping the bowels working and moving other food quickly through the body
17. the state of no longer having sth or as much of sth
18. to be different from each other in size, shape, etc.; to change or be different according to the situation
19. to leave out sth that would normally be the next thing that you would do
20. to make or adapt sth for a particular purpose, a particular person, etc.
21. to measure how heavy sb/sth is, usually by using scales
22. to suffer or die because you do not have enough food to eat
23. to think or guess that the amount, cost or size of sth is smaller than it really is
24. very hungry
25. without enough food, education, and all the things that are necessary for people to live a happy and comfortable life

RC 2 – TRUE/FALSE/JUSTIFICATION: "COUCH POTATOES, ARISE!"

You have nothing to lose – except your bulges. But how do you get started?

Task 1 Pre-Reading

1. Think about the following:
   a. What are **couch potatoes** and what are **bulges**?
   b. Why might it be desirable to **lose your bulges**?
2. What should couch potatoes start to do and how should they go about it?

Task 2 Reading

Read the text and find out whether your ideas were correct. Study the statements in Task 3, read the text again and decide whether they are true (T), false (F) or not given (N). Ignore the words in **bold print** until you get to Task 4.

The Complete Text:

There's nothing easier than falling out of shape, especially in this age of instant entertainment on your flat-screen TV, pizza deliveries to your door and an arsenal of remotes **within easy reach**. Most of us have got leisure time **nailed**.

Climbing off the couch and getting back into condition is a trickier proposition. Trying to do it too fast can actually be dangerous. "Among those at greatest risk for heart-attack death is the habitually **sedentary person** who engages in **unaccustomed** physical **activity**," warns Barry Franklin, physiologist and chairman of the American Heart Association's Physical Activities Committee. Before starting even a minimal exercise program, therefore, you should call your doctor for a preworkout O.K. or even a checkup.

Once you've been cleared for take-off, the first step you take may be just that: a walking program that begins modestly and then builds up. Most national government guidelines recommend at least 30 minutes of **moderate**-intensity activities, including walking, most days of the week. In a campaign to get its people on their feet, Germany's Ministry of Health has set them a target of 3,000 extra steps a day, and is handing out free pedometers to help keep count. Launching the campaign in May, Health Minister Ulla Schmidt was keen to assure people that "Exercise can be integrated into everyday life, and doesn't need to be exhausting. Exercise is fun."

Fun or not, such small starts can yield big dividends. A good walking program may improve overall measures of physical health as much as 15% in just three months. Since the human body after age 25 experiences, on average, about a 1% **falloff** in fitness for every additional year of life, the **numbers** are easy to **crunch**. "That's a 15-year functional rejuvenation," Franklin says.

If you're aiming for more – weight loss, a competitive edge in sports – there are other avenues to becoming active again. Depending on how many years you've logged on the couch, high-impact activities such as jogging may not be for you – not if your **creaky** knees, ankles and hips have anything to say about it. Best to get yourself back in shape with a low-impact activity like swimming, cycling or rowing.

Whatever you choose, begin with a shorter workout than you believe you can handle. "Consciously underdo," advises exercise physiologist Carl Foster of the University of Wisconsin-La Crosse. "We're all 19 behind our eyes, but if you jogged 16 km a day when you were in college, that doesn't mean you can do it now." Besides, once you're comfortable with a more modest workout load, you can slowly increase it – about 10% a week, Foster recommends. If time is an issue, U.S. government guidelines suggest that there are still significant health benefits to be gained if your 30 to 60 minutes of exercise is broken up into 10- or 15-minute segments throughout the day.

If you're interested in activities that require skill, be willing to bend the rules a little so you can keep up – allow the tennis ball to take an extra bounce, play half-speed hoops on just a portion of the court. Also, don't choose activities that are seasonal, expensive or too **solitary** – each one a handy excuse for not sticking with your workout program. If you can, try to work with a personal trainer at least some of the time – someone who can **rein** you **in** when you're doing something wrong, applaud when you're doing something right and, perhaps most important, make you feel guilty if you don't show up at all. Trainers are also good at knowing which muscle groups you need to strengthen for a sport you may be considering trying, and helping you exercise them into shape.

Finally, for all people new to workouts, it pays to continue to play it safe, even after your doctor has cleared you to exercise. Be alert for **lightheadedness** or pain or pressure in the chest. And if you can't speak reasonably comfortably while you're exercising, you're probably getting more **winded** than is good for you. "The risk from exercise is not too great, but it's there," says Foster. The benefits from doing it right, of course, are enormous.

By Jeffrey Kluger, Time Magazine (700 words)

Task 3 Comprehension

Read the text and decide whether the statements (1–8) are true (T) or false (F). Put a ✗ in the correct box. Then identify the sentence in the text which supports your decision. Write <u>the first four words</u> of this sentence in the space provided. There may be more than one correct answer; write down <u>only one</u>. The first one (0) has been done for you.

		T	F	Justification
0.	People who lead a sedentary life are more likely to get a heart attack.		✗	*Among those at greatest ...*
1.	Walking for about 30 minutes a day is a good way of starting your workout program.			
2.	Ulla Schmidt stressed the importance of exercising exhaustively on a regular basis.			
3.	Within a few months your physical health can be improved considerably if you stick to a good walking program.			
4.	If you have been inactive for years you should start with a more modest workout load.			
5.	People who could easily jog 16 km when they were young need not necessarily begin with a very modest workout program.			
6.	Choosing an expensive activity can help you stick with your program.			
7.	A personal trainer can give you any kind of support you might need in a given situation.			
8.	Pain in the chest or lightheadedness must be taken as serious warning signals.			

Task 4 Vocabulary

Try to explain the following words from the text.
1. within easy reach
2. to have a thing nailed
3. a sedentary person
4. unaccustomed activity
5. moderate
6. falloff
7. to crunch numbers
8. creaky
9. solitary
10. to rein sb in
11. lightheadedness
12. winded

RC 3 – MULTIPLE CHOICE: "SLICES OF LONDON – HORROR STORIES"

Task 1   Pre-Reading

Study both the title and the opening paragraph of the text and guess what the article is about.
The following words should give you some clues: **gushing – pointless – carnage – slaughterhouse**

Task 2   Reading

Read the text twice. First try to get a general idea and find out if your guesses in Task 1 were correct. The second time pay more attention to detail.

Reading this week's horror stories, full of gushing blood and pointless carnage, it's impossible not to wonder whether we're living in a city or a slaughterhouse.

Man beheaded by axeman in Swiss Cottage! London cannibal gets life for eating two men! Reading this week's horror stories, full of gushing blood and pointless carnage, it's impossible not to wonder whether we're living in a city or a slaughterhouse.

Peter Bryan, arrested in a London flat while preparing to tuck into a body part of his host, pleaded guilty at the Old Bailey on Tuesday to two counts of manslaughter. He went on to kill a second man while already in jail. Judge Giles Forrester told him, "You killed on these last two occasions because it gave you a thrill and a feeling of power when you ate flesh."

Then on Monday, a 67-year-old pensioner was nearly beheaded in a North London street, in front of neighbours and passers-by.

Violence so public, extreme and meaningless is something that until recently the average Londoner might only have expected to find in the trashier kind of horror movie (think *Hallowe'en* and its multiple spin-offs), or lurid American supermarket tabloids.

English murderers have generally aspired to be more discreet. The Denis Nilsens and Dr Crippens in our national rogues' gallery went to some trouble to pretend to be modest, unassuming men who'd peek out at life from behind net curtains and not annoy the neighbours.

But that quiet mix of hypocrisy and hideous murder behind closed doors is history now, as violence is globalised. You can get those lurid supermarket tabloid stories at the click of a mouse. You can slaver over serial killers in Russia. You can follow the bloodstains left by rapping gangstas in LA. And you can replicate it here.

My first brush with violent death and dismemberment, new-London style, came a couple of years ago. I was scared stiff when, shortly after I moved to the quiet streets of Camden, populated (as I imagined) by sweet vegetarian shrinks, body parts started turning up in rubbish bags. It turned out that one local resident wasn't quite so harmless. Anthony Hardy, later known as the Camden Ripper lived just down the road on my bus route into the congestion zone, and had chopped up three women – his preferred disposal method, black bags fly-tipped into someone else's bin.

But he was caught, and my fear passed. After a few months of sniffing cautiously

at any extra bags in our dustbins and finding nothing much worse than someone else's leftover kebab, I calmed down.

Then I got blasé. Even my husband and two toddlers being chased in a car by a road-rage weirdo armed with a kitchen knife didn't really freak me out. They got away, after all (though it would have been nice if the police had taken a vague interest). Even someone taking a shot at a neighbour cycling through the scary estate next door; or the sweet teenage son of our next-door neighbour's best friend being stabbed and killed on another local estate – just for his mobile phone. Just keep away from trouble, I thought; pretend it's not there and it will go away.

But now I'm getting ideas about a more extrovert style of man management. Pushing through the dodgy-looking crowd by Camden Town Tube last night, being streetwise and careful not to meet the eyes of the madder-looking dealers and loonies, I shifted tactfully away when an angry-looking trampy type lurched up, scratching furiously, and yelled: "I've got an itch in my balls!"

My first thought was: "This is new London. He might have an axe. Avoid him." But my second thought – a much more exhilarating one – was: "I should start carrying an axe myself."

Source: Urban Fox, Times Online Correspondent

Task 3   Multiple Choice

For each of the following questions choose the answer which fits best according to the text. Try to find reasons why the other three answers are wrong.

1. When Peter Bryan was arrested,

A he was hiding one of his victims.

B he was about to kill one of his victims.

C he was about to eat one of his victims.

D he was cutting up one of his victims.

2. Such public violence

A is something that people in London were not really confronted with in real life.

B can only be found in trashy horror movies.

C is the favourite topic of American tabloids.

D is caused by films like *Hallowe'en*.

3. English murderers used to

A attract a lot of attention.

B copy American models.

C consider themselves as modest men.

D avoid contact with other people.

4. When the authoress of this text moved to Camden, she was

A frightened when she found body parts in rubbish bags.

B shocked when one of her neighbours turned out to be a murderer.

C happy to find that most of her neighbours were vegetarian shrinks.

D not sure it had been a good decision to move to this area.

5. What does the authoress mean when she says she got blasé?

A She got frustrated by the violence around her.

B She was relieved because the Camden Ripper was caught.

C She could stay away from trouble.

D She became accustomed to the violence around her and pretended that it was not really there.

6. Why do you think the authoress came to the conclusion that she should start carrying an axe herself?

A Because it seemed to be the logical reaction to all the violence.

B Because she was attacked by a tramp.

C Because there are too many dealers and loonies these days.

D Because she met someone carrying one.

7. Which set of adjectives best describes how the attitude of the authoress changed due to the confrontation with violence and death?

A tolerant → fearful → determined

B open-minded → shocked → brave

C naïve → ignorant → realistic

D idealistic → upset → disillusioned

Task 4　Vocabulary

Look at the following list of adjectives and try to find synonyms in the text.
Then – with the help of a dictionary if necessary – come up with possible antonyms (opposites).

Adjective	Synonym	Antonym
culpable		
diplomatic, thoughtful		
experienced, clever		
humble		
innocuous		
inspiring, stimulating		
jaded, hardened		
of poor quality, with no value		
outgoing		
revolting, repulsive		
senseless		
strange, odd		
tactful		
wary		

Task 5　Topic-related Vocabulary

Complete the table below with suitable words.

Verb	Person	Action
assail		
		attack
	blackmailer	
		break-in
		bribery
	burglar	
chase		
counterfeit		
		fraud
	embezzler	
	forger	
hijack		
	kidnapper	
		killing
molest		
	mugger	

Verb	Person	Action
murder		
		perjury
	pickpocket	
		rape
rob		
		arson
shoot sb/at sb		
	shoplifter	
	smuggler	
stab		
	stalker	
	thief (pl: -ves)	
strangle		
		swindle
take sb hostage		
	vandal	

RC 4 – MULTIPLE MATCHING: "SURVIVING AGAINST ALL ODDS"

We all imagine how we would react in a traumatic situation, but some lucky people often survive unimaginable incidents and live to tell the tale.

Task 1   Pre-Reading

1. Without looking at task 2, what unimaginable incidents can you think of? Jot them down.
2. How would you react in such situations?
3. What are you afraid of? Make a list!

Task 2   Reading

Read the following first-hand accounts and see if you can decide which real life traumas they are describing from the Trauma List. Look for content clues and underline any phrases which refer to the correct trauma. Before continuing with Task 3, check your results with the key.

1. Going over Niagara Falls in a barrel   _____
2. Parachute failure   _____
3. Being struck by lightning   _____
4. A plane crash   _____
5. A shark attack   _____
6. A tornado   _____
7. An avalanche   _____

Vocabulary:		
85 mph: 136.7 kph **dumpster**: a small truck that can carry heavy loads	**to black out**: to become unconscious **staple**: a small metal clip	**30 feet**: 9.1 m **100 mph**: 160.93 kph

A "I heard this loud noise like a garage door slamming and it was completely dark. Then all of a sudden I could see these big white things out of my left eye. I heard the crunching ... but it didn't hurt. Something in the brain clicks so you don't feel it till later ... When I saw the water it was three feet below but ... we were moving fast. I tried to pull my head out. It all lasted about eight to twelve seconds. They took me to hospital in a helicopter. I had ... 40 stitches in the front of my head and ... 30 in the back. They had no mirrors at the hospital." Rodney Orr is describing.

B "People began to scream. My body was thrown against the window ... I shook, I cried and I cursed. I wanted to live, and I wanted to die quickly. I cried for my life that would never be. I didn't cry for those I would leave behind ... I looked at the ground as it reached up for us ... The sound of metal twisting and tearing ripped through my head ... We slid like a car out of control on the ice ... I opened my eyes to find the sun shining on my face. There was nothing in front of me ... I jumped to the ground unharmed but more than 30 people died." Ellen Hassman is describing.

C "It takes 2.3 seconds ... As I went over I didn't see a thing, didn't smell a thing, didn't hear a thing ... Hitting the bottom is like getting your car up to 85 mph* and ramming it into the biggest tree possible. My mouth hurt most ... The scariest part was the weight of the water ... Once we hit the bottom, water started coming in like crazy. We got pushed underneath for ten or fifteen seconds. What we did was illegal ... We made it, though." Geoffrey Petkovich is describing.

D "There's a low, ever-louder howl, like a freight train, and you feel the shuddering ground. First a sheet of rain spread against the side of the trailer like machine-gun fire. I could hear trees snapping and debris shooting through the trailer ... The roof metal began ripping off ... Just as I felt the entire trailer lift off the ground and begin to rotate I blacked out*. I woke up 20 minutes later face down outside the house. The evening was completely quiet: no wind, no cars, no insect noises ... I had gone through the wall, been thrown 30 feet* up into a tree and dropped to the ground ... Surgeons pinned, strapped and sewed me back together." John L. Neldigch is describing.

E "There was no warning. It was instant. All of a sudden I was rolled up in a ball doing somersaults. Then it was over and I was buried ... It was totally dark. My mouth was packed with snow. It was hard to breathe ... I didn't know which direction was up ... I thought, 'Maybe I'm already dead.' ... I was screaming ... I was out of my mind ... When I cried I realised the tears were running up towards my hair so I knew I was upside down. ... I started digging ... and continued for 22 hours. It was another 14 hours before the rescuers found me. ... The whole experience has made me a better person." Lester Morlang is describing.

F "We were standing there, talking ... That's about the last thing I recall ... I was absolutely frozen, just as cold as I had ever been in my entire life, but then part of me was incredibly hot, too. I saw these red flashing lights, and I kept thinking, 'It's a fire truck! It's a fire truck!' Then there was the most incredible noise I'd ever heard ... I felt as if I had been crushed between two dumpsters*... Every bit of my body was in absolute pain ... My hair hurt. My eyelashes hurt ... I had a wound in my head that needed eight staples*. Now I have a hard time with math – addition and subtraction." Max Dearing is describing.

G "I was being whipped in a circle, like in a washing-machine at full speed. In less than a second I was lifted almost horizontal, parallel to the ground, and moving in a circle at more than 100 mph*... My body was rotating ... like a helicopter blade. The blood was rushing from my head and I couldn't move my arms ... I knew I was going to pass out in a few seconds ... Finally I caught the cord in my fingertips and the secondary opened. I had the worst headache any human has ever experienced ... Most people on the ground never realised I was in trouble." Ray Maynard is describing.

Source: CURRENT, Mary Glasgow Magazines

Task 3 Multiple Matching

Read the short accounts again, then choose the correct texts (A–G) to answer the questions. You will have to use some texts more than once. Write your answers in the spaces provided.

Who:

is reported to have been taken to the hospital?	1. ____	2. ____	
had injuries in the head?	3. ____	4. ____	
was enclosed by darkness?	5. ____	6. ____	7. ____
cried?	8. ____	9. ____	
was not injured at all?	10. ____		
lost consciousness for a short time?	11. ____		
feared to faint?	12. ____		
was turned over and over again?	13. ____	14. ____	
started the adventure on purpose?	15. ____		

Task 4 Topic-related Vocabulary

Complete this table and write the following words and phrases in the most appropriate column:

Not afraid	Afraid	Very afraid	How do you react?

brave	fearful	fearless	terror
horror	bold	intrepid	anxious
unafraid	to freeze	to jump	to shiver
to tremble	to terrify sb	courageous	scary *(infml)*
apprehensive	to feel panic	a fear of sth	scare/scared
panic-stricken	to be scared of	dread/to dread	a look of terror
to fear sth *(fml)*	very frightened	to show no fear	to scare sb/sth
to watch in horror	fright/frightening	terrified/terrifying	to be frightened of
to be terrified (of)	to frighten sb/sth	to have goose-flesh	to make your blood run cold
to be scared to death	to have goose-pimples	to feel panicky *(infml)*	butterflies in your stomach *(infml)*
to shake (with fear)	to have goose-bumps (AE)	to live in dread/fear of sth	to be scared stiff (of) *(infml)*
		to frighten the life out of sb	to make your hair stand on end

afraid (not before a noun!):
to be afraid (of), to be afraid to do sth, a frightened child

RC 5 – MULTIPLE MATCHING AND MULTIPLE CHOICE: "GLOBAL WARMING MAKING HURRICANES STRONGER"

Task 1   Pre-Reading

What kind of weather do you like most? Why? What kind of weather do you hate? Why?
How might hurricanes affect people's lives? What should you do when a hurricane is coming?

Task 2   Reading

Read the article about the influence of global warming on hurricanes. Six sentences have been removed from the article. Choose the correct sentence (A–H) for each gap. Write your answers in the spaces provided. There are two extra sentences which you do not need to use.

A	Hurricanes are ranked on an intensity scale 1 to 5.
B	If early storms turn out to be more powerful than originally thought, Emanuel's findings on global warming's influence on recent tropical storms might not hold up, they said.
C	"When I look at these results at face value, they are rather alarming," said research meteorologist Tom Knutson.
D	"It is premature to conclude that greenhouse warming has already had a discernible impact on Atlantic hurricane activity."
E	Forecasters expect the stormy trend to continue for another 20 years or more.
F	Especially in the Atlantic and Caribbean basins, pools of warming seawater provide energy for storms as they swirl and grow over the open oceans.
G	The use of satellites and modern remote sensing help to prognosticate the trail of a hurricane.
H	Most forecasts don't have climate change making a real difference in tropical storms until 2050 or later.

Study: Global Warming Making Hurricanes Stronger

Is global warming making hurricanes more ferocious? New research suggests the answer is yes. Scientists call the findings both surprising and "alarming" because they suggest global warming is influencing storms now – rather than in the distant future.

However, the research doesn't suggest global warming is generating more hurricanes and typhoons.
The analysis by climatologist Kerry Emanuel of the Massachusetts Institute of Technology shows for the first time that major storms spinning in both the Atlantic and the Pacific since the 1970s have increased in duration and intensity by about 50 percent.

These trends are closely linked to increases in the average temperatures of the ocean surface and also correspond to increases in global average atmospheric temperatures during the same period.

1 _____   "These are very big changes."

Knutson, who wasn't involved in the study, works in the National Oceanic and Atmospheric Administration's Geophysical Fluid Dynamics Laboratory in Princeton, N.J.

Emanuel reached his conclusions by analyzing data collected from actual storms rather than using computer models to predict future storm behavior.

Before this study, most researchers believed global warming's contribution to powerful hurricanes was too slight to accurately measure. **2** _____

But some scientists questioned Emanuel's methods. For example, the MIT researcher did not consider wind speed information from some powerful storms in the 1950s and 1960s because the details of those storms are inconsistent.

Researchers are using new methods to analyze those storms and others going back as far as 1851. **3** _____

"I'm not convinced that it's happening," said Christopher W. Landsea, another research meteorologist with NOAA, who works at a different lab, the Atlantic Oceanographic & Meteorological Laboratory in Miami. Landsea is a director of the historical hurricane reanalysis.

"His conclusions are contingent on a very large bias removal that is large or larger than the global warming signal itself," Landsea said.

Details of Emanuel's study appear Sunday in the online version of the journal Nature.

Theories and computer simulation indicate that global warming should generate an increase in storm intensity, in part because warmer temperatures would heat up the surface of the oceans. **4** _____

Emanuel analyzed records of storm measurements made

by aircraft and satellites since the 1950s. He found the amount of energy released in these storms in both the North Atlantic and the North Pacific oceans has increased, especially since the mid-1970s.

In the Atlantic, the sea surface temperatures show a pronounced upward trend. The same is true in the North Pacific, though the data there is more variable, he said.

"This is the first time I have been convinced we are seeing a signal in the actual hurricane data," Emanuel said in an e-mail exchange.

"The total energy dissipated by hurricanes turns out to be well correlated with tropical sea surface temperatures," he said. "The large upswing in the past decade is unprecedented and probably reflects the effects of global warming."

This year marked the first time on record that the Atlantic spawned four named storms by early July, as well as the earliest category 4 storm on record. **5** _____

In the past decade, the southeastern United States and the Caribbean basin have been pummelled by the most active hurricane cycle on record. **6** _____

Even without global warming, hurricane cycles tend to be a consequence of natural salinity and temperature changes in the Atlantic's deep current circulation that shift back and forth every 40 to 60 years.

Since the 1970s, hurricanes have caused more property damage and casualties. Researchers disagree over whether this destructiveness is a consequence of the storms' growing intensity or the population boom along vulnerable coastlines.

"The damage and casualties produced by more intense storms could increase considerably in the future," Emanuel said.

Source: Associated Press

Task 3 Vocabulary

a. What adjectives can be combined with *"hurricane"* and *"storm"*? Look for examples in the text. Do you know more?

hurricane: _____

storm: _____

b. Match the words in list A with a word in list B. Sometimes there is more than one combination possible.
example: *the storm spins*

A	B
average	duration
dissipated	energy
ocean	intensity
release	speed
storm	spins
upward	surface
wind	temperature
	trend

c. Match the following words with their meaning. There are more words than meanings! One word matches with one meaning only. Write the correct number next to the meaning.

1. to be contingent on	_____ to beat, to hit someone/something hard
2. to generate	_____ to depend on something that may or may not happen in the future
3. to heat up	_____ to remain strong and working effectively
4. to hold up	_____ to move around quickly in a circular movement
5. to predict	_____ to produce, create something
6. to pummel	_____ to investigate, to study something intensively
7. to research	_____ to say that something will happen
8. to swirl	

Task 4 Multiple Choice

Read the text again, then choose the correct answer (A, B, C or D). Put a ✔ in the correct box.

1.	Global warming is affecting storms	**A** **B** **C** **D**	now but not in the future. in the future but not now. sooner now than in the future. now as well as in the future.						❑ ❑ ❑ ❑
2.	Global warming is producing	**A** **B** **C** **D**	more storms. fewer storms. no effect on the number of gales. no effect on the gale force.						❑ ❑ ❑ ❑
3.	Storms twirling in	**A** **B** **C** **D**	the Atlantic the Pacific either the Atlantic or the Pacific the Atlantic and Pacific	❑ ❑ ❑ ❑	have increased in	**A** **B** **C** **D**	length and severity by half. length by half. severity by 60 percent. strength slowly.	❑ ❑ ❑ ❑
4.	The severity and length of the storms	**A** **B** **C** **D**	are loosely related to are not connected with are partly connected with are directly related to	❑ ❑ ❑ ❑	the growth in the temperatures of the ocean surface and global temperatures.				
5.	Emanuel	**A** **B** **C** **D**	developed computer models to predict changes in hurricane intensity. inferred his conclusions from examining facts collected from actual storms. preferred examining facts collected from actual storms to using computer models. did some research on severe local storms.						❑ ❑ ❑ ❑
6.	Emanuel's results were appreciated by	**A** **B** **C** **D**	everybody. hardly anybody. the MIT. a few scientists.						❑ ❑ ❑ ❑
7.	In the Atlantic and Caribbean	**A** **B** **C** **D**	warm tropical oceans supply storms with energy. cold open oceans supply storms with energy. warm seawater evaporates and is absorbed by the air. cooler water from deeper in the ocean rises up.						❑ ❑ ❑ ❑
8.	Since the 1970s the energy set free in storms	**A** **B** **C** **D**	has waned. has risen. has decreased. has been conserved.						❑ ❑ ❑ ❑
9.	The temperatures of the Atlantic are	**A** **B** **C** **D**	considerably increasing. slightly increasing. stay about the same. significantly decreasing.						❑ ❑ ❑ ❑
10.	**A** **B** **C** **D**	The energy of the storms and low pressure The duration of the storms and tidal surges The energy of the storms and the surface temperatures of the sea The duration of the storms and the temperature of the sea							❑ ❑ ❑ ❑
11.	These devastating hurricanes will	**A** **B** **C** **D**	not stop in the 21st century. not stop in the next 20 years. stop in the next 40 to 60 years. stop in the next ten years.						❑ ❑ ❑ ❑
12.	Saltiness and temperature differences in the ocean	**A** **B** **C** **D**	never change. hardly ever change. change once in a blue moon. change regularly.						❑ ❑ ❑ ❑
13.	In the future hurricanes will cause	**A** **B** **C** **D**	more damage farther north. considerable damage to property and loss of life. minor damage to property and loss of life. a lot of pain and misery.						❑ ❑ ❑ ❑

RC 6 – MULTIPLE MATCHING AND NOTE FORM: "FACTSHEET: CHILD SOLDIERS"

Task 1 Pre-Reading

What do you know about child soldiers? What does their everyday life look like? What might be the reasons why children become child soldiers? Do you think they are enjoying themselves? Why (not)?

Task 2 Reading 1

First of all, read the definition of a child soldier and compare it with your ideas.

Who is a child soldier?

A child soldier is any person under 18 years of age who is part of any kind of regular or irregular armed force or armed group in any capacity, including but not limited to cooks, porters, messengers and anyone accompanying such groups, other than family members. The definition includes girls recruited for sexual purposes and for forced marriage. It does not, therefore, only refer to a child who is carrying or has carried arms.

Task 3 Multiple Matching

Read the text below, then choose the correct heading A–L for each section of the text. Write your answers in the spaces provided. There is one extra heading which you do not need to use.

1	

It is estimated that some 300.000 children – boys and girls under the age of 18 – are today involved in more than 30 conflicts worldwide. Children are used as combatants, messengers, porters and cooks and for forced sexual services. Some are abducted or forcibly recruited, others are driven to join by poverty, abuse and discrimination, or to seek revenge for violence enacted against them or their families.

Children are more likely to become child soldiers if they are separated from their families, displaced from their homes, living in combat zones or have limited access to education. Children may join armed groups as the only way to guarantee daily food and survival.

In some situations, the involvement of children in conflicts as soldiers may even be accepted or encouraged. Children may "voluntarily" take part in warfare, not realizing the dangers and abuses they will be subjected to. Most likely these children are responding to economic, cultural, social and political pressures.

The particular situation of girls in conflicts continues to require further attention. The potential risk of sexual violence, abuse and exploitation of children and women increase during armed conflicts, and specific measures must be taken to ensure their security and to strengthen their decision-making abilities. Still, in many instances, programmes to demobilize and reintegrate child soldiers fail to identify appropriate strategies for gaining access to these girls and young women. Ways must also be found to address the needs of girls abducted during war to serve as sexual slaves and who may have no alternative to remaining under the custody of their abductors.

2	

Ending the use of child soldiers can be extremely challenging, particularly when children are enlisted for combat by armed, non-governmental groups. In addition, modern conflicts are characterized by governmental breakdown, making it difficult to identify and influence those recruiting and using children as soldiers.

3		4	

In 2002 the Optional Protocol to the Convention on the Rights of the Child on the involvement of children in armed conflict entered into force. It outlaws the involvement of children under age 18 in hostilities, raising the previous standard of age (15 years) set by the Convention and the 1949 Geneva Conventions and their 1977 Additional Protocols. As well as requiring States to raise the age for compulsory recruitment and direct participation in conflict to 18, the Optional Protocol requires State parties to raise the minimum age for voluntary recruitment beyond the current minimum of 15.

Another milestone was set in July 2002 when the Statute of the International Criminal Court entered into force, making the conscription, enlistment or use of children under 15 in hostilities by national armed forces or armed groups a war crime.

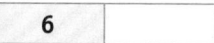

Violations of the laws of war that affect children need to be properly monitored and reported, so that perpetrators can be held accountable before tribunals or other truth and reconciliation mechanisms. This applies to the recruitment and use of children as soldiers, particularly in light of the provision in the Statute of the International Criminal Court. Adequate monitoring will also promote better understanding of and data on the numbers and situation of child soldiers.

During conflict, the capacity of families and communities to protect and care for children is undermined. Nonetheless, their efforts to ensure that their children do not become involved in violence are important and must be supported. The protection of children by families and communities is the frontline in the war against recruiting children into armed groups. Capacity also involves focusing efforts and resources on the most underserved regions and population groups, including displaced populations, to guarantee equal access to quality services, in particular education.

A protective environment for demobilized child soldiers must include strategies to prevent their re-recruitment. It should also lay the groundwork for the eventual return to their families and communities.

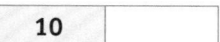

This includes advocacy on behalf of children at the international, national and community level. This could include, for example, promoting ratification of the Optional Protocol on the involvement of children in armed conflict and advocating for national law reform and sensitization campaigns. It could also mean engaging in dialogue with non-governmental armed groups to uphold international standards for child protection and securing their commitment to end the recruitment and use of children in hostilities.

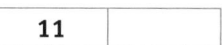

Giving children a voice – and listening to them – will allow children to have a say in their own protection and in the life of their community and country.

11

This includes providing protection to former child soldiers during demobilization and social reintegration programmes (education and vocational training) and providing psychosocial support (peer-to-peer support, community-based support and psychosocial counselling). It also means promoting family reunification as a key factor for social reintegration and ensuring follow-up care for demobilized children, focusing on long-term social reintegration.

Source: UNICEF

List of Headings

A	Attitudes, customs and behaviours, and practices	G	Legislation
B	Building a protective environment for children	H	Monitoring
C	Capacity	I	Services for victims of abuse
D	Children's life skills and participation	J	The facts
E	Elements already in place	K	The situation of girls
F	Governmental and non-governmental commitment	L	UNICEF's response

Task 4 Note form

Read the text again, then answer the questions using a maximum of 4 words. Write your answers in the spaces provided.

1. Give reasons why children become child soldiers.	
2. What do child soldiers not understand?	
3. Why is the situation of girls a special one?	
4. What does governmental breakdown make even more difficult?	
5. According to the new law, what is the minimum age to take part in conflicts?	
6. To what extent does monitoring help the situation?	
7. What should families and communities avoid for children?	
8. What is understood by a "protective environment"?	
9. How can the children help themselves?	
10. What can be done for the victims?	

Task 5 Vocabulary 1

Find the words in the text which have these meanings (the first letter is given):

1. someone who is involved in fighting in a war: **c** _ _ _ _ _ _ _ _
2. someone whose job it is to carry people's bags or other loads or to look after a building by cleaning it: **p** _ _ _ _ _ _
3. to take someone away by force, to kidnap: to **a** _ _ _ _ _ _
4. to persuade people to join the army, to conscript: to **r** _ _ _ _ _ _
5. cruel, violent treatment of someone, misuse: **a** _ _ _ _ _
6. to make a proposal into a law, to pass a law: to **e** _ _ _ _
7. fighting, a fight/battle: **c** _ _ _ _ _ _
8. to force a group of people to move away from the place where they normally live: to **d** _ _ _ _ _ _ _
9. to send home the members of an army, especially at the end of a war: to **d** _ _ _ _ _ _ _ _ _
10. without being forced, done willingly: **v** _ _ _ _ _ _ _ _
11. the activity of fighting in a war: **w** _ _ _ _ _ _
12. to be forced to suffer or experience something very unpleasant: to be **s** _ _ _ _ _ _ _ _ _   to
13. a situation in which you treat someone unfairly in order to get an advantage for yourself: **e** _ _ _ _ _ _ _ _ _ _ _
14. when someone is kept in prison while waiting for trial: **c** _ _ _ _ _ _
15. to completely stop something by making it illegal: to **o** _ _ _ _ _
16. unfriendly, aggressive feelings or behaviour, full of anger: **h** _ _ _ _ _ _ _
17. when people are ordered to serve in the army: **c** _ _ _ _ _ _ _ _ _ _
18. an action that breaks a law: **v** _ _ _ _ _ _ _ _
19. to carefully watch and check a situation over a period of time to see how it develops: to **m** _ _ _ _ _ _
20. someone who commits a crime or does something morally wrong: **p** _ _ _ _ _ _ _ _ _
21. responsible for the effects of your actions: **a** _ _ _ _ _ _ _ _ _ _
22. a court with the official authority to deal with a particular problem: **t** _ _ _ _ _ _ _
23. a situation in which two countries become friendly with each other again after quarrelling: **r** _ _ _ _ _ _ _ _ _ _ _ _
24. the place where the enemies are facing each other in a war: **f** _ _ _ _ _ _ _ _
25. to make a written agreement official by signing it: to **r** _ _ _ _ _
26. to publicly support something that should be done: to **a** _ _ _ _ _ _ _
27. advice and support given to someone with problems: **c** _ _ _ _ _ _ _ _ _ _

Task 6 Vocabulary 2

1. Complete the following collocations:

- ■ to _____ the groundwork

- ■ to _____ a say

- ■ to _____ revenge

2. Find at least 5 synonyms for *"war"*:

- ■ _____

- ■ _____

- ■ _____

- ■ _____

- ■ _____

Task 7 Vocabulary 3

Complete this table.

Noun (person)	Noun (abstract)	Verb	Adjective
		combat	
	abduction		—
recruit, recruiter			—
—		integrate	—
—		reunify	—
—	ratification		—
advocate			—
abuser			
		violate	—
	perpetration		—

RC 7 – TRUE/FALSE/JUSTIFICATION: "MALALA YOUSAFZAI"

Reading

Read the text about a courageous Pakistani schoolgirl. Decide whether the statements (1–8) are true (T) or false (F). Put a ✗ in the correct box. Then identify the sentence in the text which supports your decision. Write the first four words of this sentence in the space provided. The first one (0) has been done for you.

One day in November 2007, on an editing console in the Dawn television news bureau in Peshawar, Pakistan, the bright brown eyes of a young girl popped from the computer screen. Just three hours to the northeast, in the Swat Valley, the mountain town of Mingora was under siege. Walking by the desk of the bureau chief, a reporter named Syed Irfan Ashraf stopped to take a look at the edit, which was being translated into English for that night's news, and heard the girl's voice. "I'm very frightened", she said crisply. "Earlier, the situation was quite peaceful in Swat, but now it has worsened. Nowadays explosions are increasing. We can't sleep. Our siblings are terrified, and we cannot come to school." She spoke an Urdu of startling refinement for a rural child. "Who is that girl?", Ashraf asked the bureau chief. The answer came in Pashto, the local language: *"Takra jenai"*, which means "a shining young lady." He added, "I think her name is Malala".

The bureau chief had driven to Mingora to interview a local activist, the owner of the Khushal Girls High School & College. On the roads, Taliban soldiers in black turbans pulled drivers out of cars at checkpoints, searching for DVDs, alcohol, and anything else in violation of Shari'a, or strict Islamic law. In a lane near the market, a low wall protected the two-story private school. Inside, the bureau chief visited a fourth-grade class, where several girls shot up their hands when asked if they wanted to be interviewed. Seeing girls speak out in public was very unusual, even in the Swat Valley, a cultivated, 3,500-square-mile Shangri-la with 1.5 million inhabitants. That night, the brown-eyed girl's sound bite led the news.

Later that evening the bureau chief ran into the school's owner, Ziauddin Yousafzai, who said, "The girl who spoke on your broadcast. That Malala is my daughter". The highly educated Yousafzai clearly understood that in the rigid class system of Pakistan he was an invisible member of the rural underclass, unseen by the elite of Lahore and Karachi. For his family, a moment on national news was huge. Like his daughter, Ziauddin spoke excellent English. Ashraf, who had been a professor at the University of Peshawar, could not get the image of Malala's piercing gaze out of his mind. "She was an ordinary girl, but on-camera extraordinary", he said. His beat at Dawn television included covering the bombings that were devastating remote villages all through Swat, and he determined to meet Malala and her father the next time he was on assignment in Mingora.

Last autumn, I contacted Ashraf at a computer lab in Carbondale, Illinois, where he is studying for a doctorate in media studies at Southern Illinois University. On October 9, he had seen in a news flash the horrifying image of Malala Yousafzai lying bandaged on a stretcher, after having been shot by an unknown extremist on her school bus. For the next three days, Ashraf did not leave his cubicle as the world grieved for this teenager who had stood up to the Taliban. Then he wrote an anguished column in Dawn, Pakistan's most widely read English-language newspaper, which seemed like a profound *mea culpa*. Ashraf was savage regarding his role in Malala's tragedy. "Hype is created with the help of the media while the people wait for the dénouement", he wrote. He decried "the media's role in dragging bright young people into dirty wars with horrible consequences for the innocent". On the telephone he told me, "I was in shock. I could not call anyone". He described his mute agony watching the TV coverage. "It is criminal what I did", he said in an apoplectic tone. "I lured in a child of 11."

Ashraf had watched the news as Malala was later rushed to a hospital in Birmingham, England, where army trauma victims are treated. She was mysteriously separated from her family for 10 days. Many wondered why no relative had been allowed to travel with her. In Pakistan, thousands held candlelight vigils and carried posters that read: WE ARE ALL MALALA. Before she was flown to Birmingham, General Ashfaq Kayani, the Pakistan Army chief and former head of the all-powerful Inter-services Intelligence agency (ISI), had gone to the hospital in Peshawar where she struggled for life on a ventilator. The question arose: Why would the most powerful man in Pakistan's military rush to the provincial capital? Other girls had been assaulted, and the government had hardly reacted.

Source: Marie Brenner, Malala Yousafzai (750 words)

		T	F	Justification
0.	Recently the adverse conditions in the Swat Valley have improved.		✗	*Earlier, the situation was ...*
1.	Malala's mastery of the language was unexpected for the reporter.			
2.	A few students were very eager to talk to the reporter.			
3.	The head of the school belonged to the hidden top echelons of society in this area.			
4.	What the reporter remembered best about Malala was her uncompromising look.			
5.	The reporter was relentless because he had made Malala famous.			
6.	According to the reporter, the influence of the media can damage the reputation of smart adolescents.			
7.	When Malala was taken to a health center, she was always accompanied by a parent.			
8.	People wondered why the General of the Army came to a local hospital to visit Malala.			

RC 8 – NOTE FORM: "A VERY SHORT STORY"

Task **Reading**

Read the story by Ernest Hemingway. Complete the sentences, using a maximum of 4 words. The first one (0) has been done for you.

Ernest Hemingway – A Very Short Story

One hot evening in Padua they carried him up onto the roof and he could look out over the top of the town. There were chimney swifts in the sky. After a while it got dark and the searchlights came out. The others went down and took the bottles with them. He and Luz could hear them below on the balcony. Luz sat on the bed. She was cool and fresh in the hot night.

Luz stayed on night duty for three months. They were glad to let her. When they operated on him she prepared him for the operating table; and they had a joke about friend or enema. He went under the anaesthetic holding tight on to himself so he would not blab about anything during the silly, talky time. After he got on crutches he used to take the temperatures so Luz would not have to get up from the bed. There were only a few patients, and they all knew about it. They all liked Luz. As he walked back along the halls he thought of Luz in his bed.

Before he went back to the front they went into the Duomo and prayed. It was dim and quiet, and there were other people praying. They wanted to get married, but there was not enough time for the banns, and neither of them had birth certificates. They felt as though they were married, but they wanted everyone to know about it, and to make it so they could not lose it.

Luz wrote him many letters that he never got until after the armistice. Fifteen came in a bunch to the front and he sorted them by the dates and read them all straight through. They were all about the hospital, and how much she loved him and how it was impossible to get along without him and how terrible it was missing him at night.

After the armistice they agreed he should go home to get a job so they might be married. Luz would not come home until he had a good job and could come to New York to meet her. It was understood he would not drink, and he did not want to see his friends or anyone in the States. Only to get a job and be married. On the train from Padua to Milan they quarrelled about her not being willing to come home at once. When they had to say good-bye, in the station at Milan, they kissed good-bye, but were not finished with the quarrel. He felt sick about saying good-bye like that.

He went to America on a boat from Genoa. Luz went back to Pordonone to open a hospital. It was lonely and rainy there, and there was a battalion of arditi quartered in the town. Living in the muddy, rainy town in the winter, the major of the battalion made love to Luz, and she had never known Italians before, and finally wrote to the States that theirs had only been a boy and girl affair. She was sorry, and she knew he would probably not be able to understand, but might some day forgive her, and be grateful to her, and she expected, absolutely unexpectedly, to be married in the spring. She loved him as always, but she realized now it was only a boy and girl love. She hoped he would have a great career, and believed in him absolutely. She knew it was for the best.

The major did not marry her in the spring, or any other time. Luz never got an answer to the letter to Chicago about it. A short time after, he contracted gonorrhea from a sales girl in a loop department store while riding in a taxicab through Lincoln Park.

Source: Ernest Hemingway, In Our Time (645 words)

0	The others left the rooftop, when _____.	*it got dark*
1	When Luz made him ready for the operation, he was afraid of _____.	
2	It was impossible for him and Luz to register for marriage because they did _____.	
3	He received Luz's messages only _____.	
4	After the war Luz decided against _____.	
5	Because he and Luz had a fight before they parted, he _____.	
6	After Luz returned to her job, she _____.	
7	When Luz sent him a farewell letter, she already realized he _____.	
8	The story ends with Luz neither hearing from him nor _____.	

RC 9 – NOTE FORM: "DEAD POETS SOCIETY"

The new term has just started at Welton Academy, a private boarding school for boys in New England. It is the year 1959. Neil Perry and his friends are just introducing themselves to a new fellow student, when suddenly they are interrupted by an unexpected visitor.

Task 1 Pre-Reading

1. **If you have read the book or seen the film**, try to remember the scene and who the unexpected visitor is. What is his relationship to Neil and his friends and what does he want? How do the boys react to his presence?
2. **If you have not read the book or seen the film**, read the first two paragraphs to find out who this unexpected visitor is. Make sensible guesses as to why he has come and how the boys react to his presence. Bearing in mind that this is the year 1959 and that the setting is a private boarding school for boys, what do you think the relationship between Neil and his visitor is like?

Task 2 Reading

Read the extract from the novel and answer the questions below it, using a maximum of 4 words.

There was another knock on the door. "It's open," Neil called. But it wasn't another of their buddies this time.

"Father," Neil stammered, his face turning white. "I thought you'd left!"

The boys jumped to their feet. "Mr. Perry," Meeks, Charlie, and Knox said in unison.

"Keep your seats, boys," Neil's father said as he walked briskly into the room. "How's it going?"

"Fine, sir. Thank you," they answered.

Mr. Perry stood face to face with Neil, who shuffled uncomfortably. "Neil, I've decided that you're taking too many extracurricular activities. I've spoken to Mr. Nolan about it, and he's agreed to let you work on the school annual next year," he said, and then walked toward the door.

"But, Father," Neil cried. "I'm the assistant editor!"

"I'm sorry, Neil," Mr. Perry replied stiffly.

"But, Father, it's not fair. I ..."

Mr. Perry's eyes glared at Neil, who stopped midsentence. Then he opened the door and pointed to Neil to leave the room.

"Fellows, would you excuse us a minute?" he asked politely. Mr. Perry followed Neil closing the door behind him.

His eyes raging, Mr. Perry hissed at his son. "I will not be disputed in public, do you understand me?"

"Father," Neil said lamely, "I wasn't disputing you. I ..."

"When you've finished medical school and you're on your own, you can do as you please. Until then, you will listen to ME!"

Neil looked at the floor. "Yes, sir. I'm sorry."

"You know what this means to your mother, don't you?" Mr. Perry said.

"Yes, sir." Neil stood silent in front of his father. His resolve always crumbled under the threats of guilt and punishment.

"Oh well, you know me," Neil said, filling the pause. "Always taking on too much."

"Good boy. Call us if you need anything." He turned without further comment and walked off. Neil looked after his father, feeling overwhelmed with frustration and anger. Why did he always let his father get to him like that?

He opened the door to his room and walked back in. The boys tried to look as if nothing had happened, each waiting for the other to speak. Finally Charlie broke the silence.

"Why doesn't he ever let you do what you want?" he asked. "And why don't you just tell him off! It couldn't get any worse," Knox added.

Neil wiped his eyes. "Oh, that's rich," he sneered. "Like you tell YOUR parents off, Mr. Future Lawyer and Mr. Future Banker!" The boys studied their shoes as Neil stormed around the room angrily. He ripped the school annual achievement pin from his blazer and hurled it furiously at his desk.

"Wait a minute," Knox said, walking toward Neil. "I don't let my parents walk on me."

"Yeah," Neil laughed. "You just do everything they say! You'll be in daddy's law firm as sure as I'm standing here." He turned to Charlie who was sprawled across Neil's bed. "And you'll be approving loans till you croak!"

"Okay," admitted Charlie. "So I don't like it any more than you do. I'm just saying ..."

"Then don't tell me how to talk to my father when you're the same way," Neil snapped. "All right?"

"All right," Knox sighed. "Jesus, what are you gonna do?"

"What I have to do. Chuck the annual. I have no choice."

"I certainly wouldn't lose any sleep over it," Meeks said cheerfully. "It's just a bunch of people trying to impress Nolan."

Neil slammed his suitcase shut and slumped onto his bed. "What do I care about any of it anyhow?" He slammed his hand into his pillow, lay back silently, and stared with glazed eyes at the ceiling.

The boys sat around glumly, feeling Neil's disappointment and sadness.

Source: N. H. Kleinbaum, Dead Poets Society (about 600 words)

0.	Who did Neil expect when there was a knock at the door?	*another of their buddies*
1.	How did Neil feel in the presence of his father?	
2.	Which extracurricular activity did Mr Perry want his son to drop?	
3.	How did Mr Perry feel when Neil disputed him in public?	
4.	What was Neil's reaction to his father's threats of guilt and punishment?	
5.	What did his friend Knox think Neil should do?	
6.	What did Charlie's parents expect their son to become?	
7.	What did Neil decide to do?	
8.	Who was Mr Nolan?	
9.	What – according to Meeks – did the people who worked on the annual really want to do?	
10.	How did all the boys feel at the end of this scene?	

Task 3 Vocabulary

Choose the correct definitions for these words from the extract.

1.	briskly	A	to tear sth or to become torn, often suddenly or violently
2.	to shuffle	B	to begin to fail or get weaker or to come to an end
3.	an annual	C	to put, push or throw sth into a particular place or position with a lot of force
4.	resolve	D	to sit or fall down heavily
5.	to crumble	E	practically and confidently; showing a desire to get things done quickly
6.	to rip	F	strong determination to achieve sth
7.	to hurl	G	to give up or stop doing sth
8.	to approve	H	sadly, quietly and unhappily
9.	to croak	I	to move from one foot to another; to move your feet in an awkward or embarrassed way
10.	to chuck	J	to die (*very informal!*)
11.	to slump	K	to think that sb/sth is good, acceptable or suitable; to officially agree to a plan, request
12.	to slam	L	a book that is published once a year, with the same title each time, but different contents
13.	glumly	M	to throw sth/sb violently in a particular direction

INTRODUCTION

Ein Teilbereich der neuen **Standardisierten Reifeprüfung in Englisch** ist die Überprüfung des Hörverständnisses, **Listening Comprehension (LC)**. Die Art der Aufgabenstellungen sind mit der *Cambridge First Certificate*-Prüfung vergleichbar. Das bedeutet, dass du innerhalb von **45 Minuten** verschiedene Aufgaben zu vier unabhängigen Texten zu lösen hast. Es darf bei der **LC** kein Wörterbuch verwendet werden.

	Mögliche Aufgabenstellungen
Multiple Matching	Gezielt Informationen heraushören und den richtigen Fragen zuordnen
Multiple Choice	Verständnisfragen zum Inhalt des Hörtextes mit jeweils 4 Antwortmöglichkeiten
Note form	Sätze vervollständigen, Fragen beantworten mit bis zu maximal vier Wörtern

In diesem Übungsbuch geht den eigentlichen Hörverständnisaufgaben immer eine kurze *introduction* voraus. Diese soll dich auf das Thema des Hörtextes einstimmen und dich dazu anregen, dir schon vor dem Hören zu überlegen, worum es gehen könnte.

10 GOLDEN RULES FOR LISTENING COMPREHENSIONS

Hier findest du eine Reihe von allgemeinen Richtlinien, die dir helfen sollen, **LCs** richtig anzupacken.

1. Thinking Ahead
Bevor du die Aufgabenstellung genauer studierst oder dir den Text anhörst, solltest du immer versuchen, Vermutungen über den Inhalt des zu bearbeitenden Textes anzustellen.
- Worum geht es?
- Verrät dir der Titel Näheres?
- Was weißt du über das Thema, das da auf dich zukommt?
- Welche englischen Wörter oder Phrasen könnten vorkommen?

2. Understanding The Tasks
Lies dir alle Aufgabenstellungen genau durch und versichere dich, dass dir völlig klar ist, was du zu tun hast.

3. Predicting
Das sorgfältige Durchlesen der gesamten Angabe lässt dich nun sicher schon genauer erahnen, worum es in der Hörübung geht. Versuche dir auch darüber klarzuwerden, welche Informationen gefragt sind oder fehlen. Bei Übungen, in denen einzelne Wörter einzusetzen sind, solltest du dir überlegen, welche Wortart ergänzt werden muss, damit die Sätze vollständig werden.

4. Listening – ❶
Hör dir die Aufnahme an und beantworte so viele Fragen wie möglich. Achte auf *key words*! Verfalle nicht in Panik, wenn es dir nicht gelingt, alle Aufgaben zu lösen – du hörst den Text ohnehin ein zweites Mal.
Wenn du ein *summary* schreiben musst, so empfiehlt es sich beim ersten Zuhören nur in jede zweite Zeile zu schreiben, damit du anschließend beim zweiten Durchgang genug Platz hast, deine Notizen zu ergänzen. Oder du kannst natürlich auch das Blatt in zwei Spalten teilen und beim zweiten Zuhören in der rechten Spalte die ersten Notizen auffüllen.

Abkürzungen

Versuche beim Zuhören lange Wörter abzukürzen und verwende gewisse Kürzel (zB **+** für „und" oder → für „in der Folge" oder „daraus folgt").

5. Completing Your Notes

Bevor du den Text noch einmal abspielst, vervollständige deine Notizen:

- Ergänze, was du dir zwar gemerkt, aber noch nicht aufgeschrieben hast.
- Schreibe abgekürzte Wörter aus.
- Korrigiere unleserlich geschriebene Passagen jetzt, wo du noch weißt, was du damit gemeint hast.

6. Listening – ❷

Beim zweiten Zuhören ergänze, was dir noch fehlt, und entscheide dich in Zweifelsfällen jedenfalls für eine Lösung – hoffentlich die richtige.

7. Completing And Eliminating

Vervollständige wiederum deine Aufzeichnungen und versuche auch den Umkehrschluss: Frage dich nicht nur, warum eine bestimmte Antwortmöglichkeit hier passt, sondern auch, warum die anderen falsch sind.

8. Checking Correctness

Zum Abschluss lies dir noch einmal alle Übungen genau durch und überprüfe Grammatik, Rechtschreibung und auch Satzzeichen.

9. Guessing The Answer

Lasse nie eine Frage unbeantwortet oder eine Lücke ungefüllt, auch wenn du die richtige Lösung einfach nicht heraushören konntest. Raten ist besser als nichts ankreuzen oder einfügen!

10. Checking Completeness

Wirf noch einen letzten Blick zurück, ob du auch wirklich alle Fragen beantwortet und alle Aufgaben gelöst hast.

Wenn du eine LC durchgemacht hast, dann solltest du sie dir noch einmal anhören und dabei im Lösungsheft das *tapescript* mitlesen. So werden manche unklare Stellen im Nachhinein klar und dein Hörverständnis von mal zu mal besser!

LC 1 – NOTE FORM: "DIALECTS AND STANDARD ENGLISH"

Introduction

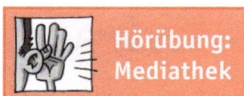

You are going to hear an interview with Professor David Crystal and Professor Edgar Schneider about the importance of standard language and dialect as well as linguistic identity.

First study the task below, then listen to the recording twice. While listening, answer the **questions 1–7 using a maximum of 4 words**. The first one (0) has been done for you.

0.	What is sometimes impossible to understand for speakers of Standard English?	*(the) New Englishes*
1.	What is "Singlish"?	
2.	What used to happen to dialects for many centuries?	
3.	What is the English language doing at the moment?	
4.	Why do accents and dialects come into being?	
5.	Why do we need standard languages?	
6.	Why are people in Singapore increasingly adopting English as their first language?	
7.	What might Singapore become in the long run?	

 # LC 2 – NOTE FORM: "SEXY ADS?"

Introduction

You are going to hear an interview with advertising researcher John Morris about young women's reactions to current beauty ideals.

First study the task below, then listen to the recording twice. While listening, write your answers in the spaces provided using a maximum of four words. The first one (0) has been done for you.

A recent study shows that the attitude that **(0.)** *'sex sells'* may no longer apply to young women.

The models in the study had to be classified according to **(1.)** _____.

It turned out that just two categories of models remained, which were then referred to as **(2.)**

_____ and **(3.)** _____.

The women's **(4.)** _____ to the models was explored with the

help of a technique called 'AdSAM'.

The women used **(5.)** _____ to communicate how they felt about the different models.

It turned out that most of the women in the study reacted with a feeling of **(6.)**

_____ to very sexy models.

John Morris believes that women in general don't find sexy imagery very **(7.)** _____

and are consequently not willing **(8.)** _____ the brand associated with it.

It seemed that the women in the study labelled the models as sexy-sensual not so much because they really

saw them that way but because they had been **(9.)** _____.

College women are an important target group for advertisers, because they have the **(10.)**

_____.

LC 3 – MULTIPLE MATCHING: "YOUNG PEOPLE AND THE EU"

Introduction

Five young people have been interviewed about how they see current developments in the EU.

First study the task below, then listen to the recording twice. While listening, match the speakers 1–5 with the statements A–G. There are two extra statements that you should not use (–). Write your answers in the spaces provided. The first one (0) has been done for you.

Speaker 1	G
Speaker 2	
Speaker 3	
Speaker 4	
Speaker 5	

A	Certain countries don't seem to be welcome in the EU.
B	Countries with a record of human rights abuses should not be accepted in the EU.
C	Only the EU can guarantee a peaceful future.
D	The EU has made life more expensive.
E	The EU offers some wonderful opportunities for young people.
F	The people of Turkey are sceptical about the euro.
G	Young people in the EU have to face certain disadvantages.

 # LC 4 – MULTIPLE CHOICE: "THE UN CLIMATE CONFERENCE IN NAIROBI"

Introduction

You are going to listen to a recording about three different perspectives on the UN climate conference.

First study the task below, then listen to the recording twice. While listening, choose the correct answer (A, B, C or D). Put a   in the correct box. The first one (0) has been done for you.

		Nairobi was chosen as the location of the conference because of
	A	its wish to promote Kenya internationally.
0. ✗	B	*the increasing needs of the Third World.*
	C	sending too many greenhouse gases out into the air.
	D	its climate.

		Sarah Higgins
	A	lives four hours away by car from Nairobi.
1.	B	lives in a beautiful, mountainous region close to Nairobi.
	C	moved from Sweden to Kenya 30 years ago.
	D	has been living in Kenya for more than three decades.

2.		**Sarah Higgins and her husband have succeeded in**
	A	planting a lot of trees.
	B	buying a flower farm.
	C	installing sprinkler systems.
	D	helping all the other farmers around them.

3.		**According to Sarah,**
	A	the protection of environment is given careful attention.
	B	the government does its best.
	C	the educational process is slow.
	D	there are a lot of resources for underdeveloped countries.

4.		**Achim Steiner of the UN Environment Program supports solutions that**
	A	are fast.
	B	use high tech products.
	C	are expensive, but effective.
	D	people take responsibility for themselves.

5.		**The local farmers face difficulty because**
	A	their own actions have failed.
	B	they do not have enough means to adjust.
	C	they have no information on climate change.
	D	they have no access to credit.

6.		**The public has come to see that**
	A	the governments will decide on new emission standards.
	B	they will not get money for new projects.
	C	the governments need to take action.
	D	the Adaptation Fund will be administered by the First World.

7.		**Kofi Annan delivered one important message:**
	A	Decision makers on a global level urgently need to combat climate change.
	B	Investing in Africa's infrastructure would create jobs.
	C	We must seek solutions to stop the global CO_2 emissions.
	D	Ignoring the needs of the developing world is unfair and short-sighted.

LC 5 – NOTE FORM: "AN INTERVIEW WITH SOMEONE WHO FOUNDED A MAGAZINE"

Introduction

Listen to part of an interview with someone who founded a magazine. Before listening think about possible motives for founding a new magazine. What kinds of magazines might be missing today?

You are going to listen to an interview with Tony Elliott, who founded *Time Out*, a new magazine. First study the task below, then listen to the recording twice. While listening, write your answers in the spaces provided using a maximum of four words. The first one (0) has been done for you.

0.	What does *Time Out* feature?	*what's going on*
1.	In 1968, where could you find the information where events happened?	a) b)
2.	Whom did he create the magazine for?	
3.	Where did they sell the new magazine at first?	a) b)
4.	When Tony took control of the magazine at university what did he transform it into?	
5.	What was Tony believed to do during the summer holidays?	
6.	What did he do instead?	
7.	How often are most magazines published?	
8.	What led to the magazine becoming a weekly?	
9.	What was the attitude of publishers as well as advertisers to Tony's readership like?	
10.	Who is primarily the readership of Time Out?	

LC 6 – NOTE FORM: "THE EUROPEAN DREAM – A MODEL FOR THE WORLD?"

Introduction

Hörübung: Mediathek

You are going to listen to a recording about the differences between the American and the European Dream. First study the task below, then listen to the recording twice. While listening, answer the questions in the spaces provided using a maximum of four words. The first one (0) has been done for you.

0.	Why has the American Dream lost its importance?	*Americans are overworked/underpaid*
1.	Why would Jim Hill from Nevada like to return to Europe?	
2.	How would an American now define the American Dream?	
3.	In contrast to the individuality in the American Dream, what does the European Dream emphasize?	
4.	Why do the Americans have a better life?	
5.	In what respect have the Europeans surpassed the Americans? Give one example.	
6.	In what subjects at lower levels of education do European children outdo the Americans?	
7.	When would you prefer to go to a clinic in the US?	
8.	Name one advantage of the European health care.	
9.	Why is America placed 27th in infant mortality?	
10.	How do Europeans contribute to sustain the environment?	

LC 7 – MULTIPLE MATCHING: "CHOOSING THE RIGHT HOLIDAY"

Introduction

You are going to listen to five people, who have been interviewed about their preferences when choosing the right holiday. First study the task below, then listen to the recording twice. While listening, match the five speakers with the statements A–G. There are two extra statements that you should not use. Write your answers in the spaces provided. The first one has been done for you.

Anita	C
Kirti	
Claire	
Kirk	
Oliver	

A	You will never feel bored in Vienna, the city of music, art and unforgettable architecture.
B	Deep-Ocean Travel is planning two unique journeys to the ocean floor.
C	The English Lake District is a natural adventure park and offers new activities every day.
D	Tallin has got one of the best preserved old towns in Europe.
E	You will be entertained with numerous activities onboard your Caribbean cruise ship.
F	Northern England offers you both adventure activities and comfortable holiday accommodations.
G	*Earthwatch Expedition* supports a project which protects the cheetah in Namibia.

INTRODUCTION

Ein weiterer Teilbereich der schriftlichen Neuen Standardisierten Reifeprüfung ist der **Language in Use**-Teil (LiU). Ähnliche Aufgabenstellungen kannst du auch bei den *Use of English*-Aufgaben der *Cambridge First Certificate*-Prüfungen finden. Du hast 45 Minuten Zeit, um vier verschiedene Aufgaben zu lösen.

Diese vier Texte sind ungefähr 200–350 Wörter lang und haben zwischen 10 und 14 Lücken. Du findest immer ein Beispiel zu Beginn der Aufgabe. Auch bei diesem Teil ist die Verwendung des Wörterbuches nicht erlaubt.

	Mögliche Aufgabenstellungen
Multiple Choice	Du wählst die richtige von 4 Möglichkeiten aus. Achte sowohl auf Bedeutungsunterschiede von Vokabeln als auch auf grammatikalische Feinheiten.
Word formation	Der Stamm eines Wortes steht in Klammer und durch Anhängen von Vor- und Nachsilben musst du die richtige Form bilden, die in den Text hineinpasst. Normalerweise musst du Nomen, Adjektive, Adverbia oder Verbformen bilden. Achte vor allem auf negative Vorsilben, wie zB un-, im-, il-, dis- oder Nachsilben wie zB -ment, -ion, -or, -er ... oder den Plural eines Wortes. Lies den Text genau, denn auch der Inhalt des Textes rund um die Lücken gibt dir Entscheidungshilfen.
Banked gap-filling	Du wählst die richtige Antwort aus einer „bank" aus – da stehen alle möglichen Antworten plus zwei Distraktoren, die im Anschluss an den Text in alphabetischer Reihenfolge angeordnet sind. Die Wörter dieser „bank" können 1–3 Wörter lang sein.
Open gap-filling	Die Vorgansweise ist die gleiche wie beim banked *gap-filling* mit dem Unterscheid, dass es keine „bank" gibt. Du musst also ein passendes englisches Wort finden, das in die Lücke passt. Es fehlt immer nur ein Wort.
Editing	In einen Text sind zusätzliche Wörter eingefügt worden. Finde diese unnötigen bzw. falschen Wörter heraus. Es kann immer nur ein Wort pro Zeile sein. Ein paar Zeilen sind richtig.

7 GOLDEN RULES FOR LANGUAGE IN USE

1. **Reading the text**
   Lies den Text einmal durch, damit du weißt, worum es geht. Beachte die Lücken vorerst gar nicht.

2. **Reading the text again**
   Schau genau auf die Wörter, die vor und nach der Lücke stehen, ob sie dir einen Hinweis geben, welches Wort du brauchst. Probier die Lücken zu vervollständigen.

3. **Word formation**
   Verändere das Wort durch Hinzufügen der notwendigen Vor- und/oder Nachsilben.

   Multiple Choice
   Schau dir die 4 Möglichkeiten genau an und versuche die „falschen" drei zu eliminieren. Dafür kann es sowohl grammatikalische als auch lexikalische Gründe geben.

4. **Reading the text**
   Überprüfe nochmals, ob deine Antworten im Kontext dazu passen, wenn du den kompletten Text liest.

5. **Making a guess**
   Lass keine Lücke leer. Wenn du dir unsicher bist, rate.

6. **Checking the spelling of your answers**
   Achte auf die richtige Schreibweise, vor allem bei word formation ist dieser Punkt wichtig.

7. **Checking completeness**
   Kontrolliere, ob du alle Aufgaben/Lücken gelöst hast.

LIU 1 – MULTIPLE CHOICE: "RULE NUMBER 1: FOLLOW ALL RULES"

You are going to read a text about an American who does not follow an important rule in a bar. Some words are missing from the text. Choose the correct answer A, B, C or D for each gap 1 to 12 in the text. Write your answers in the boxes provided. The first one (0) has been done for you.

I did a foolish thing (**0**) _____ evening. I went into one of our local bars and seated myself without permission. You just don't do this in America, but I had an important recurring thought that I wanted to (**1**) _____ down before it left my head (…), and anyway the place was practically empty, so I just took a table near the door.

After a couple of minutes the hostess – the Customer Seating Manager – came (**2**) _____ me and said in a level tone, "I see you've (**3**) _____ yourself."

"Yup," I replied proudly. "Dressed myself too."

"Didn't you see the sign?" She tilted her head at a bog sign that said "Please Wait to Be Seated."

I (**4**) _____ in this bar about 150 times. I have seen the sign from every (**5**) _____ but supine.*

"Is there a sign?" I said innocently. "Gosh, I didn't notice it."

She sighed. "Well, the server in this section is very busy, so you may (**6**) _____ wait some time for her to get to you."

There was (**7**) _____ customer within 50 feet, but that wasn't the point. The point was that I (**8**) _____ a posted notice and would have to serve a small (**9**) _____ in purgatory in consequence.

It would be entirely (**10**) _____ to say that Americans love rules, but they have a certain regard for them. They behave towards rules in much the way the British behave towards queues – as something that is fundamental to the maintenance of a civilized and (**11**) _____ society. I had, in effect, queue-jumped the "Wait to Be Seated" sign.

Source: Bill Bryson, Notes from a Big Country

0.	A	another	**B**	the other	C	every	D	all
1.	A	scribble	B	draw	C	get	D	bring
2.	A	down on	B	on to	C	up for	D	up to
3.	A	sat	B	seated	C	seat	D	sit
4.	A	was	B	had been	C	have been	D	were
5.	A	angle	B	angel	C	sphere	D	window
6.	A	be able to	B	can	C	have to	D	must
7.	A	none	B	nobody	C	any other	D	no other
8.	A	had disregarded	B	have disregarded	C	had regarded	D	regarded
9.	A	command	B	question	C	speech	D	sentence
10.	A	right	B	logical	C	wrong	D	impossible
11.	A	primitive	B	orderly	C	order	D	tribal

0.	1.	2.	3.	4.	5.	6.	7.	8.	9.	10.	11.
B											

---

* lying on your back

LIU 2 – WORD FORMATION: "WE THE PEOPLES OF EUROPE"

You are going to read a review of a book about the European Union. Some words are missing from the text. Use the words in brackets to complete each gap 1–12 in the text. Write your answers in the spaces provided at the end of the text. The first one (0) has been done for you.

The European Union now stands at a crossroads – The Irish "no" to the referendum on the Treaty has seen to that – and must rethink how it is to proceed. Are the bureaucrats of Brussels going to be allowed to fudge the treaty yet again and blackmail Ireland into (**0**) _____ (hold) another referendum and ensuring that the next time round the Irish people vote "yes"? Or will the EU leaders accept that the Treaty is (**1**) _____ (honest) and undemocratic, and examine the fundamental problems that (**2**) _____ (threat) the future of what is perhaps the most important and (**3**) _____ (courage) political experiment of the last century? The Treaty represents an attempt to combine a Constitution and a set of working (**4**) _____ (regulate) and is, in consequence, a mess. The Constitution of the EU should be as short as possible and should set out the principles by which the EU will operate: democracy, free movement of people, observance of human rights, (**5**) _____ (free) of speech and the press and so on. This must be (**6**) _____ (accept) to all EU members. Second, there must be a set of regulatory laws of rules that govern the ways in which 27 countries work together and these must be flexible to accommodate the (**7**) _____ (vary) that are inevitable in a community (**8**) _____ (consist) of 27 countries and 475 million people.
Above all, if the EU is to work to the advantage of all its members it must be (**9**) _____ (true) democratic. Democracy is not just about periodic (**10**) _____ (elect); it is about people taking part in decision-making (**11**) _____ (process) and feeling that their voices are both heard and taken into account. For this state of affairs to be (**12**) _____ (achieve), the EU must rethink itself from the grassroots up.

Source: North-South Publication, October 2008

0. *holding* _____

1. _____

2. _____

3. _____

4. _____

5. _____

6. _____

7. _____

8. _____

9. _____

10. _____

11. _____

12. _____

LIU 3 – BANKED GAP-FILLING: "RUNNER HOBBLES HOME AFTER 5 YEARS AND 20,000 MILES"

You are going to read a text about a woman who ran across the globe. Some parts of the text are missing. Choose from the list A–P the correct part for each gap in the text. There are two extra parts that you should not use. Write your answers in the boxes provided. The first one (0) has been done for you.

Having clocked up 20,000 miles on a five-year-journey run around the globe with nothing but her cart for company, Rosie Swale-Pope is entitled to put her (**0**) _____ up.

Crutches held aloft, the 61-year-old grandmother of two returned to an (**1**) _____ welcome in Tenby yesterday, as her mission to run solo across the northern hemisphere came to a triumphant end. Hundreds of well-wishers turned out to cheer their (**2**) _____ as she crossed the pink ribbon.

It was in her Welsh hometown in 2003 that Mrs Swale-Pope had (**3**) _____ her journey to highlight awareness of prostate cancer after her husband, Clive, died of the disease.

Yesterday, nearing the line, she modestly described her feat as "just a fun run that's got out of hand". The adventure had (**4**) _____ her across Europe and into Russia, where she survived two Siberian winters, the US and Canada.

She camped in blizzards and (**5**) _____ frostbite, broken ribs and double pneumonia. She was (**6**) _____ by a bus, was almost swept to her death in a swollen river and had to outpace bears, wolves and (**7**) _____ .

As she returned across less fearsome Welsh terrain, (**8**) _____ in her legs caused by stress fractures compelled a stay in a Haverfordwest hospital that she insisted be kept brief, and she hobbled the last stretch on crutches. She nevertheless looked fit and (**9**) _____ yesterday as she arrived in the seaside town.

"I'm pleased I fractured my hip because it's made it more (**10**) _____ and I got here just fine," she said. "I thank the (**11**) _____ consultant of Withybush Hospital for letting me go. I looked in his eyes and said, 'I've got to do it'."

She was joined at the last stage by Tenby Aces Cycling Club and the Trots Running Club, and the throngs greeting her included new friends that she had (**12**) _____ on her way and who had arrived from Alaska and Chicago.

Clutching a glass of champagne, she said: "I can't believe you've all turned out for me. I'm overwhelmed. It's a journey that came out of (**13**) _____ and pain and heartache, but it's a journey that has turned to joy."

Source: THE TIMES, August 26, 2008

A	begun	E	feet	I	made	M	sorrow
B	done	F	head	J	painkiller	N	suffered
C	enthusiastic	G	heroine	K	pains	O	taken
D	exciting	H	hit	L	robbers	P	well

0.	1.	2.	3.	4.	5.	6.	7.	8.	9.	10.	11.	12.	13.
E													

LIU 4 – EDITING: "ABOUT A BOY"

You are going to read an extract from the novel *about a boy*. In most lines of the text there is a wrong word. Write the wrong word in the space provided after each line. Some lines are correct. Indicate these lines with a tick . There are two examples at the beginning.

Once or twice Will decided he couldn't face it and went shopping or to the cinema; but	✔	0.
most of the time he was in home at four-fifteen, waiting for the buzzer – sometimes	*home*	00.
because he couldn't be bothered to go out, sometimes because he felt he owed to Marcus		1.
something. What and why he owed him he didn't know of, but he could see he was serving		2.
some purpose in the kid's life at the moment, and as he served no second purpose in		3.
anybody else's he was hardly going to die of compassion fatigue. It was still a bit of a drag,		4.
though, having some kid inflict himself on you every afternoon. Will who would be relieved		5.
when Marcus found a purpose to the life somewhere else.		6.
On the third or fourth visit he has asked Marcus about Fiona, and ended up wishing he		7.
hadn't, because it was quite clear that the boy was messed up about it. Will couldn't blame		8.
him on, but couldn't think of anything to say that would be of even the smallest		9.
consolation or value, so he ended up simply swearing sympathetically and, given Marcus's		10.
age, down inappropriately. Will wouldn't make that mistake again. If Marcus wanted to		11.
talk about his suicidal mother, when he could do it with Suzie, or a counsellor, or someone		12.
like that, someone capable of something more than an obscenity.		13.

Source: Nick Hornby, about a boy

LIU 5 – OPEN GAP-FILLING: "I'M A STRANGER HERE MYSELF"

You are going to read a text about Bill Bryson's return to the USA. Some words are missing from the text. Write the missing words (1–12) in the spaces provided. The first one (0) has been done for you.

When we moved to this little town in New Hampshire, people received us as if the one thing that had kept them from total happiness to this point was the absence of us in their lives. They brought (**0**) _____ cakes and pies and bottles of wine. Not one of them said, "So you're the people (**1**) _____ paid a fortune for the Smith place," which I believe is the traditional greeting in England. (**2**) _____ next-door neighbors, upon learning that we were intending to (**3**) _____ out to eat, protested that it was too, too dreary to dine in a restaurant on one's first night in a new town and insisted we come to them (**4**) _____ dinner there and then, as (**5**) _____ feeding six extra mouths was the most trifling of burdens.

When word got (**6**) _____ that our furniture was on a containership making its way (**7**) _____ Liverpool to Boston, evidently by the way of Port Said, Mombasa, and the Galapagos Islands, and that we were temporarily (**8**) _____ anything to sleep on, sit on, or eat from, a stream of friendly strangers (some of whom I have not seen (**9**) _____) began traipsing up the walk with chairs, lamps, tables, even a microwave oven.

It was dazzling, and it (**10**) _____ remained so. At Christmas this year we went to England for ten days and returned home (**11**) _____ at night and hungry to find that a neighbor had stocked the fridge with (**12**) _____ essentials and goodies and filled vases with fresh flowers. This sort of thing happens all the time.

Source: Bill Bryson, I'm a Stranger Here Myself

0. *us*

1. _____   **7.** _____

2. _____   **8.** _____

3. _____   **9.** _____

4. _____   **10.** _____

5. _____   **11.** _____

6. _____   **12.** _____

LIU 6 – MULTIPLE CHOICE: "THE 'DIRT' ON CLEAN"

From Roman baths to today's hand wipes, a new book tells the fascinating (and often gross) history of cleanliness

You are going to read a text about the history of cleanliness. Some words are missing from the text. Choose the correct answer A, B, C or D for each gap 1–10 in the text. Write your answers in the boxes provided. The first one has been done for you (0).

"When people hear that I've written a history of cleanliness, they often (**0**) _____ that I'm a clean-freak," says Canadian writer Katherine Ashenburg, author of Clean: An Unsanitised History of Washing. "I'm (**1**) _____ not. My interest in writing the book didn't stem from cleanliness so much as from my (**2**) _____ about the everyday lives of people in past ages."

But in her new book, Ashenburg certainly dishes the dirt on clean. (**3**) _____ our ancestors' bathing habits might disgust us, our bathing habits would also disgust them. "The thought of a daily hot shower would have filled the 17th century Frenchman with fear," she says. That's because after the Black Plague in the 14th century, the French thought that hot baths made (**4**) _____ ill – and for 200 years Europeans avoided hot baths just like the plague. And while some cultures consider body odour (**5**) _____, others find it sexy. Before a return to Paris, for instance, Napoleon ordered his wife Josephine to 'stop washing'! Ready for more dirt on clean? Read on.

For the modern, middle-class North American, 'clean' means that you shower and apply deodorant (**6**) _____ day without fail. For the aristocratic seventeenth-century Frenchman, it meant that he changed his linen shirt daily and dabbled his hands in water but never touched the rest of his body with water or soap. For the Roman in the first century, it involved two or more hours of splashing, soaking and steaming the body in water of various temperatures, raking off sweat and oil with a metal scraper, and giving himself a final oiling – all done daily, in (**7**) _____ and without soap.

Even more than in the eye or in the nose, cleanliness exists in the (**8**)_____ of the beholder. Every culture defines it for itself, choosing what it sees as the perfect point between squalid and over-fastidious. The modern North American, the seventeenth-century Frenchman and the Roman were each (**9**) _____ that cleanliness was an important matter of civility and that his way was the royal road to a (**10**) _____ groomed body.

Source: Current, Mary Glasgow Magazines, Sept/Oct 2008

0.	A	assign	B	assume	C	associate	D	assert
1.	A	deeply	B	deferentially	C	defiantly	D	definitely
2.	A	question	B	interest	C	curiosity	D	knowledge
3.	A	during	B	while	C	before	D	when
4.	A	one	B	someone	C	no one	D	none
5.	A	offensive	B	offensively	C	offended	D	offendingly
6.	A	every other	B	each other	C	every and each	D	each and every
7.	A	partnership	B	accompaniment	C	company	D	assembly
8.	A	brain	B	head	C	mind	D	spirit
9.	A	convicted	B	considered	C	confirmed	D	convinced
10.	A	precisely	B	properly	C	cleanly	D	tidily

0.	1.	2.	3.	4.	5.	6.	7.	8.	9.	10.
B										

LIU 7 – WORD FORMATION: "DO CELEBRITIES INFLUENCE YOU TO TAKE DRUGS? – A UN REPORT THINKS SO"

You are going to read a text about the influence celebrities have on young people when it comes to drug abuse. Some words are missing from the text. Use the words in capital letters to form words to fill gaps 1–10. Write your answers on the lines provided at the end of the text. Write only one word on each line. There is an example at the beginning (0).

"They're trying to make me go to rehab/I said no, no, no," sings Amy Winehouse in her award-winning song Rehab. ... Everyone seems to know about the British star's non-stop battles with alcohol and drug (**0**) _____ . News writers and paparazzi record each mishap on a daily basis – one journalist calls Winehouse a 'tattooed train wreck'. **USE**

And now even the United Nations has got in on her act: "Amy Winehouse may adopt a defiant pose and slur her way through Rehab, but does she realise the message she sends to others who are vulnerable to (**1**) _____ and who cannot afford expensive treatment?" asks Antonio Maria Costa, executive director or the UN's Office on Drugs and Crime. **ADDICT**

His words reflect the 2008 annual report from the UN International Narcotics Control Board (INCB). Without (**2**) _____ out any celebrities by name, for the first time ever the report claims that drug-abusing singers, actors and sport stars (**3**) _____ drug use – especially cocaine. And they encourage (**4**) _____ teens to use drugs: "Celebrity drug offenders can profoundly influence attitudes, values and behaviour towards drug abuse, (**5**) _____ among young people," the report states. **SINGLE / GLAMOR / IMPRESS / PARTICULAR**

What's more, it claims, the criminal justice system treats celebs far more leniently than ordinary (**6**) _____ , who often face stiff penalties and even jail time: "Celebrities should not be treated any more leniently than any other non-celebrity," says the report's author Hamid Ghodse. **OFFEND**

While the song Rehab describes Winehouse's (**7**) _____ to enter a rehabilitation centre, she has in fact checked herself into rehab several times without success. And while she's been arrested more than once for (**8**) _____ drug possession, Winehouse has so far escaped with little more than a fine. **REFUSE / SUSPECT**

Amy is not alone: in 2005, British tabloids splashed front-page photos of supermodel Kate Moss using cocaine – yet she was never charged with (**9**) _____ of an illegal drug. Instead, she (**10**) _____ entered rehab, and her career has thrived since the publicity. **POSSESS / VOLUNTARY**

Source: Current, Mary Glasgow Magazines, Sept/Oct 2008

Write your answers here:

0. *abuse*

1. _____   **6.** _____

2. _____   **7.** _____

3. _____   **8.** _____

4. _____   **9.** _____

5. _____   **10.** _____

LIU 8 – BANKED GAP-FILLING: "UP CLOSE AND PERSONAL"

You are going to read a text about new methods in advertising. Some words are missing from the text. Choose the most appropriate word from the list A–P for each gap 1–13. There are two extra words which you do not need to use. Write your answers in the boxes provided. The first one has been done for you (0).

The words 'donuts' and 'cutting edge' are rarely seen in the same sentence, but in Buffalo, New York, the ring-shaped snacks are at the center of an (**0**) _____ that could influence shopping (**1**) _____ in the future. Two Dunkin' Donuts stores will soon be testing a system that can (**2**) _____ your face and play an ad on a digital screen that is (**3**) _____ to your age, gender, and demographic group.
This is the first time such a system has been used by a mainstream(**4**) _____ in the U.S. It works in the same way as systems used by police and immigration (**5**) _____ to identify criminals in crowds. A camera above a screen (**6**) _____ an image and analyzes facial features such as the eyes, nose, and bone structure. The information is then used to (**7**) _____ ads to be played on the screen as you look at products or at the cash register.
"It's in the region of 85 percent (**8**) _____, which is a very high level of precision for advertisers and marketers," says Barry Salzmann, head of YCD Multimedia, which (**9**) _____ the display platform. "What we're doing basically is creating the shopping environment of the future. Imagine you walk in, and instead of seeing (**10**) _____ materials, it's all digital screens." Those who have seen the movie Minority Report, in which Tom Cruise is followed by ads wherever he (**11**) _____, won't find this hard to imagine.
So are we now facing a future – some say it could be the norm in 20 years – in which we are (**12**) _____ with personalized messages about deodorant and other things and in which we can't hide anywhere?
When asked about these (**13**) _____ displays in real life, John Underkoffler, the science and technology expert who worked on the Steven Spielberg film, said there's really no going back.

Source: Spotlight, Dezember 2008

A	accurate	**E**	advertiser	**I**	agencies	**M**	bombarded
B	captures	**F**	experiences	**J**	experiment	**N**	goes
C	high-tech	**G**	invented	**K**	printed	**O**	scan
D	select	**H**	store	**L**	targeted	**P**	wants

0.	1.	2.	3.	4.	5.	6.	7.	8.	9.	10.	11.	12.	13.
J													

LIU 9 – EDITING: "WHEN GIRLS GET VIOLENT"

You are going to read a text about a girl called Amy who was abused by her stepfather. In most lines of the text there is one unnecessary or wrong word. Write this word in the space provided at the end of each line. Tick any lines that are correct ( ). There are two examples at the beginning: (0) and (00).

0. With her bright smile and clear, perfect skin, it's both difficult to believe *both*

00. that Amy, 18, was once a gang member in the poor London ✗

1. neighbourhood in where she grew up. It's even harder to imagine _____

2. that she was well known for her violence. But when at an early age, _____

3. Amy's life was already be set on a troubled course. From the age _____

4. of four, she was beaten and raped by her stepfather, someone _____

5. who was seen as an important man in the community. "I did felt   _____

6. nobody would believe me if I told how every day he came for and   _____

7. forced me to have sex," she says. She thinks her mother may   _____

8. have been aware but 'chose not to have see'.   _____

9. Alone and unhappy at home, she turned around to drugs at a very   _____

10. early age. "I was six when I tried weed and skunk," Amy says,   _____

11. "and the wonderful thing was that they have sedated me so that   _____

12. I could block out what was being going on with my stepfather.   _____

13. I was coming up for ten when someone gave me charlie (cocaine),   _____

14. and then when I began smoking crack. That was extraordinary because   _____

15. we were all filled as with this uncontrolled sense of power. I felt as if   _____

16. no one who would ever break me again.   _____

Source: Spotlight, Oktober 2008

LIU 10 – OPEN GAP-FILLING: "DO WE HAVE A ROYAL TRADITION?"

Read the text below. Some words are missing from the text. Complete the text using one word in the spaces provided. The first one (0) has been done for you.

Do we have a royal tradition?
by Amy Argetsinger

We were supposed to be the land without kings, but from the (**0**) _____ start, we've cultivated a number of dynasties. John Adams, for example, was our second president, and his son, John Quincy Adams, became our sixth. Franklin Roosevelt, the 32nd president, was a distant cousin of Teddy Roosevelt, the 26th.

It was the Kennedys, (**1**) _____, who first brought us the sense that politics could be a family business. And (**2**) _____ some voters were suspicious about handing so much power to one family, others loved the idea, especially after the death of President John F. Kennedy. It was (**3**) _____ if they believed the leadership qualities they missed so much might also be found (**4**) _____ men with his same teeth and hair and confident style.

With the Bush family, though, the men who (**5**) _____ to the top offices – George Bush and his sons George W. Bush and former Florida Governor Jeb Bush – were very different from each other. The only things they had in (**6**) _____, really, were their basic conservative politics and their last name. But maybe that was all voters needed: to them, Bush was a brand. They knew what they were getting when they voted for that name.

When Hillary Clinton (**7**) _____ for Senate, and later for president, it was the first time in this country that a woman had followed so successfully in her husband's political (**8**) _____. Hillary Clinton is as different from her husband as the Bushes are from each other, yet she had been (**9**) _____ an important part of Bill's White House that voters understood that she, too, could offer more (**10**) _____ whatever they had liked previously.

Source: Spotlight, Jänner 2012

0. *very*

1. _____	**6.** _____
2. _____	**7.** _____
3. _____	**8.** _____
4. _____	**9.** _____
5. _____	**10.** _____

WRITING

PARAGRAPHS

Paragraphs (Absätze) sind die Bausteine jedes Textes. Daher solltest du – ganz egal, welche Textsorte du verfasst – immer besonderes Augenmerk auf gut durchdachte *paragraphs* legen. Damit dir das auch gelingt, werden hier ein paar wichtige Richtlinien zusammengefasst.

- Unterteile jeden Aufsatz immer in sinnvolle *paragraphs*.
- Sammle zunächst deine Gedanken in Stichwortform.
- Sortiere sodann deine Ideen, Argumente und Beispiele immer, bevor du überhaupt zu schreiben beginnst.
- Versuche deine *paragraphs* durch geeignete *link words and phrases* (Verbindungswörter, Überleitungen) zu verbinden, damit dein Text ein zusammenhängendes Ganzes wird (siehe Seite 173).
- Auch die *introduction* (Einleitung) und die *conclusion* (Schlussfolgerung) deines *essays* (Aufsatzes) sollten als *paragraphs* erkennbar sein und zum einen auf das Thema hinführen bzw. zum anderen vorher Gesagtes zusammenfassen und abrunden.

 Oft ist es leichter, eine treffende *introduction* erst ganz am Schluss zu formulieren, wenn dein Text bereits fertig vorliegt.

- Auch vom Schriftbild her sollten *paragraphs* auf den ersten Blick erkennbar sein – am besten durch leichtes Einrücken der ersten Zeile.
- Bemühe dich auch um die richtige *punctuation* und denke daran, dass es neben Punkt und Beistrich auch noch Strichpunkt, Bindestrich, Ausrufungszeichen und Doppelpunkt gibt. Diese Satzzeichen können deinem Text noch mehr Zusammenhalt und auch Dramatik verleihen, wenn du sie geschickt einsetzt.

Innerhalb eines *paragraphs* spielt auch noch der *opening sentence* (erste Satz) eine wichtige Rolle. So wie die *introduction* das Gesamtthema der Aufgabenstellung umreißt, sollte der *opening sentence* des *paragraphs* auf den Inhalt desselben verweisen.

Ein möglicher Aufbau eines *paragraphs* könnte zum Beispiel so aussehen:

sentence 1: *opening/topic sentence*
sentence 2: *illustrations*
sentence 3: *examples of illustrations*
sentence 4: *illustration*
sentence 5: *result of illustrations*

FORMAL AND INFORMAL LANGUAGE

Je nachdem, welche Art von Text du verfasst, musst du auch auf die Wahl der passenden Sprache achten. So verlangen etwa Berichte und Beschwerdebriefe eine sehr formelle Sprache, während persönliche Briefe oder Notizen in einem informellen Stil geschrieben werden.

Wichtige Unterscheidungsmerkmale zwischen *formal* und *informal language*

Formal	Informal
longer sentences	shorter sentences
impersonal tone	personal tone
full verb forms (e.g.: do not)	shortened verb forms (e.g.: don't)
polite phrases	not especially polite phrases
passive verbs	active verbs
single-word verbs (e.g.: to postpone)	phrasal verbs (e.g.: to put off)
pronouns included	pronouns sometimes left out
avoidance of slang	some slang may be used

Konkrete Beispiele

Formal	Informal
At your earliest convenience.	As soon as you can.
I am writing to enquire whether progress is being made.	I was wondering how things are going.
We are looking forward to receiving your prompt reply.	Hoping to hear from you soon.
I apologise for the delay in writing.	Sorry I haven't written earlier.
Please give my regards to your parents.	All the best to your mum and dad.
I am extremely grateful to you.	Thanks a lot.
It gives me great pleasure to ...	I'm very pleased to ...
We would be most grateful if you ...	Please will you ...

Welche Texte verlangen welche Sprache?

Formal

formal letters:
- complaint
- application (jobs, courses ...)
- apology
- request for information
- resignation
- business letters

reports, compositions, minutes of meetings, reviews

Informal

personal letters:
- general
- pen friend
- thank-you
- invitation

postcards, notes, messages, emails

FORMAL LETTERS

Beim Verfassen eines *formal letter* (formellen Briefes) ist zunächst einmal das korrekte Layout zu beachten.

> Adresse (nicht der Name!) des Absenders
> Telefonnummer
>
> Name, Titel/Position des Adressaten
> (im Zweifelsfall: *The Manager*)
> Firmenname
> Adresse
>
> Datum
>
> (1) Dear Sir or Madam,
> (2) Dear Mr/Mrs/Miss/Ms Smith,
>
> **Briefinhalt**
>
> - *Introduction:* Halte deine Einleitung kurz (1–2 Sätze) und erwähne den Grund deines Schreibens.
> - *Body of letter:* Lies dir die Aufgabenstellung genau durch, denn du musst in deinem Brief auf alle angeführten Punkte eingehen. Zähle deine Argumente in logischer Reihenfolge auf und verbinde sie durch entsprechende *link words*. Achte darauf, deinen Text in passende *paragraphs* zu unterteilen. Erkläre, was du dir als Reaktion auf deinen Brief erwartest.
> - *Conclusion:* Beende deinen Brief mit einer höflichen Floskel, die deine Vorfreude oder Erwartungshaltung auf die Antwort oder Reaktion auf dein Schreiben ausdrückt.
> (1) Yours faithfully,
> (2) Yours sincerely,
>
> Unterschrift
> (Titel) Name – leserlich!
> Position
>
> *Enc(s)* (Liste der Beilagen)

(1) ... wenn der Name des Adressaten unbekannt ist, (2) ... wenn der Name des Adressaten bekannt ist

Formal letters werden natürlich – wie der Name schon sagt – stets in *formal language* abgefasst!

All diese Konventionen bezüglich Layout und Sprache sollten im Geschäftsleben auf jeden Fall beachtet werden, wenn man mit seinem Anliegen ernst genommen werden will und den Adressaten nicht verwirren, verärgern oder gar beleidigen will.

PS
Eben dieses (ein Postskriptum) solltest du in einem *formal letter* unbedingt vermeiden, denn es vermittelt nicht den Eindruck eines gut durchdachten und klar aufgebauten Briefes!

Nützliche, allgemeine Phrasen für *formal letters*

Introduction:	I am writing to ...
	I am interested in ...
	I would like to ...
	I apologise for the delay in writing.
Body of letter:	firstly, secondly, thirdly ...
	furthermore, besides, moreover, in addition
	more importantly, most importantly
	however, notwithstanding, nevertheless
	finally, lastly
Conclusion:	I hope you will ...
	I look forward to hearing from you soon/shortly.
	We look forward to receiving your prompt reply.
	I thank you in advance for your time and attention and look forward to your reply.

Passende Phrasen für bestimmte *formal letters*

Apology:	I am writing to apologise for ...
	I am extremely sorry to cause you this inconvenience.
	I assure you nothing like this will ever happen again.
Request for information:	I would be most grateful if you could ...
	I would like to request further information about ...
	I am writing to enquire about ...
	It would be helpful if you could ...
	Would you be so kind as to ...
Application:	I am interested in applying for the post of ... which was advertised in ... on ...
	In response to your letter of 26 March, I am writing to ...
	I wish/would like to apply for the post of ... which was advertised in ... on ...
	My qualifications and experience make me a particularly suitable applicant for this post.
	As you can see from my enclosed CV, I have ... years' experience in ...
	At present I am employed as a ... by ..., a position I have held for ... years.
	In the course of my present job, I have been responsible for ...
	My duties have included ... as well.
	From ... to ... I was employed as a ... with ...
	I attended the ... , where I obtained the Matura in ...
	I am used to working under pressure/as a part of a team/to a deadline.
	I am familiar with recent developments in ...
	I also have some knowledge of ...
	I am especially keen to work for a company such as yours because ...
	I will gladly supply you with any further information you may need.
Complaint:	I am writing to express my concern about ...
	I am writing to complain about ...
	I would like to point out that ... and must insist that you look into the matter further.
	I shall have no option but to ...

Letter to the editor: Sir, ... – Yours faithfully, ...

I feel compelled to comment on your article ...

I am writing in response to ...'s article on ... that appeared in ... on ...

I read with interest the article by ... that appeared in ... on ...

I am writing because I strongly object to the comment made by ... concerning ...

I totally agree with ...

I was pleased to see your paper devote so much space to the topic of ...

Your coverage of ... was ...

I have been a lifelong supporter of ...

As a father of six, I know from experience ...

It is high time ...

I hope you will take this letter seriously.

I hope you have now gained some insight into how your readers think about this.

Stop writing/printing such ...

INFORMAL LETTERS, NOTES AND MESSAGES

Informal letters, notes und *messages* sind an Personen gerichtet, die man kennt, daher gibt es nicht so strenge Vorgaben bezüglich Layout, und die Verwendung von *informal language* ist hier angebracht. Vorsichtig sollte man jedoch auf jeden Fall bei *slang* und *colloquial expressions* sein – was in einem Brief an einen guten Freund sprachlich völlig in Ordnung ist, könnte einen Vorgesetzten doch verärgern.

Aufbau und Layout von *informal letters*

Adresse des Absenders
(nicht der Name!)
Telefonnummer
Datum (1)

Dear ...,

Briefinhalt

- *Introduction:* Üblicherweise leitet man solche Briefe mit einem kurzen Verweis auf den letzten – brieflichen oder persönlichen – Kontakt mit der angesprochenen Person ein. Man bedankt sich für erhaltene Post und Neuigkeiten oder erinnert sich an ein vergangenes Treffen. Wenn man lange nicht von sich hat hören lassen, entschuldigt man sich und erklärt den Grund.
- *Body of letter:* Lies dir die Aufgabenstellung genau durch, denn du musst in deinem Brief auf alle angeführten Punkte eingehen. Führe den Grund deines Schreibens an, und präsentiere die zu vermittelnden Informationen in logischer und strukturierter Reihenfolge. Verbinde sie durch entsprechende *link words*. Achte darauf, deinen Text in passende *paragraphs* zu unterteilen. Eventuell erkläre, was du dir als Reaktion auf deinen Brief erwartest.
- *Conclusion:* Meistens drückt man am Ende des Briefes seine Vorfreude oder Erwartungshaltung auf die Antwort oder Reaktion auf sein Schreiben aus. Gegebenenfalls runden Grüße an gemeinsame Bekannte oder Freunde den Brief ab.

Yours, (2)

Unterschrift

(1) Hier sind Abkürzungen durchaus üblich: *Mon, Tues, Wed, Thurs, Fri, Sat, Sun, Jan, Feb, Aug, Sep, Oct, Nov, Dec*
(2) Oder eine andere passende Abschlussphrase – je nachdem, wie nahe einem der Adressat steht.

Notes und Messages

Notes und *messages* konzentrieren sich auf das Wesentliche. Datum und Uhrzeit stehen meist am Anfang, die Anrede beschränkt sich auf den Namen des Adressaten ohne *Dear*. Ebenso entfallen Abschlussfloskeln. Vergiss keine relevanten Informationen und achte auf den richtigen Tonfall, je nachdem, an wen du schreibst. Unvollständige Sätze sind typisch für diese Texte; das bedeutet, dass Pronomen, Artikel oder sogar Verben ausgelassen werden können.

Wie klingt und schreibt man weniger formell?

Refer to common friends:	Say hello to Susan for me.
	Give my love to Pat.
Refer to something your friend knows:	As you know ...
	I'm sure you remember ...
Be friendly and include jokes:	How's your diet going?
Use personal constructions:	I hope you don't mind my saying, but ...
	... if you know what I mean!
Use exclamation marks:	How terrible!
Use dashes:	I'm fed up with this job – I want to quit!
Use abbreviations:	etc.
	a.m., p.m.
Use contractions:	*I'll* instead of *I will*
Use ellipses:	Glad you could come.
	Remember me?

Nützliche Phrasen für *informal letters, notes and messages*

Form of address (neutral):	Dear ...
Form of address (affectionate):	Dearest ...
	My dear ...
Letter openings:	How are you? I'm fine.
	Thanks very much for your letter. It was good to hear from you.
Apologising:	I'm really sorry I haven't written for so long/lately but ...
	I just haven't been able to get round to writing recently.
	I have been so busy at work.
	Sorry it's been so long since I last wrote, but ...
Saying why you are writing:	You asked me to ...
	I've managed to find out some information about ... for you.
	About your ...
Expressing your opinion:	As I see it ...
	Actually, ...
	I'd say, ...
Expressing surprise:	Believe it or not ...
	You'll never believe this, but ...
	Guess what!
Reassuring:	Just you wait and see. I'm sure everything will be alright.
	Don't worry about ...
Giving advice:	If I were you, I'd ...
	Have you ever thought of ...?
	What about ...?
	I think you should ...
Changing the subject:	Anyway, ...
	By the way, ...
	Before I forget, ...
	That reminds me ...

Listing reasons:	To start with ...
	And another thing ...
	What's more ...
	Plus ...
Refusing politely:	I'd love to ..., but I'm afraid I won't be able to make it.
	I really don't think there's much chance of ...
	It's nice of you to offer, but I don't think we'll need ...
	Thanks anyway.
Letter endings (general):	Write back soon.
	Do write again soon.
	Look forward to seeing you soon.
	Give my regards to your ...
Letter endings (intimate friends):	Love, ...
Letter endings (more affectionate):	All my love, ...
	Lots of love, ...
	Love and kisses, ...
Letter endings (friends or colleagues):	All the best, ...
	Best wishes, ...
Letter endings (not a personal friend):	Yours, ...
	Regards, ...

Task 1   Formal letters

a. You are going to attend university in Boston for a year, as an exchange student. Your mother has an ex-colleague there, a Dr Susan Bond, who might be able to help you with accommodation and all the necessary preparations. Write to Dr Bond, introduce yourself, explain your situation and ask for help.

b. Study this advertisement and write your letter of application.

Quaint souvenir shop in the heart of Edinburgh needs assistants for the summer.

As our shop is very popular with tourists from all over the world, you should have a good level of spoken English and be fluent in at least two other languages, preferably German and Italian. Working experience appreciated but no prerequisite. Explain why you think you are particularly suitable for this job.

(The Treasure Chest 95, Queen Street, Edinburgh EH1 1EE/Scotland)

Task 2   Informal letters

a. Your British pen-friend has invited you and your family to England for the summer. Write a letter thanking him for the invitation and giving details as to the time and length of your stay. Tell him what you would like to do and which places you would love to see.

b. Your American friend wants to know more about typical Austrian food and would like to try and make a traditional dish. Write a letter telling your friend about traditional Austrian cooking and food. Also include instructions on how to prepare one special dish.

Task 3   Notes and messages

a. Write a note to some friends of yours to thank them for the wonderful weekend you spent at their house in the country. Tell them what you enjoyed most about your stay and how you are planning to return the favour.

b. You were alone at home when your aunt called for your mother because she would like her to baby-sit next Friday. Your aunt has been invited to dinner and does not want to leave her ten-year-old son alone at night. You promised that your mother would ring her back.
Write a note to your mother in which you tell her about the call and remind her that she promised to go to the cinema with you on Friday night. Try to come up with a solution that is acceptable to everyone.

ARTICLES

Articles sind Texte, die für Zeitungen, Magazine oder Journale geschrieben sind und zwar mit dem Ziel, Fakten und Ideen auf interessante Weise zu vermitteln. Man unterscheidet prinzipiell zwischen *serious articles* und *popular articles*. Erstere findet man in Wissenschaftsmagazinen, und sie ähneln einem *discursive essay*. *Popular articles* hingegen versuchen durch auffällige Bilder oder Schlagzeilen, Aufmerksamkeit und Interesse zu wecken. Der Stil des *article* wird bestimmt durch das Thema und das Medium, für das er gedacht ist.

Beim Verfassen eines *article* solltest du unbedingt folgende Punkte beachten:

Keep a distance: Bleibe unpersönlich und sprich nicht von dir und deinen Meinungen.

Be interesting and relevant: Wenn dein Artikel nicht durchgängig interessant bleibt, wird ihn niemand lesen wollen. Bemühe dich daher und
- formuliere einen auffälligen Titel, um Aufmerksamkeit zu erregen;
- beginne mit einer guten Einleitung, die neugierig macht: *a definition of the topic, a bizarre statement, a description or image, a quotation, a question, a story, a surprising fact, astonishing statistics, a proverb;*
- präsentiere konkrete Fakten, Zahlen und Bilder;
- vermeide Verallgemeinerungen und klischeehafte Darstellungen;
- stelle Gerüchte, Meinungen und Vermutungen nicht als Fakten dar: *the alleged/suspected murderer* ist besser als *the murderer*, *the king is said to have a mistress* ist besser als *the king has a mistress;*
- organisiere deine Ideen in logischer Reihenfolge;
- überrasche deine Leser und erzähle ihnen etwas Neues;
- höre rechtzeitig zu schreiben auf, bevor du dich wiederholst oder langweilig wirst. Auch darfst du die vorgegebene Maximallänge nicht überschreiten;
- überprüfe zuletzt, ob dein *article* auch wirklich zu seinem *title* passt und ob alle angesprochenen Punkte darin auch tatsächlich relevant für das Thema sind.

Keep your readers in mind: Denke immer daran, wer deine Leser sind.
- Wie alt sind sie und welcher Nationalität gehören sie an?
- Aus welcher Berufsgruppe oder sozialen Schicht kommen sie?
- Was ist ihr Bildungsniveau und was interessiert sie?
- Was wissen sie schon über das Thema und was muss noch erklärt werden?

Remember your aim: Vergiss nie das genaue Thema und was du mit deinem *article* erreichen willst:
- Willst du informieren oder überreden?
- Willst du unterhalten oder warnen?
- Willst du Empfehlungen oder Ratschläge abgeben?
- Oder eine Kombination aus diesen?

Choose the correct language: Wie formell dein *article* geschrieben sein muss, hängt vom Thema und dem Publikationsmedium ab (*serious article* oder *popular article*).

Pay attention to layout: Am Anfang deines *article* steht natürlich der *title*. In manchen Fällen wird es aber auch angebracht sein, *subtitles* einzufügen. Und natürlich – wie immer – darfst du nicht auf entsprechende *paragraphs* vergessen.

Close your article: Wenn es dir nicht gelingt, für deinen *article* einen gelungenen Abschluss zu finden, so trübt das den Gesamteindruck, den dein Text hinterlässt. Du könntest also
- sprachlich oder inhaltlich an den Anfang zurückkehren, damit sich der Kreis schließt;
- mit einer ernsten Fragestellung oder einem humorvollen Zitat ausklingen;
- in einer kurzen Zusammenfassung deine wichtigsten Punkte unterstreichen;
- einem passenden Bild das Schlusswort sozusagen überlassen.

REPORTS AND PROPOSALS

Ein *report* ist für gewöhnlich länger und detaillierter als ein *article* und richtet sich an Leser, die mit dem Thema vertraut sind. Einerseits liefert ein *report* eine sachliche Beschreibung einer Situation oder eines Ereignisses, andererseits kann er auch Empfehlungen für zukünftige Handlungen beinhalten. Verfasser kann nicht nur eine Person, sondern auch eine Gruppe von Personen sein, Zielgruppen können entweder die Leser einer Zeitung oder Arbeitgeber, Kollegen, Sponsoren etc. sein. *Formal language* ist hier angebracht und ein sachlicher Titel sowie eventuell passende Untertitel.

Ein *proposal* hat ein ähnliches Layout wie ein *report*, doch während ein *report* vergangene oder gegenwärtige Ereignisse beschreibt, hat ein *proposal* zukünftige Handlungen zum Thema, für die es Vorschläge und Empfehlungen abgibt.

Beachte beim Verfassen eines *report* oder *proposal* folgende Richtlinien:

What is the purpose?

Verlangt die Aufgabenstellung, dass du
- Empfehlungen abgibst?
- Vorschläge machst?
- Informationen weiterleitest?
- Fakten oder Situationen beurteilst?

Who are your readers?

Deine Leser sind normalerweise jene Leute, die den *report* oder das *proposal* angefordert haben, also eine übergeordnete Stelle, eine offizielle Institution, Arbeitskollegen etc.

What style should be used?

- Sei sachlich und unpersönlich; vermeide zu viele Aussagen in der Ich-Form.
- Konzentriere dich auf das, was wichtig ist, und lasse unnötige Ausschweifungen und Details weg.

What information should be included?

Sammle alle relevanten Punkte und ordne sie. Ergänze die notwendigen Erklärungen und Beschreibungen. Schließe ab mit einer Empfehlung.

How should your text be structured?

Verwende klare und eindeutige Überschriften, die dem Leser helfen, sich zu orientieren, zum Beispiel:
- *Introduction*
- *Positive Aspects/Negative Aspects*
- *Advantages/Disadvantages*
- *Merits/Drawbacks*
- *Facts and Figures*
- *Consequences*
- *Possible Solutions*
- *Recommendations*
- *Conclusion*

What phrases can be used?

Einleitung:
- *This report intends to/aims at/examines …*
- *This report is intended to …*
- *This report will consider/analyse/compare …*
- *The aim of this report is to …*

Gründe und Folgen anführen:
- *For this reason/these reasons …*
- *As/Since …*
- *Consequently …*

Vorschläge machen und abschließen:
- *In view of this I (would) recommend …*
- *We (would) suggest that …*
- *It is recommended that …*
- *To summarise/On balance/In short …*

Task 1 **Articles**

a. Your school magazine has asked for articles about their readers' frightening experiences. Write an article describing such an experience, but do not exaggerate too much.

b. An English student magazine has a section called **My Idol,** in which readers' articles are published. Write an article about a person who has or has had an important influence on your life.

Task 2 **Reports**

a. A group of English exchange students are going to study at your school for a month. An information brochure is being prepared and you have been asked to write a report for the section about leisure facilities. Describe what is available and list advantages and disadvantages.

b. A company asked you to try out a product (e.g. a new cosmetic product, a gadget, a car ...). Now they would like you to write a report on this product for their consumer magazine.

Task 3 **Proposals**

a. As a member of an environmentalist group you are right now working on a campaign to reduce the use of cars. Write a proposal to the mayor of your town suggesting new legislation and promotional measures.

b. Certain things at your school need to be improved. As a member of the students council write a proposal for your headmaster pointing out desirable changes and putting forward new ideas.

PUBLIC INFORMATION

Brochures	Leaflets	Information sheets
Kurze Werbe- oder Informationsdokumente, die gratis verteilt werden. Sie enthalten oft Illustrationen.		Ungefaltete Blätter, mit wenigen oder gar keinen Illustrationen.
Brochures sind kleine, reich illustrierte Büchlein.	*Leaflets* bestehen meist nur aus einem Blatt Papier und sind oft dreifach gefaltet. Text und Illustrationen halten sich die Waage.	

Beim Verfassen solcher Werbe- und Informationsschriften musst du ein paar Richtlinien beachten. Vor allem sollte dir klar sein, dass solche Folder oder Broschüren nur dann Beachtung finden, wenn sie ansprechend aussehen.

Writing good leaflets, brochures, information sheets	
Zielgruppe und Absicht:	Wie bei jeder anderen Textsorte auch, musst du immer im Hinterkopf behalten, für wen und warum du schreibst. Willst du informieren, warnen, überreden oder etwas verkaufen?
Inhalt:	Sammle deine Ideen, bevor du zu schreiben beginnst, und ordne sie.
Titel und Überschriften:	Neben einem auffälligen Titel ist natürlich das entsprechende Layout sehr wichtig. Unterteile deinen Text in passende Teile mit markanten Unterüberschriften.
Text:	Kurze und einfache Sätze sind besser als lange, komplizierte Konstruktionen.
Buchstaben:	Verwende große, auffallende Buchstaben für Überschriften und wichtige Informationen.
Layout:	Übersichtlichkeit ist wichtig und kann zum Beispiel durch Aufzählungen und Nummerierungen erreicht werden.

Tasks

a. You are working at a summer camp for 8 to 12-year-olds and have been put in charge of one activity or sport. Write a leaflet introducing the children to the activity/sport. Explain the necessary equipment, rules, safety precautions and give useful advice.

b. Produce a brochure presenting your home town to English-speaking visitors. Offer general information as well as specifics (e.g. history, places to see, accommodation, entertainment, customs, etc.)

DESCRIPTION

Focusing on details is the key to descriptive writing!

Wer gut beschreiben will, muss zunächst gut beobachten. Beobachten kann man mit allen fünf Sinnen – beschränke dich daher nicht nur auf visuelle Beschreibungen! Überlege auch, wie etwas riecht, schmeckt, sich anfühlt oder klingt. Bedenke, dass du gedankliche Bilder entstehen lassen möchtest.

 ***Show* your readers what something/somebody is like, rather than *tell* them!**

Weiters solltest du immer deine Zielgruppe (Leserschaft) im Hinterkopf behalten und was du mit deinem Text bezwecken willst. Ganz bestimmt möchtest du vor allem deine Leser bei der Stange halten. Das gelingt dir, indem du alles vermeidest, was sie langweilen könnte. Hier findest du eine Liste der DOs and DON'Ts, die dir dabei helfen.

DON'Ts	DO'S
Sprich nicht zu viel über dich selbst.	Denke vielmehr stets an deine Leser und ihre Interessen.
Sei nicht langweilig und zu berechenbar.	Überrasche deine Leser. Verrate nicht alle interessanten Punkte gleich am Anfang, sondern Stück für Stück und hebe dir auch etwas für den Schluss auf.
Schreibe nicht einfach drauflos.	Sammle und organisiere deine Gedanken, zum Beispiel chronologisch oder nach ihrer Wichtigkeit. Nimm deinen Leser mit auf deine Erzählreise, indem du seinen Blick lenkst, damit er mit dir die Dinge wahrnimmt: ■ *The first thing you see is ...* ■ *Next you will notice ...* ■ *Finally, ...*
Verfasse keine zu langen *paragraphs*.	Teile deinen Text lieber in eher kürzere *paragraphs* ein, denn das ist erzähltechnisch besser und lässt deine Beschreibung lebendiger werden.
Bleibe nicht an der Oberfläche stecken.	Beschreibe die Situation/das Ereignis in allen Details: ■ *What can be seen/heard/smelled/tasted/felt?* ■ *What is the setting like (size, temperature, colours ...)?* ■ *How do the people involved feel and what are they thinking?* Dein Leser soll das Gefühl bekommen, er erlebt die Situation.
Verwende keine Verallgemeinerungen und knappen Formulierungen wie: *a tree* *She was a beautiful woman.*	Nenne die Dinge beim Namen, gehe ins Detail und sei so präzise wie möglich: *an old oak tree* *She was a stunning beauty with jet black hair and eyes the colour of the deep blue sea.*
Vermeide Wortwiederholungen: *ugly ... ugly ... ugly ...* *house ... house ... house ...*	Suche nach sinnverwandten Wörtern: *ugly ... unsightly ... unattractive ... hideous ...* *home ... cabin ... mansion ... cottage ...*
	Dafür gibt es eigene Wörterbücher der Synonyme und Antonyme!
Beginne nicht jeden Satz auf die gleiche Weise.	Variiere deine Satzanfänge, damit nicht alle Sätze gleich klingen. Gute *link words and phrases* findest du auf den Seiten 152–154.
Beschränke dich nicht auf eher langweilige Ausdrücke, die wenig Emotion oder Zusatzinformation vermitteln wie: *look*	Überlege vielmehr, wie genau in diesem Fall jemand „schaut" und verwende so genannte *strong action verbs* wie zum Beispiel: *peep, stare, glare, gaze, glimpse, scrutinize ...*
Deine *description* sollte nicht sachlich und trocken sein.	Verwende geeignete Stilmittel wie: ■ *analogies, similes and metaphors* ■ *personification* ■ *alliteration*
Vermeide Passivkonstruktionen.	Aktive Verben machen *descriptions* lebendiger.

Wenn du *descriptions* verfasst, stelle dir vor, du malst für deinen Leser ein Bild, das er selber nicht sehen kann. Das gelingt dir, indem du Substantive durch passende Adjektive ergänzt. Wenn du mehrere Adjektive vor einem Hauptwort verwenden möchtest, musst du dabei eine bestimmte Reihenfolge einhalten:

1	2	3	4	5	6	7	8	9	10
Determiner	**Opinion**	**Size**	**Age**	**Shape**	**Colour**	**Origin**	**Material**	**Compound**	**Noun**
a	*lovely*	*large*	*antique*	*round*	*brown*	*Italian*	*wooden*	*dinner*	*table*

 Natürlich wirst du nie so viele Adjektive hintereinander vor ein Substantiv setzen, das würde zu unnatürlich klingen! Außerdem kann manchmal eine Kurzbeschreibung fast noch einprägsamer sein als eine lange Aufzählung von beschreibenden Adjektiven!

Eine präzise Beschreibung: *a Brad Pitt look-alike*
erreicht mehr als eine lange Formulierung: *a tallish young broad-shouldered man with short blond hair and deep blue eyes*

Bilder in den Köpfen deiner Leser entstehen auch, wenn du Adverbien geschickt verwendest oder überhaupt passende, ausdrucksstarke Verben (*strong action verbs*) einsetzt. Ein einfaches Beispiel soll dir das zeigen:

Variante 1: *They came into the room.* **Eher einfallslos!**
Variante 2: *They entered the room aggressively.* **Besser!**
Variante 3: *They stormed into the room.* **Zweifellos am bildhaftesten!**

Tasks

a. Pick any photograph from a newspaper, magazine or your family album that you like very much and describe it in as much detail as possible.

b. You have lost one of your favourite possessions and the people at the lost property office have asked you to write a detailed description of it so that they can help you find it.

DISCURSIVE COMPOSITION

Ein *discursive essay/composition* (auch oft *discussion essay* oder *for and against essay* genannt) ist ein erörternder Texttyp, in dem der Verfasser das Thema/das Problem/den Sachverhalt von **beiden** Seiten beleuchtet und seine persönliche Meinung dazu vermittelt. Man betrachtet das Thema von mehreren Standpunkten und schreibt ausgewogen die Vor- und Nachteile. Das Thema ist scharf umrissen und meist sehr kontroversiell – gutes Sachwissen ist Grundvoraussetzung!

Eine geordnete Struktur ist bei dieser Textsorte ganz besonders wichtig:

■ eine klare Einleitung
■ Hauptteil (Vor- und Nachteile strikt voneinander getrennt behandeln, nicht vermischen)
■ ein klares Ende

Style:	Formal language
What are you writing about?	Was genau ist das Thema, die Fragestellung? Was steht zur Debatte? Diskutiere alle Aspekte des Themas gründlich.
A persuasive argument:	Du solltest nicht einfach auf deiner Meinung bestehen, sondern deine Argumente darlegen und durch Daten und Fakten unterstützen, die den Leser überzeugen. Je mehr, desto besser.
Use reliable sources:	Vertrauenswürdige Quellen sind zB Statistiken, (Zeugen)Aussagen, Enzyklopädien, Bücher, Zeitungen (quality papers), das World Wide Web (vernünftig auswählen), Interviews mit Experten, Meinungsumfragen, Experimente usw.
Focus on logical arguments:	Vermeide irrelevante und unlogische Beweise. Vermeide jene Argumente, die bei jedermann beliebt, aber nicht aussagekräftig sind.
First and last paragraph:	Wähle deinen ersten und letzten Absatz sorgfältig aus.
Planning the composition:	Sammle möglichst viele Ideen und Gedanken (brainstorming) und ordne sie in einer Mind map oder in Tabellenform (Vorteile – Nachteile). Siehe unten.
Revise, edit and re-write:	Lies dir deinen Text noch einmal gut durch, bessere Struktur- und Rechtschreibfehler aus und schreibe, falls notwendig, Absätze nochmals um.

Mind map

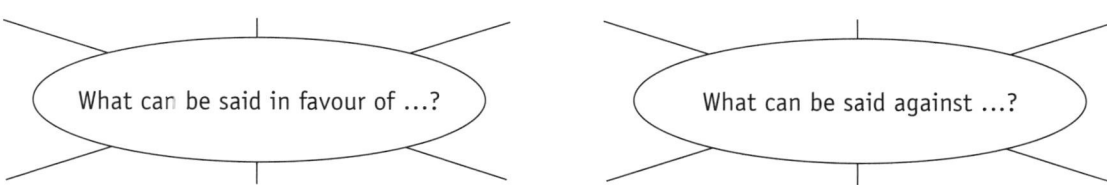

Tabellenform

First area	Second area	Third area	Fourth area

You will find a lot of useful phrases for discursive essays at the end of the book. ► Link words, p. 173 f.

A good way of structuring your discursive essay:

Opening paragraph:	■ Führt in das Thema ein und erklärt die Fragestellung. ■ Zeigt, dass es zwei Seiten zum Thema gibt. ■ Kann auch ein allgemeiner Kommentar sein. ■ Kann Hintergrundinformationen geben. ■ Könnte das Thema auch ein bisschen einschränken, falls es sonst zu umfangreich wäre. ■ Sollte den Leser dazu verlocken, weiterlesen zu wollen. ■ Sollte nicht Beispiele aufzeigen. ■ Sollte nicht verschwommen, verworren sein. ■ Du kannst auch aufzeigen, was du in deinem Essay beabsichtigst zu schreiben.

Advantages:	■ Die eine Seite (Vorteile) wird im Detail ausgeführt.
	■ Jede Idee/jeder Punkt wird in einem eigenen, gut aufgebauten Absatz behandelt. Jeder Absatz beginnt mit dem topic sentence. (Siehe paragraphs S. 50)
	■ Die Argumente werden strukturiert, zB vom Allgemeinen zum Spezifischen oder umgekehrt, vom wenig zum höchst Interessanten, ...
	Die Punkte können je nach Themenstellung zum Beispiel Folgendes behandeln:
	■ einen historischen Rückblick
	■ die betroffenen Personen
	■ die derzeitige Situation
	■ mögliche Auswirkungen
	■ Erklärungen, Beispiele, Fakten, Gründe, Vergleiche, Kontraste, ...
Disadvantages:	■ Die andere, gegenteilige Seite wird ebenso genau dargestellt.
	■ Auch hier vergiss nicht, strukturiert und in Absätzen zu schreiben.
Closing paragraph:	■ Fasst deine wichtigsten Argumente kurz in ein bis zwei Sätzen zusammen.
	■ Drückt klar deine eigene Meinung aus.
	■ Vermittelt eine zufriedenstellende Schlussfolgerung.
	■ Rundet deine Argumentation ab, sollte aber keine weiteren, neuen Argumente beinhalten.

Advantages und *Disadvantages* können auch in umgekehrter Reihenfolge behandelt werden. Du entscheidest, wo die beiden Punkte am besten platziert werden sollten. Die Vor- und Nachteile sollten immer klar und logisch nachvollziehbar ausgedrückt werden und durch gut ausgesuchte Beispiele und überzeugende Gründe unterstützt werden.

Dein *discursive essay* kann also folgendermaßen aussehen:

Opening paragraph		
paragraph 1 (...): advantages/ agree	paragraph (...): disadvantages/ disagree	Argument 1: advantage + disadvantage
		Argument 2: advantage + disadvantage
paragraph 2 (...): diasadvantages/ disagree	paragraph 2(...): advantages/ agree	Argument 3: advantage + disadvantage ...
Closing paragraph		

Tasks

Write texts of 200–250 words. Don't spend more than 50 minutes on these texts.

1. EDUCATION

Your class had a discussion on different kinds of schools. At the end of the lesson the teacher asked you to **write a discursive composition** on the following statement:

Homeschooling is considered the right choice for more and more families.

Use these questions to help you:
■ Can you imagine being homeschooled? Why? Why not?
■ Think of positive as well as negative reasons for homeschooling.
■ Who can homeschool?
■ Do homeschooled children have the same academic performance as regular students?
■ How do homeschooled children socialize?
■ Is homeschooling legal? What are the conditions of homeschooling?
■ What are the effects on the family as a whole (household, time management, ...)

2. SPORT

You see this notice in the international sports magazine XTREME SPORTS:

What's so extreme about extreme sports?

A new extreme sport is born almost every week, each more bizarre and dangerous than the last. Extreme sports, such as skydiving, BASE-jumping, hang-gliding, buildering, extreme snowboarding, ..., have been growing since the late 1980s at the expense of traditional sports.

Write a discursive composition weighing the pros and cons of extreme sports. The top ten replies will be included in the next edition of our magazine.

3. GLOBALIZATION

Your school is producing a special issue of its school magazine for your European partner schools. It will feature articles on the topic: Is globalization a good or a bad thing?

Write a discursive article for your school magazine on the following statement by Thomas L. Friedman:

"Globalization is in so many ways Americanization: globalization wears Mickey Mouse ears, it drinks Pepsi and Coke, eats Big Macs, does its computing on an IBM laptop with Windows 98. Many societies around the world can't get enough of it, but others see it as a fundamental threat."

4. GAP YEARS

Your class has been discussing the advantages and disadvantages of gap years. Your teacher has asked you to write a discursive composition on the following statement

Should teens take a gap year after school? Is a gap year a good idea?

Write a discursive composition weighing the pros and cons of taking a year off.

Use these questions to help you and weigh the pros and cons of each of them:

- What are the aims of this year? Travelling, earning money, volunteering?
- Does the relationship with parents change, for the better or the worse?
- What about gap years later in life, having a career break?

OPINION ESSAY

In einem *opinion essay* (auch *argumentative essay* genannt) wird von dir erwartet, dass du deine Meinung zu einem bestimmten Thema darlegst und den Leser von der Richtigkeit deines Standpunkts überzeugst. Die Struktur und die Merkmale des *opinion essay* sind der des *discursive essays* sehr ähnlich. Der einzige, aber entscheidende Unterschied liegt darin, dass du in einem *opinion essay* nur **eine**, nämlich deine **Meinung** darlegst.

State your thesis:	Stelle deine Behauptung/Meinung (thesis) auf, die du erklärst und verteidigst.
Take a clear position:	Äußere ganz klar, welche Position du zu diesem Thema einnimmst. Du bist entweder dafür **oder** dagegen.

A good way of structuring your opinion essay:

Opening paragraph:	■ Definiert das Problem.
	■ Sollte klar, kurz und interessant sein.
	■ Kann auch ein allgemeiner Kommentar sein.
	■ Erwähnt eine ungewöhnliche oder verblüffende Tatsache.
	■ Stellt eine rhetorische oder provokante Frage.
	■ Spricht den Leser an.
	■ Drückt die *thesis statement*, die wichtigste Idee, aus.
Main Body:	■ Jede Idee/jeder Punkt wird in einem eigenen, gut aufgebauten Absatz behandelt. Jeder Absatz beginnt mit dem topic sentence. (Siehe paragraphs S. 50)
	■ Jede Idee unterstützt die *thesis*.
	■ Die zahlreichen Argumente werden strukturiert, z.B. vom Allgemeinen zum Spezifischen oder umgekehrt, vom wenig zum höchst Interessanten, ...
	■ Erklärungen, Beispiele, Fakten, Gründe, Vergleiche, Kontraste, ...
	■ Kann auch den entgegengesetzten Standpunkt aufzeigen, der aber unglaubwürdig ist.

Closing paragraph:	■ Kann sich auf die Einleitung bzw. die Aufgabenstellung beziehen.
	■ Fasst deine wichtigsten Argumente kurz in ein bis zwei Sätzen zusammen.
	■ Formuliert nochmals deine Meinung in anderen Worten.
	■ Vermittelt eine zufriedenstellende, klare Schlussfolgerung.
	■ Rundet deine Argumentation ab, sollte aber weitere, neue Argumente vermeiden. Der Schluss bleibt dem Leser in Erinnerung!

Dein opinion essay kann also folgendermaßen ausschauen:

Introduction	
Main body: Paragraph 1	Pattern of exposition in paragraphs: **General to specific** Specific to general
Paragraph 2	Least to most interesting, logical, ... Problem to solution
Paragraph 3	Question to answer
Conclusion	

Tasks

Write texts of 400 words. Don't spend more than 100 minutes on these texts.

1. IMMIGRATION:

You have had a class discussion on immigration from less developed countries into your country. One of your fellow students said this:

The adverse effects of immigration on our country far outweigh the benefits. Our schools are filled with children who can't speak the language, our streets are filled with dangerous gangs of immigrant youth, and our social service programmes are going bankrupt at the expense of the large, poverty-stricken families crossing the border every day.

Do you agree or disagree with this opinion stated here? State your thesis. Don't forget to balance your ideas. Think of various aspects in favour of or against immigration. Think of persuasive and logical arguments. Plan and structure the composition and each paragraph. Revise and edit your statement.

Give your opinion on this question. **Write an opinion essay.**

2. ENVIRONMENT:

Your class has been doing a project on environmental problems. As a round-up of this project, your teacher has asked you to prepare for a discussion on the following statement:

Your future is growing dimmer and dimmer.
Is sustainable development a solution to make the Earth worth living on again?
Does the solution lie with young people?

Write this opinion essay.

Think about the topic thoroughly. The following questions should help you:
What environmental problems test the Earth's limits?
What kind of future awaits you? What will it look like? Will your future be worth living?
What can be done to stop this development?
What is environmental education? Are you not educated well enough to do something? Would better education alter destructive behaviour?
Make suggestions of a sustainable course. Is it in young people's hands?

3. REALITY TV SHOWS:

When *The Truman Show* was released, it seemed like a gross exaggeration of anything that could be permitted in a civilized society. Does it now sound like an idea for the next show?
Write an opinion essay on the following statement:
"Reality TV shows are becoming more and more popular around the world because ordinary people who are eager for fame will do desperate things and jump at any chance to achieve it."

4. CLIMATE CHANGE AND HUMAN RIGHTS:

You see the following announcement on the Internet:

	2009 Student Conference on Human Rights will take place from 8–10 December. Theme: **Climate Change and Human Rights.** **Registration** *for the discussion forums is now open.*

At the 12th Annual United Nations Student Conference on Human Rights (UNSCHR) participants will explore the timely issue of "Climate Change and Human Rights". The goals of this event are to promote awareness and prompt action. Secretary-General Ban Ki-moon has referred to climate change as "the moral challenge of our generation". Is climate change a threat to human development?

Write your contribution to the discussion forum and express your thoughts and ideas on:
- Relationship between climate change and human rights
- Impact of climate change on human development
- Impact on developing countries/the poor
- What do we need to do about climate change and human rights?

Write this opinion essay.

5. ADVERTISING:

*"Have It Your Way", "Just Do It", "Ipod, Therefore I Am",
"Reach Out and Touch Someone", "It's Everywhere You Want To Be",
"Finger Lickin' Good", "Got Milk?", "Can't Beat the Feeling"*

We have heard these slogans many times during the course of a day in some fashion or other. What they all have in common is that they are directed toward teenagers. Teenagers are probably more influenced by advertising than any other age group, and they are really not aware of it.

Your class has been discussing the impact that advertising has on teenagers. Give your opinion considering the following:
- Are teenagers aware of the impact that advertising has on them?
- Why do advertisers target this particular age group?
- Are teenagers "impulse" purchasers?
- What must advertisements geared toward teenagers incorporate?

Write your opinion essay.

6. MEDIA:

You have seen this notice in an international magazine:

Do young people realize the amount of influence the media has on them?
From television to magazines, teenagers just seem to eat it all up. In this day and age, individuality is in. Stereotypes are cast out. However, the concept of individuality is also (unsurprisingly) an influence of media on young people. Think of all the movies and television programs which highlight individuality as a cool concept.
Write us an article with a snappy title giving your opinions. The best article will be published and the writer will receive € 500.

Write your opinion essay for the magazine.

SUMMARY

Eine gute Zusammenfassung (*summary*) ist eine kurze, präzise Version eines längeren Textes **in eigenen Worten**, sodass die Kernaussage, die wichtigsten Punkte des Originals, die Meinung des Autors und die gedankliche Struktur eines Textes erhalten bleiben. Man berichtet nur, man gibt wieder, was jemand anderer geschrieben hat – kürzer und in eigenen Worten. Ein *summary* ist objektiv und formell.

Die Schwierigkeiten, ein *summary* zu schreiben, liegen darin, die inhaltlichen Aussagen nicht zu verändern, jedoch mit eigenen Worten auszudrücken. Weiters sollte man die Länge des Originals kürzen, aber dabei keine essentiellen Informationen vergessen, um ein klares Bild vermitteln zu können. Der Zweck eines *summary* ist es, den Inhalt eines Textes jemandem zu vermitteln, der den Originaltext nicht kennt und nicht gelesen hat. Wenn du *summaries* üben möchtest, so kannst du dafür ganz einfach die Texte aus dem Kapitel *Reading Comprehension* heranziehen.

Folgende Schritte helfen dir sicherlich, ein gutes *summary* zu schreiben:

Information:	Autor und Titel (ev. Quelle) solltest du als erstes herausfinden.
First reading – skimming:	Überfliege den Text, um die Kernaussage zu entschlüsseln – unterstreiche sie!
Writing the central idea:	Fasse die Kernaussage des Textes in ein bis zwei Sätzen zusammen.
Second reading:	Jetzt solltest du sorgfältig lesen und auch die Details verstehen: Während des zweiten Lesens unterstreiche Details, markiere sie mit einem Highlighter oder mache dir am Rand Notizen.
Dictionary:	Schlage unbekannte Wörter in einem guten Wörterbuch nach, sodass du die Sätze des Autors und wie sie zueinander in Beziehung stehen gut verstehst.
Paragraphs:	In guten Texten ist immer **ein** Argument bzw. eine Idee in **einem** Absatz ausgedrückt.
Writing the main points:	Fasse jeden Absatz in ein bis zwei Sätzen zusammen, die den Hauptpunkt enthalten.
First draft:	Schreibe deinen ersten Entwurf, ein Konzept.
Starting point:	Im ersten Satz deines *summary* gib Autor, Titel und Kernaussage an.
Final summary:	Die Kernaussage des Originals sollte am Anfang genau festgehalten werden. Dann folgen die unterstützenden Argumente.
Same order:	Die Ordnung der Absätze sollte beibehalten werden.
Your own words:	Du musst deine eigenen Worte verwenden.
Checking:	Überprüfe die inhaltliche Genauigkeit deiner Version.
Revising:	Runde die Kanten ab und verwende *links, connectives,* um die Sätze sinnvoll miteinander zu verbinden.
Proofreading and spellchecking:	Kontrolliere noch einmal grammatikalische Korrektheit, Rechtschreibung und Satzzeichen.
Writing a clean draft:	Verfasse eine Reinschrift.

■ Lies das Original sorgfältig und genau durch und vergiss dabei nie die Absicht/die Zielsetzung des Autors.
■ Beim Unterstreichen behalte das Zusammenfassen im Hinterkopf: Du sollst die wichtigsten Gedanken eines Textes sinngemäß wiedergeben.
■ Der erste Satz könnte zum Beispiel so lauten:
    According to X in his article "title" ...
    In his article "title" X states that ...
■ Du gibst die Meinung des Autors wieder: e.g. *the author believes, argues, claims etc.*
■ Kürze auf ein Drittel bis ein Viertel, manchmal sogar auf ein Zehntel.
■ Das *summary* muss ein in sich eigenständiger Text sein.
■ Gib keine persönlichen Kommentare oder Meinungen ab.
■ Verwende keine direkte Rede.
■ Vermeide Wortwiederholungen, bleibe sprachlich nicht zu nahe am Text.
■ Lasse genaue Details, Beispiele und unwichtige Beschreibungen weg.
■ Ist deine Version zu lang, kürze lieber Wörter statt Ideen.
■ Achte auf ein gutes Layout.
■ Schreibe in der *present tense* (bei historischen Werken – *past tense*).

	Paraphrasing	Summarising	Précis
Was?	Umschreibung eines Textes oder einer Textstelle mit anderen Worten ohne die Originalbedeutung und die Autorenmeinung zu verändern (*in your own words*). ■ Klarer und leichter verständlich ■ Verändert die Wortwahl, nicht die Bedeutung ■ Ca. gleich lang wie das Original	Die Kernaussage und die unterstützenden Argumente werden in eigenen Worten wiedergegeben. Dies setzt sehr gutes Textverständnis und Paraphrasieren voraus. ■ Viel kürzer als das Original ■ Beispiele und Unwichtiges werden weggelassen	Exakte Wiedergabe der Logik, Organisation, Betonung, Entwicklung und Argumente des Originals, in viel kürzerer Form. ■ Ton, Emotionen, Laune beibehalten ■ Keine Interpretation ■ Keine eigene Meinung ■ Klare Ausdrucksweise, effektive Satzkonstruktionen ■ Um 75–80% kürzen, bei langen Werken: 200 Wörter insgesamt
Wie?	Lies den Text sorgfältig durch und unterstreiche die wichtigen Wörter. Finde Synonyme und Umschreibungen. Vereinfache Satzstruktur und Vokabular, ohne die inhaltliche Bedeutung zu verändern.	Siehe vorherige Seite.	Ist noch präziser als ein *summary*: Genaue Anordnung der Originalpunkte und der Verhältnisse der Punkte zueinander, wie der Autor es geschrieben hat, werden beibehalten – aber mit eigenen Worten.

REVIEW

Ein *review* (Rezension, Kritik) ist eine kritische Analyse, ein Kommentar, eine kritische Bewertung eines Textes, Werkes, einer Ausstellung, Vorführung etc. und nicht nur eine einfache Zusammenfassung des Inhalts. Eine Rezension spiegelt die persönliche Meinung des *reviewers* wider und soll den Leser auch davon überzeugen. Thema eines *review* kann sowohl ein *fiction* als auch ein *non-fiction* Buch sein. Die Vorschläge, die du hier findest, sind nicht auf alle Bücher und Filme zutreffend. Wähle aus, was für deine Zwecke am brauchbarsten ist.

Before you start writing: ■ Es ist sicher von Vorteil, dir Notizen zu machen, während du das Buch liest, den Film ansiehst etc. Beobachte und lies genau (inklusive Vorwort)!
■ Welches Thema/welcher Schwerpunkt soll im *review* im Vordergrund stehen?
■ Für welche Altersgruppe/Zielgruppe ist der *review*? (ein Schülermagazin, für Erwachsene, für Kinder etc.) Das hat Auswirkungen auf Wort- und Themenauswahl.
■ Stelle dir vor, du trittst mit dem Autor in Dialog, in eine Diskussion, du kannst ihm zustimmen, aber auch widersprechen, ihn loben oder kritisieren.
■ Stelle dir vor, du erzählst einem Freund eine Geschichte.

Introduction: Die Einleitung gibt allgemeine Informationen über das Werk. Eine witzige Bemerkung, ein guter Spruch erregen hier Aufmerksamkeit.

Book review	Film review
■ Autor, Titel des Buchs, Genre, ev. Verlag, Ort und Datum der Herausgabe ■ Für welche Leserschaft ist er beabsichtigt? ■ Definiere deine Hauptaussage (*thesis*), das Hauptthema, die Problemstellung (*thesis statement*: Warum hat der Autor dieses Buch überhaupt geschrieben?) ■ Hintergründe zum Buch	■ Filmtitel, Regisseur, Schauspieler, Genre, eventuell wo man den Film sehen kann, für welches Zielpublikum, Filmgesellschaft etc. ■ Ist der Film eine Adaption eines Romans? Entspricht er dem Original? ■ Deine *thesis*: dein Argument zum Thema des Films ■ Aussage des Films (*message*) ■ Hintergrundinformationen über den Film oder wie er beworben wurde

Body:	
Book review	**Film review**
1. Deskriptiver Teil (*summary, outline*) **Fiction** ■ *Setting: When? Where?* ■ *Main characters* ■ *Storyline: Outline the plot, but do not give away the ending.* ■ *Perspective* **Non-fiction** ■ Kurzer Überblick über die Hauptaussage mit unterstützenden Argumenten ■ Thema und Zielsetzung des Buches ■ Stellt der Autor eine explizite These auf? ■ Welche Quellen, Beweise benutzt der Autor? ■ Wie wird das Material verwendet, um die These zu bestätigen? ■ Zur Diskussion steht nicht das Thema, sondern **wie** es behandelt wird. ■ *"This book shows ..., The author argues ..."*	**1. Deskriptiver Teil (*summary, outline*)** ■ *Setting: When? Where? Important?* ■ *Main characters – actors (Are they believable, realistic, good? Do they change?); acting* ■ *Storyline: Outline the plot, but do not give away the ending.* ■ *Director:* Hat er gute Regiearbeit geleistet? Ist der Film zu schnell, zu langsam? Guter Kameraeinsatz? ■ *Soundtrack:* Unterstreicht die Musik die Handlung? Ist die Musik gut? ■ *Cinematography:* Licht, Farben, Kameraführung, Kostüme, Ton, Musik, *special effects,* etc. ■ *Themes, symbols:* ein provokantes, klares Thema in Verbindung mit bestimmten Filmqualitäten, welche Bedeutungen werden damit (Licht, Ton, Dialoge, etc.) erreicht? ■ Kontraste, Gegensätze und Parallelen betrachten, Veränderungen beachten.

Tipp 1: Das Thema nicht nur mit einem Wort beschreiben, sondern vorbringen, wie und warum es Thema ist.
Tipp 2: Alle Thesen/Argumente mit genügend Beweisen aus dem Buch/Film untermauern.
Tipp 3: Beschreibe eine Szene. Was war so gut? Damit kannst du auch deine Argumente unterstützen.
Tipp 4: Baue ein paar kurze Zitate ein, so kann sich der Leser ein Bild über den Stil des Werkes machen.

2. Analysierender und evaluierender Teil Kritische Analyse und Bewertung des Inhalts ■ Absicht des Autors herausarbeiten ■ Stärken und Schwächen des Buches ■ Ist das Buch interessant? ■ Ist das Buch gut strukturiert? Illustriert? ■ Ist es gut geschrieben? Guter Titel? ■ Ist es objektiv? ■ Welche Möglichkeiten eröffnet es? ■ Lässt es etwas aus? Gibt es Fehler? ■ Zitate und Verweise, um dein Thema zu veranschaulichen ■ Bezug auf andere Werke des Autors bzw. auf sein Leben, falls relevant ■ Vergleiche mit ähnlichen Werken/anderen Autoren zu diesem Thema ■ Wie wird das Ziel erreicht? Deine Meinung, Bewertung ■ Stimmst du zu? Warum (nicht)? ■ Inwiefern hat es dich betroffen/verändert?	**2. Analysierender und evaluierender Teil** Kritische Bewertung ■ Heben die filmischen Qualitäten (*cinematography*) die Themen, die Stimmung ... hervor? ■ Stimmt er nachdenklich? ■ Hat dich der Film gefesselt? Was genau? ■ Für welches Publikum ist er geeignet? ■ Vergleiche mit anderen Filmen ■ Rating: Wie viele Sterne ☆ vergibst du? Deine Meinung, Bewertung ■ Hat dir der Film gefallen? Hat er dich provoziert? Fasziniert? ■ Was war gut? Was schlecht? Führe Gründe an. ■ Was hat dir gefallen?/nicht gefallen? War es die Atmosphäre? Der Schauplatz? War die Handlung fließend? Die Charaktere? Begründe!

Conclusion
Zusammenfassung und Verbindung der wichtigsten Argumente Ausgleich zwischen Stärken und Schwächen des Buches/Filmes herstellen Dein endgültiges, eindeutiges Urteil Positive oder negative Empfehlung *(recommendation)* – Gib immer eine Begründung an!

Editing Revising Proofreading	■ Enthält der *review* die wichtigsten Schritte? Überprüfe die Vollständigkeit nochmals anhand der oben genannten Liste. Hast du die wichtigsten Ideen/Punkte genau und klar zusammengefasst? ■ Ist er gut geschrieben? Hast du dich klar und eindeutig ausgedrückt? Sind die ersten Sätze fesselnd? ■ Ist er gut strukturiert? Lies dir einen Absatz nach dem anderen durch. Ist jede Idee in einem eigenen Absatz enthalten? ■ Hast du das geschrieben, was du sagen wolltest? ■ Ist er genau? Ist ein Satz oder Absatz nicht ganz klar, dann formuliere ihn um, vereinfache. ■ Ist er interessant für den Leser? ■ Grammatik-, Rechtschreibfehler, Satzzeichen und Tippfehler überprüfen.

A few more tips:

Title:	Denke dir einen fantasievollen Titel aus, der andeutet, worum es in dem Buch/Film geht!
Length:	500–750 Wörter (Artikel: 100–250, Buch: 250–800 W.) *Rule of thumb:* Die erste Hälfte bis zwei Drittel des *reviews* fasst Ideen des Autors zusammen, ein Drittel soll der Evaluation des Buchs gewidmet sein.
Present tense:	Verwende stets die *present tense*, denn die Handlung passiert immer wieder, wenn man das Buch liest oder den Film sieht.
Structure:	Entweder kommt zuerst die Inhaltsangabe, dann die Evaluation, oder man vermischt die beiden Teile und führt Beispiele aus dem Inhalt an, um Kommentare zu unterstreichen. Die positiven und negativen Punkte sollten nacheinander behandelt werden: zB zwei Absätze positive, dann 2 Absätze negative Punkte. Nicht durchmischen!
Paragraphs:	Pro Absatz nur eine Idee behandeln! Die Absätze/Ideen sollten logisch und flüssig ineinander überführen: verwende Links! (Siehe Seite 152)
Language:	Eine präzise, gute und sorgfältige Wortwahl ist sehr wichtig.
Tone, Style:	können variieren
Avoid:	■ *informal language*: *slang expressions*, Verkürzungen (*contractions*) ■ Wiederholungen ■ irrelevante Informationen über den Autor, die nicht zum Thema passen ■ lange Zitate ■ die 1. Person: „*This is a good book.*", nicht "*I think this is a good book.*"

Tasks

a. Choose two different films or plays you have recently seen, a comedy or children's film and a thriller or horror film. Did you generally like them or dislike them? Before you start, take some notes, including a synopsis of the plot and a list of positive **and** negative points. Don't forget to mention the title, actors, director, producer, and the message of the film. Evaluate and recommend them.
Write the two reviews, each about 250 words, for a family magazine. Write in paragraphs. Check your reviews carefully.

b. An international youth magazine has just started a new series called "The best computer game I have ever played". Each week another review is published in the magazine. You decide to write a 250-word review for this series. Don't forget to follow the instructions on "How to write a review"!

c. Choose one of the class readers you read in the 7th or 8th form. Write a book review of about 300 words for a British teen magazine.

A review consists of description **and** opinion!
There must be a difference in vocabulary and also content.

EMAILS

E-Mails und Briefe haben in gewissen Punkten Ähnlichkeiten, allerdings gibt es auch ein paar Unterschiede. Wie Briefe sollten auch E-Mails gut organisiert sein, die Sprache sollte klar und präzise sein, die Grammatik korrekt und das Vokabular passend. Anders sind hingegen der Stil und das Register. Der Betreff (*subject line*) ist aus zwei Gründen wichtig: Er teilt dem Empfänger mit, worum es geht, und man findet das E-Mail leichter im Posteingang.

Es gibt auch noch entscheidende Vorteile des E-Mails gegenüber dem Brief bzw. dem Telefon: Das E-Mail ist schnell abgeschickt und man kann auch eine schnelle Antwort erwarten. Außerdem kann man nie zum falschen Zeitpunkt anrufen, und die Nachricht ist schriftlich und nicht nur mündlich eingegangen.

Ob ein E-Mail in *formal* oder *informal language* verfasst sein soll, hängt einerseits vom Empfänger (schreibe ich einem guten Freund oder einem eher unbekannten Geschäftspartner) und andererseits von der Art der Mitteilung ab (eine Anfrage oder eine Entschuldigung ist formeller als eine Verschiebung eines Treffens).

		formal	*informal*
Subject line	Kurz und prägnant		
Salutation	Kann *informal* oder *formal* sein	Dear ... How are you?	Hi/Hello/Hey ... How's it going? How was the holiday?
Opening sentence	Erklärt den Grund, warum man schreibt	I'm writing to (inform you) ... Many thanks for ... I'll be away from the office ... I have to change our meeting. Could you (please) send me ... I'm writing to confirm your order of ... I would like to ... We would also appreciate ...	(Just) a quick note to (tell you) ... I'm writing to ... Thank you for ... I would like to ... I'm off to ... Would it be OK if ... Hope you ... Speak to you ...
Body		Attached you'll find ...	We're meeting ... Is that OK?
Conclusion	Drückt Erwartungen aus	Looking forward to your reply. We look forward to ... Thank you for your cooperation.	Hope to hear from you soon. See you then! Enjoy yourself! Have a nice day!
Close	Wie **salutation** *formal* oder *informal*	Yours sincerely/Regards/Kind regards/ Best wishes	Regards/Best wishes/Bye/ All the Best/Best/See you/name

Typisch sowohl für *emails* als auch für SMS sind Emoticons. Hier ein paar Beispiele:

:-)	Smiling, I'm happy	;-)	I've made a joke, just kidding	:*)	Clowning, sending a kiss	|-O	Yawning
:-(	Sad, I'm unhappy	:-o	I'm angry or shocked, Wow!	:-||	Angry	:Q	What?

E-Mails können auch viele Akronyme und Abkürzungen enthalten. Hier ein kleiner Überblick über die häufigsten:

w/e	weekend	AFAIK	As far as I know	CB	Call back
FAQ	Frequently asked questions	ATB	All the best	NP	No problem
BBL	Be back late(r)	B4	before	SRY	Sorry
asap	As soon as possible	BTW	by the way	KISS	Keep it simple, stupid
CUL8R	See you later	F2F	face to face	BB	Bye bye
bw	Best wishes	Fwd	forward	G2G	Got to go
GR8	great	HAND	Have a nice day	SIT	Stay in touch
Re	regarding	IMO	in my opinion	Thx/TX	Thanks
MSG	message	MYOB	Mind your own business	WU	What's up?
OIC	Oh I see	PCM	Please call me	X	Kiss
FYI	For your information	pls	please	XLNT	Excellent
rgds	regards	REQ	request	XOXOX	hugs and kisses
IC	I see	RUOK	Are you okay?	YR	Your
ie	in other words	WALOR	What a lot of rubbish	2NITE	Tonight

VOCABULARY

BEZIEHUNGEN UND SOZIALE NETZWERKE

Some important terms

Immediate (Nuclear) and Extended Family Work

ancestor/descendant	significant other	godfather/child ...	to adopt
parents/children	fiancé(e)	guardian	to bring up
siblings	bride/groom	orphan	to raise
(baby/twin) brother/	relative/relation	bachelor	to live together
sister	aunt/uncle/cousin	spinster	(best) friend
daughter/son	niece/nephew		acquaintance
father/mother	in-laws		boss
grandchild/daughter/son	son (sister ...)-in-law	to be: divorced / engaged / (un)married / separated / single / widowed	colleague
grandfather/mother	step-father (-daughter ...)		employee/er
great-grandchild	half brother/sister		neighbour
husband/wife (couple)	foster parents		soul mate
partner/companion	widow/er		

Task 1

Match the phrases on the left with the explanations on the right.

Part 1:

1. to drift apart		**A** to be similar to
2. to hit it off		**B** to become less close to sb
3. to settle down		**C** to begin a friendship
4. to be well matched		**D** to end a romantic relationship
5. to keep in touch with sb		**E** to have good and bad times
6. to pop the question		**F** to keep in contact with sb
7. to have ups and downs		**G** to like spending time with sb
8. to break up		**H** to propose to sb; to ask sb to marry you
9. to fall head over heels in love with sb		**I** to quickly become good friends with sb
10. to strike up a relationship		**J** to start a family
11. to enjoy sb's company		**K** to start to love sb a lot

Part 2:

1. to be in a relationship		**A** to agree on a subject
2. to work at a relationship		**B** to be romantically involved with sb
3. to make up with sb		**C** to fall in love with sb
4. to go back years		**D** to get married
5. to fall for sb		**E** to have known sb for a long time
6. to have a lot in common		**F** to not see or hear from sb any longer
7. to lose touch with sb		**G** to reconcile
8. to see eye to eye with sb		**H** to share similar interests
9. to fall out with sb		**I** to stop being friends with sb after a fight
10. to tie the knot		**J** to try to maintain a positive relationship with sb
11. to get on well with sb		**K** to understand sb and enjoy similar interests

Task 2

Fill in any missing prepositions or choose the right preposition.

to accept sb	to be divorced	to understand sb
to apologize **to/by** sb	to be honest **with/to** sb	to be jealous **about/of** sb
to be happy	to be selfish	to be wrong _____ sb
to be married **with/to** sb	to criticize sb	to date sb
to count **on/at** sb	to forgive sb	to get a divorce
to divorce sb	to get married **to/with** sb	to get **over/across** sb
to get engaged **to/with** sb	to gossip _____ sb	to have sth in common _____ sb
to go out _____ sb	to ignore sb	to keep a secret
to **have/go** on a date _____ sb	to obey sb	to pay attention **to/at** sb
to make peace _____ sb	to separate	to support sb
to propose **to/for** sb	to trust sb	
to accuse sb **about/of** doing sth	to agree **to/with** sb	

Task 3 Social networks

Match these terms to the explanations below.

flash mob	Digg	emoticon	troll	subscribe	profile page	viral
MoBlogging	blog	crowdfunding	forum	live streaming	MySpace	transparency
tweet	invite (evite)	chat	crowdsourcing	lurker	Facebook	smartphone
unfriend	tag	MisTweet	social networking	comments	engage	lifecasting

1. _____ an online journal updated regularly with entries appearing in reverse chronological order

2. _____ communicating in real-time through computers or smart phones, by writing messages back-and-forth

3. _____ small bits of feedback left by visitors of a site

4. _____ trying to find a way to solve a problem by asking a wide range of people for help via the Internet

5. _____ funding a project by raising money from a large number of people via the Internet

6. _____ social news web site that accepts links and comments on news articles from members; other members "digg" stories they like and "bury" those they don't

7. _____ a pictorial representation of a facial expression used in writing to convey the writer's emotions

8. _____ to interact with others

9. _____ the most popular social networking site in the world

10. _____ a discussion arena on websites which allows users to post messages or comment on existing comments

11. _____ a gathering organized via telecommunications, social media or emails; a large group of people assemble in a public place, perform an unusual act and then disperse

12. _____ to send an invitation to a special event through email or networking sites

13. _____ an around-the-clock broadcast of events in a person's life through digital media transmitted over the Internet; can involve wearable technology

14. _____ broadcasting live over the internet

15. _____ a person who watches the discussions on social networks but doesn't participate

16. _____ an easy way to stay connected on the go

17. _____ a regrettable Tweet after the fact

18. _____ an online social network similar to Facebook that caters to artists and bands, who enjoy the flexibility of creating an individual "look" for their page; allows users to "friend" each other and create groups

19. _____ a page hosting general and personal information about a person or organization

20. _____ a handheld device capable of advanced tasks beyond those of a standard mobile phone (email, chat, taking photos, etc.)

21. _____ socializing in an online community (create a profile, add friends, communicate with other members and add your own media)

22. _____ becoming a fan or a member of a blog (= on-line equivalent of signing up for a magazine)

23. _____ attaching a person's name to a picture of them

24. _____ not creating a myth about one's online self

25. _____ a person who posts controversial, inflammatory, irrelevant or off-topic messages in an online community in order to provoke other users into an emotional response or to disrupt normal on-topic discussions

26. _____ an updated message, in real time, allowing followers to know where you are, what you are doing, or what is on your mind, in 140 words or less

27. _____ to remove a 'friend' from your networking site

28. _____ anything that is shared in social networks and gets passed along to many people very rapidly (to go ~)

The main benefits and drawbacks of social networking

Negatives

- it's a waste of time
- it's addictive
  - users lose focus on tasks at work or chores around the house
  - they don't get enough sleep
  - they neglect their family and friends
- relationships can be ruined
- it offers a false sense of connection
- too much time and energy are focussed on casual relationships on the Internet → more important connections in real life are weakened
- it can be a great distraction at work
- loss of privacy
  - intimate details are posted
  - it's difficult to control who can actually see the things posted
  - sharing too much information (your contact information, interests, habits, and whereabouts)
    - can put your personal safety at risk – stalkers
    - can reveal things your superiors should/need not know about you
  - once sth is posted it remains available forever
- predators may target children by posing to be sb else, forming relationships with them and then convincing them to meet in person
- cyber-bullying (= online attacks to terrorize individuals) can leave deep scars or even lead to suicide

Positives

- communication among individuals increases
  - people keep socially active
  - it's easy to stay in touch with your family and friends
  - it allows contact with people from around the world
  - you can also make new friends easily by connecting with your friends' friends
  - it allows people to comment on people's statuses, join organizations, play games, etc.
- it benefits businesses economically because they can
  - find and connect with clients for free
  - post coupons
  - run promotions
  - get positive and negative feedback directly from consumers
- it can be helpful when you're hunting for a job
- it helps education by allowing teachers and coaches to post club meeting times, school projects, or homework assignments
- users can express themselves more freely
  - it can help people who have difficulties socializing in person – in front of the screen such people feel more protected and relaxed
  - they can share/vent their feelings more easily than face-to-face in real life
- it acts as a source of entertainment
- users can find support in online communities

Task 4

Choose the correct words to complete these sentences.

1. Social networking sites help people to **bend/band/bond** together online.
2. Social networking sites regularly need to **purge/position/profile** a lot of spam accounts.
3. If you want someone to join your network of friends, you send them a friend **addition/question/request**.
4. Don't change your relationship **station/status/state** without consulting the other person.
5. Don't post **embarrassing/embarrassed** photographs of other people.
6. Be **discrete/discredited/discreet** when posting messages on another person's wall.
7. The Internet **provides/proves/prevails** a false sense of anonymity and security due to a lack of physical interaction.
8. The most prevalent danger of social networking involves online **programmers/predators/practitioners** who claim to be someone that they are not.
9. A social networking service **fabricates/falsifies/facilitates** the building of social relations among people who share interests and backgrounds.

WOHNEN UND UMGEBUNG

CITY/TOWN

amenities
beggars
citizen
the city centre/the middle/heart of a city
counterurbanisation
district
downtown
estate
factory
homelessness
inhabitant

junction
kerb
metropolis
neighbourhood
overcrowding
pavement
skyscraper
slums
the people of
to make way for
to spoil the view
to wander

town: the centre/middle/edge of the town
Town or City Hall
urbanisation
vandalism
within walking distance of the centre

COUNTRY

hedge
main crops
rural life
tiny cottage
village

Task 1

Match two words, one from each list, to make common collocations. Some words must be used twice.

beauty	main	areas	of flats
block	multi-storey	belt	parks
building	no-go	bins	prices
business	open	block	redevelopment
Central	pillar	box	road/street
cycle	property	Business District (CBD)	site
department	public	car park	space
green	red-light	city	spot
home	shanty	conveniences	sprawl
inner	shopping	districts	store
land	tower	houses	tower blocks
litter	unsafe	lanes	town
low-cost	urban	mall	
low-rise			

Task 2

The following adjectives describe a city or the country. Assign them to the three lists.

positive	neutral	negative

atmospheric	filthy	peaceful	rural
bustling	hectic	picturesque	safe
clean	historic	polluted	shabby
cosmopolitan	lively	quaint	spacious
crowded	magnificent	quiet	stressful
deserted	noisy	relaxing	urban
dirty	off the beaten track	remote	
elegant	packed	run-down	

attractive/lovely/picturesque/spectacular/unspoilt countryside

MODE UND TRENDS

fashion:	the currently accepted, prevailing style
style:	a particular design of clothing (hippie, gothic, cowboy ...)
design:	a specific version of a style
fad:	an intense and widely shared enthusiasm for sth that is short-lived; a craze
trend:	a certain style in fashion that is hip or popular at a certain point in time
classic:	traditional, always fashionable/stylish, popular for a long time
avant-garde:	ahead of its time, very modern and revolutionary

Task 1

Look at these adjectives and match them with the explanations.

1.	au courant	☐	**A**	unconstrained and informal, the opposite of stiff and formal
2.	cheap and cheerful	☐	**B**	does not cost much but is attractive
3.	free and easy	☐	**C**	famous, memorable, representing a certain time and place
4.	fave	☐	**D**	currently popular
5.	essential	☐	**E**	informal, slang, short for 'favourite'
6.	trendy	☐	**F**	necessary, important, you must have it
7.	iconic	☐	**G**	not in fashion any more
8.	fashionable	☐	**H**	sth that is up-to-date and/or reflects the latest styles and trends
9.	well-dressed	☐	**I**	to be dressed attractively
10.	old fashioned	☐	**J**	what everyone else is wearing right now; a new, popular style

Task 2 Multiple choice

Choose the correct word for each sentence.

1. The fashion show this year can't hold a _____ to last year's.
(**= it's not as good**)

   A lamp
   B torch
   C candle

2. Miniskirts are the latest _____ this year.
(**= currently fashionable**)

   A rage
   B fury
   C storm

3. This dress fit like a _____ when I bought it and now it needs to be let out.
(**= fit perfectly**)

   A mitten
   B sock
   C glove

4. Mother's kilt has had its _____ – it's time to get her a new one.
(**= old, no longer useful, outdated**)

   A night
   B day
   C week

5. Your leather pants really made a _____ at the club last night.
(**= expressed your personal taste and were attention-grabbing**)

   A statement
   B comment
   C point

6. I don't care what the latest trends are – I won't dance to anyone else's _____ .
(**= I won't do what I'm told**)

   A music
   B rhythm
   C tune

7. In my opinion, those colours he's wearing don't match. But – to _____ his own!
(**= people have different tastes**)

   A each
   B every
   C any

8. Did you see Cindy last night? Once again she was dressed to _____ .
(**= wearing clothes that attract admirers**)

   A hit
   B kill
   C strike

9. Are we supposed to wear _____ clothes for tomorrow's dinner party?
(**= the kind of clothes worn for a formal event**)

   A smart
   B clever
   C bright

10. I've had my _____ of black! So from now on I'm going to wear bright colours!
(**= have had too much of it and don't like it anymore**)

   A full
   B filling
   C fill

11. I know it's stupid, but it's true: Clothes make the _____ !
(**= people will judge you by your clothes**)

   A man
   B person
   C people

12. The wonderful colours this year really catch the _____ .
(**= are exceptionally noticeable and attractive**)

   A sight
   B look
   C eye

Task 3

Choose the right word or phrase to complete the sentences.

blast from the past	casual	chic	dressed to the nines
faux pas	hand-me-downs	timeless	dress for the occasion
must-have	stylish	works wonders for	vintage
	fashionable	latest	

1. Wow! Look at Susan! She's so _____ (*wearing clothing that is popular now – 3 possibilities*)! She always keeps up with the _____ (*most recent, newest*) trends.

2. The young princess wore a beautiful, _____ (*beautiful no matter how much time passes*) gown on her wedding day.

3. Look, I've found this amazing _____ (*old, but high quality and valuable*) jacket in the shop over there.

4. We all agreed that the new Prada handbag was a _____ (*sth you absolutely must possess*) accessory.

5. When I was little, I always had to wear my brother's _____ (*clothes that are passed down from older siblings to their younger ones*).

6. You look absolutely great! This dress _____ (*improves it a lot*) your figure!

7. I'm really glad we can wear _____ (*not formal*) clothes to work.

8. These skirts are a real _____ (*sth that makes you think of the past*).

9. Wearing that black dress to her brother's wedding was an absolute fashion _____ (*mistake*).

10. My mother reminded us that this time she really expected us to _____ (*wear clothes suitable for a particular event*).

11. When Pam went on her first date with Brad she was really _____ (*wearing fashionable, fancy or attractive clothes that made her look very good*).

Task 4

Can you explain these terms?

1. a slave to fashion: _____

2. a fashion victim: _____

3. a fashionista: _____

4. a fashion icon: _____

5. a trailblazer: _____

6. knockoffs: _____

7. accessories: _____

Task 5

Can you answer these questions?

1. What is the difference between *haute couture clothing* and *ready-to-wear clothing*?
2. What do you do when you *dress up*?
3. What do you do when you *mix and match*?
4. What do you do when you *go overboard on something*?
5. What is the name of the stage that models walk along to present the latest fashion?
6. What does it mean if something in fashion is *yesterday's news*?
7. When do you say a piece of clothing *fits you* and when do you say it *suits you*?
8. What is the opposite of *to come into fashion*?

Some questions to think about:

1. Do you try to keep up with the fashion trends? Why or why not?
2. Do you think it is important to wear fashionable clothes?
3. Does fashion affect who you hang out with or date?
4. What type of clothing is considered fashionable right now?
5. Do you read fashion magazines?
6. Do you love talking about trends, designers and the latest must-have item?
7. Do you think that the clothes we wear reflect what is inside us?
8. Do you think people feel different when they wear different clothes?
9. Do you follow trends or do you have an individual style?
10. Are you fashion forward and a trendsetter?

ERNÄHRUNG, GESUNDHEIT UND SOZIALE ABSICHERUNG

Task 1 Welfare and Health Care

Match the words with their definitions.

1. access	**A** a social system in which a government is responsible for the economic and social welfare of its citizens and has policies to provide free health care, money for people without jobs, etc.
2. acute care	
3. alternative medicine	
4. ambulatory care	**B** a United Nations agency to coordinate international health activities and to help governments improve health services
5. ensure	
6. health care	**C** an expected time to live as calculated on the basis of statistical probabilities
7. health insurance	**D** any medical treatment not generally recognized as effective by the medical community at large (acupuncture, homeopathy, aromatherapy, etc.; many insurance companies do not provide coverage for these services)
8. infant mortality	
9. insured	
10. life expectancy	**E** covered by insurance
11. medicaid	**F** health care for the needy
12. uninsured	**G** insurance against loss due to ill health
13. welfare state	**H** make certain of
14. World Health Organization	**I** medical care administered for the treatment of a serious injury or illness or during recovery from surgery
	J medical care rendered on an outpatient basis, which may include diagnosis, certain forms of treatment, surgery and rehabilitation
	K not covered by insurance
	L the availability of medical care
	M the death rate during the first year of life
	N the preservation of mental and physical health by preventing or treating illness through services offered by the health profession

Task 2 Factors of good health

Fill in the missing verbs.

accepting	cutting	develop	have	improve
limiting	linked	maintained	prevent	volunteering

Health is not only (**1**) _____ and improved through the advancement of health science but also

through the lifestyle choices of the individual. People can (**2**) _____ their health via exercise,

enough sleep, maintaining a healthy body weight, (**3**) _____ alcohol use and avoiding smoking.

A thirty-minute walk every day will (**4**) _____ weight gain and may even lead to weight loss.

Reducing fat and (**5**) _____ down on sugar will help reduce cholesterol and blood pressure.

Learning to manage one's time and (**6**) _____ that there are things one cannot control will reduce

stress. Sleep can be improved by avoiding caffeine, alcohol and nicotine. Meditation is (**7**) _____

to a lot of benefits such as changes in blood pressure, brain activity and other bodily processes. Optimistic people are

less likely to (**8**) _____ health conditions like cardiovascular disease, depression and cancer.

Personal health also depends on the structure of one's personal life – maintaining strong personal relationships,

(**9**) _____ and other social activities are clearly linked to mental health and longevity. Prolonged

psychological stress, on the other hand, may (**10**) _____ a negative impact on one's health.

Task 3

Study these words and fill in the missing prepositions.

Medical conditions	Other words related to health	Related verbs
acne	**People**	to analyse sb's blood/urine sample
ache	anesthesiologist	to be allergic _____ pollen
AIDS	dentist	to be examined _____ a doctor
allergy	dietician	to be ill
arthritis	(family) doctor	to be _____ bad shape
asthma	general practitioner (GP)	to be _____ good health
backache	gynecologist	to be sick
bleeding	midwife	to bleed
blister	neurologist	to catch a cold
bruise	nurse	to catch a disease
cancer	ophthalmologist	to check _____ a hospital
chest pain	orthopedist	to check sb's blood pressure
cold	paramedic	to check sb's pulse
cough	patient	to come _____ with pneumonia
cramp	pediatrician	to cope _____ stress
cut	physician	to cough
depression	psychiatrist	to cure an illness
diabetes	surgeon	to dress a wound
earache		to exercise regularly
eating disorder	**Places**	to fall ill
eczema	chemist's/drugstore	to feel sick
fever	doctor's	to get well
flu	ER	to give birth _____ a baby

food poisoning	hospital	to give _____ smoking
fracture	operating theater	to go _____ a diet
graze	OR	to have a runny nose
hay fever	pharmacy	to heal a wound
headache	surgery	to hurt
heart attack	waiting room	to hurt one's leg
high blood pressure	ward	to inject sb _____ sth
HIV		to injure a limb
infection		to lose consciousness
infectious disease	**Treatment**	to operate _____ sb
inflammation	abortion	to prescribe pills
injury	appointment	to recover _____ an illness
lump	check-up	to regain consciousness
lung cancer	diagnosis	to sneeze
malaria	operation/surgery	to stay slim
migraine	prescription	to suffer _____ asthma
MS (multiple sclerosis)	vaccination	to take _____ a prescription
pain	X-ray	to take sb's temperature
pneumonia		to take an X-ray
rabies	**Medicines**	to treat sb
rash	antibiotics	to undergo an operation
rheumatism	bandage	to vomit
sore throat	contraception	
spots	cream	**Adjectives**
sprain	dose (of medicine)	fit
STD (sexually transmitted disease)	drugs	health-conscious
stomach ache	injection	healthy
stroke	medicine	ill
swelling	pain-killer	overweight
toothache	pill	painful
tonsillitis	plaster	sick/nauseous
tumor	shot/injection	terminally ill
virus	syringe	unhealthy
wart	syrup	unwell
wound	tablet	well
	tranquilizer	

Task 4

Try to define these words.

1. nutrients
2. carbohydrates
3. fats
4. proteins
5. vitamins
6. minerals
7. nutrient deficiency
8. food guide pyramid
9. vegetarian
10. overweight
11. obesity
12. body image

13. food allergy
14. lactose intolerance
15. lifestyle disease
16. risk factor
17. sedentary
18. wellness
19. life skills
20. coping
21. symptom
22. depression
23. eustress
24. resiliency

25. physical fitness
26. chronic disease
27. dehydration
28. sleep deprivation
29. insomnia
30. intoxication
31. drug
32. side effect
33. carcinogens
34. side stream smoke
35. mainstream smoke

Task 5   Fields of medicine

Do you know the terms?

1. ON____ ____LOGY   the field of medicine that deals with the diagnosis and treatment of cancer

2. GER____ ____ ____ ____ICS   a field in medicine that focuses on the health of older people

3. ORTH____ ____ ____DICS   a branch of medicine that tries to prevent and correct problems that affect bones and muscles

4. PE____ ____ ____ ____RICS   a branch of medicine that deals with the development, care, and diseases of babies and children

5. DER____ ____ ____ ____LOGY   a branch of medicine dealing with the skin, its structure, functions, and diseases

6. S____ ____ ____ ____RY   a branch of medicine concerned with diseases and conditions requiring operative procedures

7. PA____ ____ ____LOGY   the study of diseases and of the changes that they cause

8. I____ ____ ____ ____ ____ ____L MEDICINE   the work of a doctor who treats diseases that do not require surgery

9. R____ ____ ____ ____LOGY   a branch of medicine that uses some forms of radiation (such as X-rays) to diagnose and treat diseases

10. PS____ ____ ____ ____ ____TRY   a branch of medicine that deals with mental or emotional disorders

11. ANES____ ____ ____ ____ ____ ____LOGY   the branch of medicine specializing in the use of drugs that cause insensibility to pain

Task 6

Choose the right words to complete the sentences below.

administer	boost	discharged	dress
immunize	increase	incurable	infectious
intravenously	monitor	outpatient	preventive
rehabilitation	routine	scope	supervise

1. Dr. Stern will _____ the procedure. (watch over)

2. His _____ is going smoothly. (process of physical restoration)

3. I will have to _____ your wound. (apply bandages, medication to)

4. I'm still trying to determine the _____ of your illness. (extent)

5. These people only visit on an _____ basis. (they don't stay at the clinic)

6. That patient has been _____ from the hospital. (allowed to go home)

7. The nurse will _____ the vaccine to Mrs. Black. (give)

8. These are _____ measures. (steps taken to make sure something doesn't happen)

9. The vitamins will _____ your immune system. (improve the performance of)

10. This disease is _____. (can spread to other people)

11. This is a _____ procedure. (normal, not serious)

12. This medicine has to be given _____. (through one's veins)

13. Unfortunately, this disease is _____. (there is no cure for it)

14. We have to _____ all children against measles. (= give a vaccine to prevent infection by a disease)

15. We will have to _____ your dosage. (You will have to take more medicine.)

16. We will have to _____ your blood pressure. (pay close attention to)

SPORT

Task 1 **The role of sport in society**

Fill in the missing words.

awareness	barriers	behaviours	challenges	confidence
gaps	levels	tool	walks	work

Sports transcend all social, political and ethnic _____.

cross educational _____, religious preferences and all language groups.

unite people from all _____ of life.

bridge _____ in communities.

create bonding among people.

are a powerful communication _____.

inspire people.

encourage other healthy _____, such as avoiding alcohol and drug use.

instil _____ and discipline.

give people hope.

raise _____ of important issues.

provide entertainment.

offer positive _____.

allow people to value team _____.

Task 2 **Sport affects us all**

Form the right nouns to complete the sentences.

When participating in sport you can

improve your physical _____ (**fit**).

build and maintain healthy bones, muscles and joints.

develop _____ (**endure**) and stamina.

de-stress yourself.

ignore the stresses and demands of every-day life.

control feelings of _____ (**anxious**) and _____ (**depress**).

have fun and relax.

develop creative ideas.

develop self-confidence and _____ (**persist**).

learn to assert yourself.

develop _____ (**determine**) and _____ (**compete**).

become more disciplined and resolute.

learn _____ (**patient**) and respect.

experience a feeling of _____ (**fulfil**) and integrity.

learn how to handle _____ (**fail**) with dignity.

learn from your _____ (**lose**).

learn to perform to the best of your _____ (**able**).

utilize your free time in a meaningful way.

Some more ideas:

Spectator sports bring people together.
promote a sense of pride.
develop a feel good factor.
unite a community or a nation.

Sport is a business that creates jobs.
employs a lot of people (professional athletes, coaches, ...).
pays taxes.
provides a valued service.
boosts the economy.
helps the economy when a nation hosts a world championship (extra income due to tourists, supporters and the general advertisement of the nation).

USEFUL PHRASES

I am fond of sports like ...
I do karate/yoga.
I enjoy playing ...
I exercise regularly.
I go lift.
I go to the gym.
I prefer summer sports.
I go train.
I am not too keen on sports such as ...
I do some exercise.
I exercise for 50 minutes.
I get some exercise.

I go pump some iron.
I work on the stair climber.
I try to keep fit.
I work on the treadmill.
I do a lot of sport.
I don't usually do any exercise.
I exercise once/twice a week.
I go in for ...
I go running.
I play volleyball/tennis.
I work on the bike.
I work out.

REASONS FOR DOING SPORTS

for exercise
it gives you a change
to avoid becoming sedentary
to be active and part of a team

to compete against others

to reduce obesity/overweight
to improve your stamina and health
to develop team spirit

to look better
to lose weight
to relax
to promote friendship and fair play
to slim down

to stay fit and healthy
to push yourself

to develop self-discipline

to obtain health benefits
to overcome your fear
to explore your limits
to lower blood pressure and
    cholesterol
to reduce the risk of developing
    diseases
to have fun
to learn how to cope with setbacks

Task 3

Read the sports quotations and fill in the missing words.

A	arena	D	challenge	G	compete	J	easy win	M	fear
B	friendships	E	losses	H	parts	K	qualities	N	respect
C	setbacks	F	sweaty	I	team mates	L	victories	O	winner

"If you never lose then you can never appreciate the (1) _____." – Laura Twitchell

"The power of the human will to (2) _____ and the drive to excel beyond the body's normal

capabilities is most beautifully demonstrated in the (3) _____ of sport." – Aimee Mullins

"Victory isn't defined by wins or (4) _____. It is defined by effort. If you can truthfully say, 'I did

the best I could, I gave everything I had,' then you're a (5) _____." – Wolfgang Schadler

"It may sound strange, but many champions are made champions by (6) _____." – Bob Richards

"I love the game. It's fun to play, period. I love running around and getting (7) _____. I love trying

to lead my team. I love facing the (8) _____ of another team that's better." – Jamila Wideman

"Those who truly have the spirit of champions are never wholly happy with an (9) _____. Half the

satisfaction stems from knowing that it was the time and the effort you invested that led to your high achievement."

– Nicole Haislett

"When all is said and done, it's not the shots that won the championship that you remember, but the

(10) _____ you made along the way." – Unknown

"Sports remain a great metaphor for life's more difficult lessons. It was through athletics that many of us first came to

understand that (11) _____ can be tamed; that on a team the whole is more than the sum of its

(12) _____; and that the ability to be heroic lies, to a surprising degree, within." – Susan Casey

"If there is a mutual (13) _____ between players and coaches, that keeps the team honest and

makes for a very healthy environment which in turn promotes other important (14) _____ such as

work ethic, integrity and a positive atmosphere for competing and winning." – Jillian Ellis

"When you need a friend, you can always count on your (15) _____." – Jim Brown

SCHULE UND BILDUNG

Match the expressions 1–10 with their definitions A–T.

1.	assignment	**A**	a course or area of study
2.	boarding school	**B**	a course that offers lots of training in order to reach a goal in as short a time as possible
3.	distance learning	**C**	a grant or payment made to support a student's education, awarded on the basis of academic or other achievement
4.	educational background	**D**	a mark indicating the quality of a student's work
5.	face-to-face classes	**E**	a person who holds a university or college degree
6.	gap year	**F**	a school paid for by public funds and available to the general public
7.	grade	**G**	a task or piece of work allocated to someone as part of a job or course of study
8.	graduation ceremony	**H**	a way of studying where tuition is carried out over the Internet or by post
9.	intensive course	**I**	a school where only boys or girls attend (as opposed to a mixed-sex school)
10.	learning strategies	**J**	an academic title given by a college or university to a student who has completed a course of study
11.	private lessons	**K**	an event where successful students receive their academic degrees
12.	public schools	**L**	a school where pupils live during term time
13.	report card	**M**	past experience in education
14.	scholarship	**N**	extra lessons some pupils need to keep up with their mates
15.	school subject	**O**	techniques used to proceed in your own learning
16.	single-sex school	**P**	exclusive independent schools in the UK
17.	state school	**Q**	the money paid for a course of study
18.	tuition fees	**R**	the traditional way of studying in a classroom with colleagues and a teacher
19.	university degree	**S**	a period, typically an academic year, taken by a student as a break between school and university or college education
20.	university graduate	**T**	a teacher's written assessment of a pupil's work, progress, and conduct, sent home to a parent or guardian

1.	2.	3.	4.	5.	6.	7.	8.	9.	10.	11.	12.	13.	14.	15.	16.	17.	18.	19.	20.

Collocations

Tick all the verbs that go with the word *'exam'*.

☐ attend		☐ prepare for
☐ cram for		☐ re-sit
☐ fail		☐ retake
☐ flunk	**an exam**	☐ revise for **an exam**
☐ make		☐ sit
☐ participate in		☐ take
☐ pass		☐ do well/badly in

Task 3

Here's a list of things pupils do. Look at the pairs of words in bold print and cross out the wrong alternative for each pair.

pupils

go to school

visit/attend a school/course/classes

take/make a course/lessons

study a subject/at a university

pay/give attention

take notes

learn **from/by** heart

make/do their homework

submit/admit an assignment

memorise facts

do/make progress

revise/cram/prepare for an exam

meet a deadline

keep up **on/with** their studies

fall **after/behind** with their studies

copy from somebody

cheat **in/by** an exam

arrive late

play truant

skip school

chat **with/up** their classmates

make/do mistakes

repeat a year

take a year out

drop out **of/from** school

are kept in **for/after** school

get a detention

are suspended

are expelled **of/from** school

are home-schooled

qualify

get **thorough/through**

get a pass in …

hold a diploma

achieve/gain/score top marks/grades

pass with honours

get a place **in/at** a university

graduate from … with a degree in …

do/make their doctorate

gain/get their doctor's degree

Task 4

Can you come up with a similar list for all the things teachers do?

teachers   assign homework, _____

_____

_____

Levels of education	Types of schools	
Primary (or elementary) **education** consists of the first years of formal, structured education, usually starting at the age of 5 or 6. **Secondary education** is the stage of education following primary education and includes the final stage of compulsory education. **Higher education**, also called **tertiary**, is the non-compulsory educational level that follows the completion of secondary education. It generally results in the receipt of academic degrees.	nursery school/kindergarten primary school (BE)/ elementary school (AE) secondary school grammar school comprehensive school high school	vocational school business school teacher training school law school medial school (technical) college university
Subjects		
Accounting Art Biology Chemistry Citizenship Economics Engineering English French Geography German Greek History IT (Information Technology) Italian Latin Music Science Physical Education Physics Religious Education Social Science Spanish Mathematics		

Talking about education

Where do you go to school?	I go to ...
What school do you attend?	I attend ...
What grade are you in?	I'm in tenth grade./I'm in grade 10.
Which subjects do you have this year/term?	I have/study ... My subjects are ...
Which subjects do you like (best)?	Most of all, I like ...
Which subjects do you not like at all? .	Least of all, I like ...
What's your favourite subject?	My favourite subject is ...
How many students are there in your class?	We are (about) ... students in my class.
What time does school begin/finish?	School begins/ends at ... On ... I have school from ... to ...
How many lessons do you have per week?	I have ... lessons per week.
How long does a lesson last at your school?	A lesson lasts ..., breaks last ...
What would you like to do after school?	After school, I want to ...
What university do you want to go to?	I would like to ...
What do you want to study?	I'm thinking about studying ...

In Austria education is free of charge.
There are usually between ... and ... students in a class.
The school year is divided into ... terms.
The school year begins in ... and finishes in ...
This is similar to the school system in ...
This is different to the school system in ...

In Austria, children usually start school when they are ... years old.
In Austria, compulsory schooling begins at the age of ...
Schooling is compulsory until the age of ...
Students are required to attend school until the age of ...
School is compulsory for everybody between ... and ... years of age.
When students leave school, they are usually ... years old.

The first school that children in Austria attend is _____ school.
After _____ school they go to _____ school.
Students attend _____ school for ... years.
Students remain at _____ school for ... years.
After _____ school, students attend _____ school.
Then they start _____ school.
At the age of ..., they start _____ school.

Students in Austria have about ... lessons per day/week.
They study approximately ... subjects.
They have lessons from ... to ...
They have lessons in the mornings and afternoons.
They may have to repeat a year.
They have about ... weeks of holiday.
They are not required to wear school uniforms.

The following subjects/courses are mandatory/compulsory ...
Optional/elective subjects are ...

ARBEITSWELT

Complete the following phrases, sentences and idioms with the correct forms of the following verbs.

apply for	find	have	meet	take
be	get	look for	miss	talk
do	go	make	offer	work

_____, _____, _____, _____, _____, _____, _____ a job

_____, _____, _____, _____, _____ work

_____ for a company

_____ on, _____ maternity leave/sick leave

_____ nine-to-five / _____ a nine-to-five job

_____ a job-share

_____ time off

_____ shift-work / _____ (in) shifts / to _____ a shift worker / to _____ on day shift/night shift

_____ sb a job

He's only _____ her job.

_____ in marketing

_____, _____ a deadline

_____ on, _____ flexi-time

_____ regular/irregular/unsociable hours

_____ full-time, overtime, part-time

1. In the USA this is the first question many people ask when they meet somebody new: What do you _____ for a living? Can you really _____ a living by selling on eBay?

2. Even when they go out in the evening, they just _____ shop all the time.

3. If you want to _____ a raise or a promotion, ask for it. She was promised that she would _____ given an increment at the end of every year.

4. Do you _____ a heavy/light workload at work?

5. If you _____ a good working relationship with a colleague or your boss, it means that you _____ on good terms and can _____ effectively together.

6. "I don't want to _____ stuck behind a desk all day" can mean that you do not want to work indoors or to _____ the same thing every day.

7. You've worked hard, you've performed well, you will _____ promoted.

8. If you and your co-workers feel your place of employment treats you poorly, you may _____ on strike.

9. At fifty his life _____ stuck in a rut, he became bored and he couldn't _____ progress. So he gave up work and travelled to India.

10. People who _____ shifts have unhealthy behaviours such as eating fast food, sleeping badly and not exercising.

Task 2

Match the words on the left with the explanations on the right. Write the correct number next to the explanation. There are more words than needed.

1. administrator	_____ a person whose job it is to look after the documents in an office
2. blue-collar worker	_____ a person who pays somebody to work for him
3. boss	_____ a person who is paid regularly to work for an organization
4. candidate	_____ a person in an office who arranges meetings, makes phone calls, prepares letters
5. clerk	_____ a person who works at home and uses a computer, the internet
6. director	_____ a person whose job it is to help customers and sell things in a shop
7. employee	_____ a person whose job it is to organize and control the work
8. employer	_____ a person who spends most of his time working
9. executive	_____ a person who is in charge of an activity or a group of people
10. manager	_____ a senior manager in a business
11. sales assistant	_____ a person whose work involves physical strength or skill with their hands
12. secretary	_____ a person who works in an office rather than doing physical work.
13. supervisor	_____ a person whose job it is to manage all or part of a company
14. teleworker	_____ the person that other people have to obey.
15. white-collar worker	
16. workaholic	

job	work: uncountable	profession	trade
refers to a paid position of regular employment	refers to a means of earning income; employment	refers to a paid occupation, which involves prolonged training and a formal qualification, e.g. teaching	a job requiring manual skills and special training, a craft, e.g. carpentry, plumbing, building

Work/a job can be well-paid, badly-paid, steady, permanent, temporary, full-time, part-time, skilled, unskilled, semi-skilled, routine.

A **job** can be challenging, demanding, interesting, boring, decent, highly-paid, low-paid.
You can be self-employed, unemployed, a part-time/full-time employee/worker.

Task 3 Multiple Choice

Choose the correct answer.

1. Medicine and law are the oldest _____.

A businesses	B trades	C occupations	D professions

2. Teaching isn't just a job for her, it's a _____.

A trade	B vocation	C work	D workplace

3. Her _____ as a receptionist lasted three days.

A career	B business	C profession	D trade

4. When people talk about what they do, I always want to know *the perks of the job*. What am I interested in?

A job security	B disadvantages	C benefits	D sanctions

5. The national minimum _____ rate per hour depends on your age and if you are an apprentice.

A bonus	B benefit	C salary	D wage

Task 4 **Banked gap-fill**

Choose the correct word from the list. There are 2 extra words that you should not use. You may use some words more than once.

applicant	employees	interviewee	redundant
apply for	employer	interviewer	resign
core	employment	laid off	retire
culture	fired	life	retirement
dead-end	flexible	living	sack
dismissal	freelance	pecking	sacked
dismisses	hierarchical	pension	sick pay
downsizing	interview	pursue	socialise

1. If you _____ a job, make your application stand out.

2. Ask yourself what you can do for the potential _____, not what they can do for you.

3. A job _____ is a kind of employment test that involves an interview between a job _____ and the employer, the _____. This is how _____ are selected.

4. All job interviews might be frightening for the candidate, the _____.

5. As an assistant manager, she was quite low in the company's _____ order.

6. Many _____ working hours schemes have a period when employees must be present. This is known as _____ time, which can be 10am to 4pm.

7. If you work _____, you are self-employed and you are hired to provide your services. _____ life can be hard, e.g. long hours for little pay, no co-workers to _____ with.

8. Career development begins with thinking of how to make a _____ until the decisions what career to _____ and apply for.

9. A _____ company is very big and has many levels, each controlled by one manager.

10. Google is known for its employee-friendly corporate _____ offering a lot of perks.

11. Larger companies are more likely to experience a _____ of the workforce.

12. Hundreds of workers are to be _____/get the _____ at the Toyota plant.

13. Is it better to _____ or should you wait to be _____? When you are forced to _____, you have to leave your job. When your employer ends your employment, he _____ you from work, then makes sure the _____ is fair.

14. If you are temporarily _____ from work, there might be no work available for you to do.

15. If you are told you are to be made _____, this can be one of the most stressful things.

16. Many governments have raised the state _____ / _____ age for both men and women.

17. We are all told to work longer. When will you be able to _____?

18. There are many good reasons for taking early _____ but think carefully about how you will manage financially.

19. You get £88 per week _____ if you are too ill to work.

20. A lot of graduates end up in _____ jobs, which do not provide them with an opportunity for growth.

Task 5

When you seek a job, what qualities do you think employers are looking for?

Think about the following:

adaptable	dependable	positive attitude	trustworthy
ambitious	energetic	problem solver	versatile
appropriately dressed	enjoy working in teams	punctual	well-groomed
can-do approach	enthusiastic	reliable	well-mannered
confident	flexible	resilient	willing to learn
creative	motivated	responsible	working with integrity
dedicated	passionate	team-oriented	

Task 6

Decide what things employees like (+) and dislike (−) about their employers/jobs and give reasons:

being under stress **(−)**	lack of transparency
benefits and compensation **(+)**	monotonous, repetitive work
bonuses	no room for advancement
challenging work	pressure
flexible work schedules, flexible hours	promotion politics
generous incentive scheme	receive a promotion
high employee turnover	steady job
high levels of stress	think non-traditionally
job satisfaction, find work satisfying	too much red tape
job security	unfair pay
lack of hierarchy	work longer hours
lack of training/development	work-life balance

Some questions to think about:

Are you a workaholic?	Which qualifications are needed for a job?
Are you a team player?	What are the worst jobs for you? Give reasons.
Do you live to work or work to live?	What is your dream job? Give reasons.
What makes a job worthwhile?	

FREIZEITVERHALTEN

General

a rewarding hobby
my favourite pastime
a popular leisure activity
my chief interests
my favourite relaxation
a wonderful recreation
pursuits

Crafts

basketry
drawing
dressmaking
embroidery

flower arranging
knitting
metalwork
needlework
painting
pottery
sewing
weaving
woodworking

Outdoor activities

backpacking
birdwatching

bungee jumping
cross-country skiing
cycling
exploring different cultures
fishing
gardening
going out with friends
hang-gliding
hiking
horse-riding
hunting
ice-skating
jogging
meeting new people
mountain climbing

mountaineering
parachuting
roller-skating
sailing
scuba-diving
shopping
skiing
skin-diving
skydiving
travelling
walking
watching wildlife
water-skiing
windsurfing
yachting

Indoor activities

baking
blogging
cooking
creating things with your
   hands
dancing
designing websites
doing crossword puzzles
doing nothing
fixing things
going to the cinema
inviting friends

listening to music
meeting friends
photography
playing a musical
   instrument
playing board games
playing computer games
reading
scrapbooking
spending time with your
   family
surfing the Internet
visiting relatives
watching films

Collecting

antiques
autographs
badges
beer mats
butterflies and moths
coins
fine old books
matchboxes
phone cards
postcards
stamps
stickers

Places and events

art gallery
ballet
café
cinema
concert
exhibition
festival
opera
political cabaret
show
theatre

Task 1   Questions

Complete the questions with *what, do, which* or *are*.

1. _____ are your interests?

2. _____ you have any hobbies?

3. _____ sort of hobbies do you have?

4. _____ do you like to do in your free/spare time?

5. _____ are you into?

6. _____ are you keen on?

7. _____ is your favourite hobby?

8. _____ outdoor leisure activities do you enjoy and why?

9. _____ do you like to do on rainy days?

10. _____ do you usually do in your leisure time with your friends/with your family?

11. _____ you collect anything?

12. _____ you do anything for fun?

13. _____ do you like to do when you are alone?

14. _____ sort of things do you do to relax?

15. _____ you interested in playing basketball?

16. _____ you take painting classes/tennis lessons?

Task 2   Possible responses

Fill in the verb in the correct form and supply a preposition where necessary.

1. I am really keen _____ _____ (play) computer games.

2. I am really passionate _____ _____ (collect) fine old books.

3. I am really/quite _____ _____ (explore) different cultures.

4. I go in _____ _____ (ride) twice a week.

5. I like to devote my time _____ _____ (play) the piano.

6. I like to _____ (fix) things for fun.

7. I like/enjoy _____ (travel).

8. I'm interested _____ _____ (design) websites.

9. I'm not very competitive, I just go _____ (jog) for relaxation.

10. I spend a lot of time _____ (practise) the violin.

11. My brother and I spend a lot of time _____ (organise) our collection of action figures.

12. My hobbies are _____ (create) things with my hands and _____ (play) board games.

13. Two months ago I took _____ a new hobby: _____ (parachute).

14. When I get the time, I relax _____ _____ (watch) TV.

15. When I have some spare time, I take delight _____ _____ (arrange) flowers.

16. On a sunny day you'll always find me _____ (pluck) weeds in my garden.

17. Most days I prefer _____ (stay) _____ and _____ (do) nothing.

18. _____ (go) _____ a pub is more my kind of thing.

Task 3   Giving reasons

Match the sentence halves.

1.	... because I enjoy being physically	**A**	relieve stress.
2.	... because I like arts	**B**	active and spending a lot of time playing sports and team games.
3.	... because I'm a creative/practical person	**C**	out of the house.
4.	... because I'm an outgoing person	**D**	and I've been doing it ever since.
5.	... because it gets me	**E**	exciting/fun/fascinating/interesting/cheap/relaxing/ different/unusual.
6.	... because it gives me	**F**	expensive, and anyone can do it.
7.	... because it helps me	**G**	and I like socialising/hanging out with friends.
8.	... because it helps me to clear	**H**	me fit.
9.	... because it keeps	**I**	meditate/think.
10.	... because it's a great	**J**	stress reliever.
11.	... because it's a great way to	**K**	and I like doing things with my hands.
12.	... because it's	**L**	and craft.
13.	... because it's not very	**M**	something interesting to do with my time.
14.	... because my friend introduced me to it	**N**	my head/mind.

How often do you ...?

(at least) once/twice/three times
   a week
fairly often
more often than not
now and then
rarely
several times a week
frequently

almost every other day
from time to time
never
on a regular basis
regularly
sometimes
usually

every so often
generally
normally
once in a while.
seldom
occasionally
hardly ever

KONSUMGESELLSCHAFT

1. SHOPPING

Task 1   Jumbled words

Rearrange the letters. The sentences will help you. The bold letter is the first letter.

1.	New York is definitely the fashion mecca, but you have to know where to go for great shopping _____.	c e e e e i n p r s x
2.	Some shops purchase authentic _____, sports cards, rare coins and other collectibles.	a a b e i i l **m** m o r
3.	_____ shopping can make us laugh but it can also be a behaviour that has negative consequences on somebody's lives. The car was an _____ buy/purchase. She bought a new car on _____.	e **i** l m p s u
4.	Do you buy new or _____ items?	c d e n o **s** – a d h n
5.	Harrods is a shopper's _____.	a a d e i **p** r s
6.	She recommended this hotel to anybody wanting to stay off the _____ _____.	a **b** e e n t a h p t
7.	Dress smart when dining in _____ restaurants.	a e k m p r t **u**
8.	A 1. _____ is a business that sells goods to the consumer. A 2. _____ sells his goods to another business.	1. a e e i l **r** r t 2. a e e h l l o r s **w**
9.	Where is a good shop to buy _____ sports cars?	a a b e l n o r s y – c d e i p r
10.	The new company invested in _____ new equipment.	**c** l o s t y
11.	A lot of consumers can only admire the _____ goods through the shop window.	c d e e i s t u v
12.	_____ _____ is common practice in American movies. This means that companies pay for promoting their products to be featured in films or on TV.	c d o **p** r t u a c e e l m n p t
13.	You often get _____, just ask for them.	c **d** i n o s s t u
14.	The advancement of a product by advertising is called _____. It should make people aware and finally buy the product.	i m n o o o **p** r t
15.	What _____ are those jeans you are wearing? 7 for all Mankind or Pepe?	a **b** d n r
16.	Even when he goes out at the weekend, he just _____ shop all the time.	a k l s t
17.	Candy is _____ placed on supermarket shelves.	e i l m n n o **p** r t y

Where do you prefer to shop? Give reasons.

boutique	flea market	shopping centre/mall
chain store	high street store	street market
charity shop	online shopping	town square
(flagship) department store	outlet store	vintage store

Adjectives you can use for describing shops and displays:

amazing dazzling eye-catching	glittering gorgeous	luxurious spectacular	splendid staggering	stunning top-quality

2. SUPERMARKET TRICKS/SECRETS: Don't fall for the following supermarket tricks:
Shopping carts/trollies are getting bigger. Items for children are positioned at their eye level.
Every part of the supermarket from the parking lot to the checkout counter makes you buy more than you need.
Loyalty cards keep you as a regular customer for the store. Sweet snacks located near the cash register make a lot of people buy them. Supermarkets constantly discount products but you don't know if it's a good deal. Supermarkets are designed to make customers linger longer and so spend more money.

Task 2

Match the words with the definitions.

1. consumer	**A** _____ allow yourself to do sth that you enjoy
2. consumer society	**B** _____ enjoy sth to excess
3. contemplate	**C** _____ a person who is conscious about what he eats and where his food comes from
4. indulge in	**D** _____ try to influence, to appeal to people
5. linger	**E** _____ think carefully about doing sth
6. lure	**F** _____ unwilling to spend money, mean
7. over-indulge	**G** _____ stop yourself from doing sth that you would very much like to do
8. pricey/pricy	**H** _____ community in which the buying and selling of goods and services is the dominant economic activity
9. resist the temptation	**I** _____ stay longer than necessary
10. smart shopper	**J** _____ a person who buys and uses goods and services
11. stingy	**K** _____ tempt, persuade people to do sth by making it look very attractive
12. target at	**L** _____ expensive

Task 3

Decide if these phrases are about having a lot of money (+) or little money (–).

a life of luxury	haven't got a penny to her name	peanuts
affluent	in the red	prosperous
afford	live from hand to mouth	rolling in money
bankrupt	live in poverty	short of money
be loaded	live in the lap of luxury	spend money like water
broke	make ends meet	tighten our belts
enough to get by	make a good living	wealthy
hard up	money is tight	well-off
have money to burn	on the breadline	worth a fortune

Task 4

Match the words with the definitions.

1. bargain	**A** _____	money, property that you receive from sb who has died
2. budget	**B** _____	money in use in a particular country
3. currency	**C** _____	valuable things that you own, your possessions
4. debt	**D** _____	money that a bank charges you for lending you money
5. income	**E** _____	a financial gain, a benefit
6. inheritance	**F** _____	the amount of money available to spend on sth
7. interest	**G** _____	a legal agreement in which you borrow money from a bank in order to buy a house.
8. mortgage	**H** _____	a sum of money that you owe
9. profit	**I** _____	sth you buy more cheaply than usual
10. property	**J** _____	money that you receive from working on a regular basis

Collocations:

big, easy, private, pocket, spending accept, borrow, collect, donate, earn, get, have, hoard, invest, launder, lend sb, lose, make, owe (sb), pay (sb), pay (sb) back, raise, receive, run out of, save, set aside, spend, squander, throw away, tie up, waste, withdraw	**money**

Task 5

Look at these sentences. See if you can guess from the context what the idioms in italics mean.

1. Money *makes the world go round*.
2. She's got *more money than sense*.
3. He's a millionaire and he got lots of influence – *money talks*!
4. Be careful how you spend your money. *Money doesn't grow on trees*.
5. Babysitting is *money for jam*.
6. It *didn't cost him a penny* to go to Cambridge for the summer. He got a scholarship.
7. If you bring your car into New York City, you have to *pay through the nose* for parking it.
8. Getting a car repaired *costs you an arm and a leg*.
9. He'd love to buy a Porsche, but they *cost a fortune*.
10. This car is really *good value for money*.
11. She won the lottery and *went from rags to riches*
12. Look, they've bought a bigger car now! They're always trying to *keep up with the Joneses*.
13. There's no better place to *pick up a bargain* in one of London's street markets.
14. The kids can *shop till they drop*.

Talk about:

What are your shopping habits? (where, when, what?)
Can you imagine life without money? Discuss.
Money – the root of all evil? Do you agree or disagree?
Money can't buy happiness. Do you agree or disagree?
How important is it for you to earn a lot of money?

TRADITION UND WANDEL

Decide if these items are about traditional or modern society and match them with the appropriate category.

many possessions, inequitable distribution of wealth and resources	pay for goods and services, contracts	small-scale, derived from indigenous and ancient cultural practices
industrial production, development of large-scale societies	production for profit, growth complex division of labor (specialization, differentiation) individualized, mechanized	populous societies, centralized state governments
cult of wealth, private ownership	few possessions, similar standard of living	encountering strangers every day
machine transportation	satisfy basic needs, rituals	subsistence, sacred land
less leisure, no time, time is money; consumption replaces conversation	living in small groups, hunting, gathering and simple farming, herding, tribal warfare, short life spans	social separation, little sense of community , family pulled apart, impersonal communication
community cohesion family important face-to-face relations	consumption needs, competitive consumerism	varied but questionable diet
no strong political leaders, no strangers, encountering strangers is frightening and dangerous, everybody knows everybody else	more leisure, more time, time means lived life; spiritual focus, conversation	production for use/subsistence, simple division of labor, cooperation; family, clan, village
exploitation of nature	accumulation for redistribution, collective ownership	no work for pay, no contracts
limited but nutritious		transport by humans or animals

	traditional/tribal society	modern/complex society
life		
strangers		
production		
subsistence, economy		
consumption		
materials		
pay		
possessions		
ecology		
transport		
diet		
community, communication		
lifestyle		

Collocations

ancient, archaic, deep-rooted, living, long-established continue, follow, maintain, preserve, uphold, hand down, break (with), revive	**tradition**
considerable, dramatic, enormous, far-reaching, major, massive, profound, revolutionary, sea, sweeping, irreversible, marginal, minor, subtle, long-term, short-term, global, desirable make, bring about, cause, introduce	**change**

Traditions

Traditions are important in many families and they can continue for many generations.

- How are traditions created, how do they evolve and why might they sometimes be rejected?
- How do cultures and traditions change over time and vary within nations?
- What traditions do most people in Austria share?
- Are there rituals, music, or customs that are typically Austrian?
- How do traditions in Austria differ in comparison to those of other countries and cultures that you are familiar with?

Family traditions

special meals	rites of passage	yearly celebrations	inheritance	religious traditions	special family times

- Think of and give examples of traditions that are important to your family.
- Are there any traditions that you would like to start in your family?

Task 2

Match the words with the definitions.

1. birthright **2.** celebration **3.** ceremony **4.** custom **5.** habit **6.** heritage **7.** holiday **8.** mores **9.** ritual **10.** routine **11.** tradition	**A** _____ a day of festivity or recreation when no work is done **B** _____ a long-established custom or belief that has been passed on from one generation to another **C** _____ valued objects and qualities such as historic buildings and cultural traditions that have been passed down from previous generations **D** _____ a privilege you have because you were born into a particular position or family **E** _____ a religious or solemn ceremony consisting of a series of actions performed according to a prescribed order **F** _____ a way of behaving or doing sth that is traditional and widely accepted among a particular society **G** _____ a sequence of actions regularly followed **H** _____ the action of honouring an important day or event **I** _____ a settled or regular tendency or practice, especially one that is hard to give up **J** _____ the characteristic customs and conventions accepted by a society, group or community **K** _____ a formal religious or public occasion, celebrating a particular event or anniversary

TRANSPORT UND TOURISMUS

Some important terms

a form/means/method/mode of **transport**
air/canal/ground/land/marine/rail/railway/river/road/sea/water/passenger/freight **transport**
transport facilities/services/network/system

car hire agency
collide with
commute/commuter
congestion
cut-price fares
cycle lane
delays
destination
get a lift
get stuck in traffic
hold-up
journey
mobility

more economical
on board
parking meters
pedestrian
pedestrian crossing
public transport
queue
run on time
rush hour
speed limit
speeding
subsidising public transport
subway

the streets get packed with traffic
timetable
tour: go/be on a tour
traffic comes to a standstill
traffic jams/congestion
traffic-calming measures
traffic-free zones
travel by/on public transport
trip
unavoidably delayed
voyage

Task 1 Forms of transport

Below you will see a list of words. Put them into their appropriate box:

(car) ferry
airship
ambulance
barge
bicycle/bike
cabin cruiser
canoe
catamaran
coach
container ship
convertible
cruise ship
dinghy
estate/family/saloon/sports car
fire engine
fishing/rowing boat
four-by-fours/four-wheel drive/all-
    terrain vehicle (ATV)

(hot-air) balloon
hatchback
helicopter
horse and cart
hovercraft
hydrofoil
jet
juggernaut
kayak
lifeboat
light aircraft
limousine
liner
lorry (BE)/truck (AE)
minibus
moped
motorbike
motorboat/speedboat

mountain bike
off-road car/vehicle
oil tanker
pick-up truck
plane
punt
racing bike
raft
school/shuttle/double-decker bus
scooter
slow/express/freight train
submarine
train
tram
trawler
tug/tugboat
van
yacht

On land		On water	Air transport
2 wheels	**4 wheels**		

Task 2

Decide whether the following words refer to railway (R), buses (B) or planes (P).

a return/round-trip ticket	disembark	ride/trip/journey
a single ticket	economy class	route
aisle	first class flight	run/come every 10 minutes
arrive at platform 1	flight attendant	runway
board/boarding (pass/card)	gate	security check
buffet/restaurant car	go through customs	service
bumpy flight	hand luggage/baggage	stopover
business class	immigration officer	take-off, to take off
cabin crew	It is full up.	taxi
catch	landing	terminal
change at	lane	The children are bussed to school.
change trains	late arrival	through train
check-in desk	line	ticket office
compartment	luggage rack	to depart/leave from
conveyor belt	miss a bus	weekly/monthly/annual
departure lounge	passengers	season ticket
direct flight	platform	window seat

Task 3

Complete the table:

	bus	train	plane	taxi	bicycle	car
person	driver					driver
verb	drive					drive
noun		fare			—	—
verb		catch/take	take		go on (my)	
verb			get on/off	get in/out		
using	go by bus			go by taxi		
place		railway station			—	—

Task 4

Look at these sentences. See if you can guess from the context what the idioms in italics mean.

1. As the Vietnam war dragged on and bad news was spreading, the U.S. government stated that *there was light at the end of the tunnel*.
2. Men are often accused of having *a one-track mind*. They are always thinking about sex.
3. Her favourite places are not undiscovered but they are just a bit *off the beaten track* of mass tourism.
4. After the children had been sitting in the car for five hours, they needed to romp around for a while and *let off steam*.
5. What about *one for the road*? – No, thanks, I never drink when I'm driving.
6. Do you feel stuck in your job? What can you do best? What do you enjoy most? Get your career *on the right track*!
7. At the end of the game the baseball team *ran out of steam*.
8. The wounded soldier could get to the military hospital *under his own steam*.

TOURISM

kinds of **holidays**:

activity	camping	cycling	safari	skiing	walking
adventure	complete	hiking	sailing	summer	winter
all-inclusive	cruise	package	sightseeing	touring	

You can say:
I go on holiday/vacation/a journey/a trip/an excursion/an outing/a tour/a cruise/a safari/a world trip.
I am on holiday/take a holiday/have a holiday.   I take a vacation/a break.
I go sightseeing.   I go/travel abroad.   I travel the world/the country.
I travel by car/train/air...   I travel widely/extensively/independently.

Task 5

Match the words on the left with the correct meaning on the right. Write the number next to it.

1. B&B	**A** _____ go from one place to another, especially over a long distance
2. excursion	**B** _____ a private house where you can sleep and have the first meal in the morning
3. journey	**C** _____ go on a short journey for a particular purpose
4. marina	**D** _____ a place where private boats are kept
5. resort	**E** _____ a long sea journey
6. spa	**F** _____ people make it for pleasure and visit many places
7. tour	**G** _____ an inexpensive place where young people can stay for a short period of time
8. trip	**H** _____ a short, organized journey with a group of people
9. voyage	**I** _____ a place where a lot of people go on holiday
10. youth hostel	**J** _____ a place where people go to improve their health and appearance by swimming, drinking the water, exercising, relaxing, ...

Task 6   Banked gap fill

Choose the correct word from the list.

adventure tourism	code of conduct	full-board	mass tourism	self-catering
all-inclusive holidays	culture shock	globetrotter	package tour	sustainable tourism
alternative tourism	ecotourism	half-board	safari	

1. _____ respects local people and the traveller, culture and the environment.

2. _____ incorporates risk, physical exertion and specialised skills, e.g. white-water rafting, hiking, mountain-biking, mountaineering, tracking, canoeing or rock-climbing.

3. _____ is a form of sustainable tourism which is environmentally responsible mainly in undisturbed natural areas.

4. _____ is seen as non-traditional and generally rejects modern mass consumerism.

5. When you plan an African _____, think about the best time to go on _____ and the animals you want to see.

6. A _____ often travels to a lot of different countries.

7. _____ involves thousands of tourists going to the same location at the same time of year. It's often cheap and sold as a package deal.

8. _____, which are a form of package holiday, are getting more and more popular because of the comfort and affordability.

9. A _____ includes transportation, accommodation, meals, guides in one inclusive price.

10. After people leave their familiar environment to move or travel to another country, they have to face a lot of changes. They have a nervous feeling, called _____. It feels like homesickness.

11. When a hotel offers you breakfast and another meal, this is called _____. When all meals are provided with the room, this is called _____. The tourist prepares his own food in _____ properties.

12. Guidelines informing visitors how to behave in a responsible manner or how to engage with local people are called the _____.

Task 7 Holiday idioms

Try to guess the meaning of the following idioms in italics and paraphrase them.

1. People who only watch TV programmes about foreign countries but never travel there, are called *armchair travellers*.
2. Use a packing list, don't pack too much stuff and you'll *travel light*.
3. He's been advised to *take time off* training to recover from an injury.
4. I've visited Cornwall so often, it's become *a home from home* for me.
5. The manager was tired after organizing the campaign so he went to a luxury resort to *recharge his batteries*.
6. We had *a whale of a time* on holiday.
7. They found a nice little Indian restaurant *off the beaten track*.
8. Police should use guns only *as a last resort*.
9. We went to California last summer and *had the time of our lives*.
10. If you get the chance, go abroad. *Travel broadens the mind.*

Think about past holidays and future plans:
What places would you most like to visit? Give reasons.
What would you enjoy most?
What are the disadvantages?
What was your best/worst holiday ever?
What kind of trips/holiday have you gone on so far/are you going to plan?
Why do you enjoy going on holidays/one of your holidays?
Why would you like to visit this destination?
What are the benefits as well as the problems tourism can bring? Here are some ideas:

- **amounts and means of transport**
- **income**
- **intercultural relations**
- **consumption of resources**
- cultural diversity
- **development of domestic markets**
- **economic growth**/prosperity
- **effects on people, nature and culture**

- **inadequate preparation of travel**
- **intraregional cooperation**
- **investment in infrastructure and marketing**
- **job creation**
- **mutual understanding**
- **people's behaviour at the destination**
- profits
- social peace

LANDESKUNDLICHE ASPEKTE

Task 1 Geography

Fill in the missing words (there are 2 extra terms).

area	borders	capital	cities	comprises	islands	lies
metropolitan	municipality	occupies	population	populous	separates	

1. The U.S. _____ fifty states and a federal district.

2. The _____ of the United States is Washington, D.C.

3. London is the largest _____ area in the United Kingdom.

4. Canada's capital city Ottawa is the fourth-largest _____ in the country.

5. Canada is the world's second largest country by total _____.

6. England covers 130,423 km² of the main island of the British Isles and _____ off the north western coast of Europe.

7. England shares its _____ with Scotland to the north and Wales to the west.

8. The English Channel _____ England from continental Europe.

9. The most _____ city in the USA is New York City.

10. Canada _____ most of northern North America.

11. England also includes over 100 smaller _____ such as the Isle of Wight.

Task 2 Society and culture

Reconstruct the verbs.

1. The United States is **K __ O __ N** as a multicultural nation.

2. Nearly all Americans or their ancestors **I __ M __ __ __ __ __ __ D** within the past five centuries.

3. American culture is a Western culture largely **D __ R __ __ __ D** from the traditions of European immigrants.

4. Canadian culture has been **I __ __ __ L __ __ __ __ __ __ D** by British, French, and aboriginal cultures and traditions.

5. The term *'British'* **D __ N __ __ __ S** someone who is from England, Scotland, Wales or Northern Ireland, whereas the term *'English'* **R __ F __ __ S** to people from England.

Task 3 Population

Choose the right word in each sentence.

1. England is the second most **deeply/densely/thickly** populated country in the E.U.
2. In 2009, 1.1 million immigrants were granted legal **reservation/request/residence** in the U.S.
3. The U.S. has a very **dividing/different/diverse** population.
4. African Americans are the largest **racial/racist/race** minority group in the U.S.
5. The two largest Asian American **ethic/ethnic/ethical** groups are Chinese American and Filipino American.

Task 4 Government and politics

Match the sentence halves.

1. The basic political system in England is a constitutional monarchy and
2. England is governed directly by
3. In the House of Commons, the lower house of the British Parliament,
4. The United States is a constitutional republic and
5. The U.S. government is regulated by
6. The U.S. Constitution serves as
7. The federal government in the U.S. is composed of
8. The major parties in the U.S. are
9. Canada is governed as a parliamentary democracy and
10. The Canadian sovereign also serves as

A 532 MPs represent their constituencies.
B a constitutional monarchy.
C a representative democracy.
D a system of checks and balances.
E head of state of 15 other Commonwealth countries.
F parliamentary system.
G the country's supreme legal document.
H the Democratic Party and the Republican Party.
I the Parliament of the United Kingdom.
J 3 branches: the Legislative, the Executive and the Judicial.

Task 5 Languages

Complete the sentences by filling in the right language. You can use some more than once.

English	French	Latin	Old English	Old Norse	Spanish

1. The modern English language evolved from _____, with lexical influences from Norman-French,

   _____, and _____.

2. _____ is the main and official language of the UK.

3. _____ is the international language of business, science, communications, aviation, and diplomacy.

4. _____ is the second most common language and the most widely taught second language in the U.S.

5. Canada's two official languages are _____ and _____.

6. _____ is the mother tongue of almost 60% of the Canadian population.

Task 6 Style and food

Which of these adverbs goes into which sentence?

authentically	broadly	commonly	frequently	heavily	predominantly	widely

1. The American style of dressing is _____ casual and _____ influenced by celebrities.

2. The U.S. is _____ referred to as a *melting pot* in which different cultures contribute their own distinct

   flavours.

3. The term Western culture often refers _____ to the cultures of the U.S. and Europe.

4. A number of foods today are _____ identified as American, such as meat loaf and hot dogs.

5. If you say that sth is *as American as apple pie,* this means that it is _____ American.

6. Tex-Mex cooking in Texas and the Southwest relies _____ on shredded cheese and beans.

Task 7 Economy

Form the right words to complete the sentences.

1. London, home to the London Stock Exchange, is England's _____ centre.   **FINANCE**

2. Tourism is a _____ industry, attracting millions of visitors to England each year.   **SIGNIFY**

3. Agriculture in England is intensive and highly _____.   **MECHANISM**

4. The U.S. has a mixed _____ economy and the largest national GDP in the world.   **CAPITAL**

5. The U.S. is the third largest _____ of oil in the world.   **PRODUCE**

6. Coca-Cola and McDonald's are the two most _____ brands in the world.   **RECOGNISE**

7. Canada is one of the world's _____ nations, with a high per-capita income.   **WEALTH**

8. The Canadian economy is dominated by the _____ industry.   **SERVE**

Task 8   Customs and traditions

Fill the gaps with a suitable word.

Like any _____ country, Britain is known to be full of customs and traditions that have existed _____

hundreds of years and are famous _____ over the world. But there's _____ to British customs than

drinking tea or eating fish 'n' chips. By the way, _____ is claimed that English people drink 165 million cups

of tea every day. A typical English breakfast is said _____ consist of eggs, bacon, mushrooms, fried bread

_____ baked beans. But _____ fact, English people are more _____ to have some cereal, a

slice of toast, a cup of coffee and a glass of orange juice for breakfast. When English people are waiting for a bus

or to _____ served in a shop, they always _____ a nice queue and they can become very rude if you

" _____ " the queue. The British are not only said to _____ reserved in manners, dress and speech, they

are also famous for their politeness, self-discipline and special sense _____ humour.

A **custom** is the usual way of behaving or acting.	A **tradition** is a custom, opinion or belief handed down from one generation to another, often orally or by practice.

Task 9   Religion

Can you unscramble the words?

1. Christianity is the most widely **A C D E I P R S T** religion in England.
2. Almost 80% of **A D L S T U** in the U.S. identify themselves as Christian.
3. A lot of Americans describe themselves as **A C G I N O S T** , **A E I H S T T** , or simply having no religion.
4. Religious **A I L L M P R S U** is an important part of Canada's political culture.

KUNST UND KULTUR

the arts (pl.):   activities such as painting, writing literature, making music.
art (sg., U):   fine art, general word; e.g. the history of art, classical art, a work of art

Events and venues:		People and reactions:	Performing arts:
ballet, opera	opera house	audience, spectator, crowd	dance
concert	concert hall	**reactions:**	cinema
exhibition	art gallery, exhibition centre, museum	to boo (at)	theatre
		to applaud	ballet
film	cinema, (multiscreen) complex;	to clap	concerts
		to cheer	opera
		a success	
play	theatre	a hit	
sports event	stadium	a flop	
		The applause was very thin.	
		The performance got rave reviews.	

THEATRE

act	Interiors:	People:
curtain call	aisle	actor/actress
(dress) rehearsal	auditorium	artist
the final curtain	box	audience (with sg. and pl. verb)
interval/intermission	box office	cast
matinee	circle (balcony)	choreographer
musical	cloakroom	cinema-/concert-goer
performance: to give a good	costumes	company
performance	curtain	composer
play: tragedy, comedy, farce;	first night	conductor
scene	footlight	critic
show	foyer	dancer
to perform a play	gallery	director
to rehearse	microphone	musician
to produce/put sth on.	orchestra pit	orchestra
The curtain goes up/comes down.	props (properties)	painter
	row	playwright (dramatist)
	scenery	prompter
	seat	stage hand
	the sets	stage manager
	stage	theatergoer
	stalls	understudy
	wings	usher/usherette

Task 1 Multiple Choice

Choose the correct answer.

1. Audiences still prefer _____ in plays running for more than 2 hours.

A acts	B intervals	C matinees	D scenes

2. The final practice session prior to opening night in which the actors wear costumes and makeup is called _____.

A rehearsal	B the final curtain	C curtain call	D dress rehearsal

3. All the objects on stage used by actors are called the _____.

A props	B sets	C costumes	D wings

4. The _____ are located on the ground floor of the auditorium. These seats are close to the stage and quite expensive.

A wings	B circles	C stalls	D galleries

5. The _____ will open at 10.00 am to sell tickets of admission.

A box office	B cloakroom	C foyer	D stalls

6. Theatergoers can walk down the _____ with seats on one or both sides.

A row	B orchestra pit	C circle	D aisle

7. A woman whose job it is to show people to their seats in a theatre is called _____.

A wardrobe mistress	B usher	C usherette	D understudy

8. A _____ reminds actors what to say when they forget their words.

A	stage hand	B	director	C	dramatist	D	prompter

9. A person who directs an orchestra is called a _____.

A	composer	B	conductor	C	choreographer	D	critic

CINEMA

synonyms: film, movie/s, movie theatre, picture/s (AE), motion picture (formal AE)

Types of films:

action film	drama	musical (film)	shorts
black and white film	dubbed (foreign) film	mystery and suspense	silent film
blockbuster	epic	newsreel	thriller
(animated) cartoon	fantasy film	oldie	trailer
cliff-hanger	features	preview	travelogue
comedy (comic films)	historical film/drama	remake	war film
detective story	horror film	romantic comedy	weepy
disaster movie	juvenile film	science fiction film	western
documentary	love story	sequel	

Task 2

Find the right type of film from the list above.

a. a very frightening film that deals with the audience's fears _____

b. a film about extraterrestrial life and aliens with robots and spacecraft _____

c. a sentimental film _____

d. a sequence of slightly different drawings is filmed so the figures seem to move _____

e. a humorous film about a love story that ends happily _____

f. a film about supernatural events with an element of magic and myth _____

g. a film that provides a factual report on a particular subject _____

h. a film with an exciting plot involving crime _____

i. a long film about heroic deeds/adventures covering an extended period of time _____

j. a film about cowboys in western North America set in the 19th century _____

k. a film based on events set in the past _____

l. a film about the places visited by a traveller _____

Task 3

Match the words on the left with the explanations on the right. Write the correct number next to the explanation. There are more words than needed.

1. blockbuster	**A** _____	an advance showing to which a selected audience is invited	
2. cliffhanger	**B** _____	short parts of a film used to advertise it	
3. credits	**C** _____	a list of the persons who contributed to the creation of a film	
4. dubbed film	**D** _____	a translation of what people are saying in a foreign language film that appears at the bottom of the screen	
5. newsreel	**E** _____	the soundtrack is in a different language	
6. preview	**F** _____	chronologically follows the events of an earlier work	
7. remake	**G** _____	an earlier film is the main source but characters and plot may be changed	
8. sequel	**H** _____	a difficult dilemma faced by the main character at the end of one episode which should ensure that viewers return to see how the problem is solved	
9. subtitles			
10. trailer			

Film terms:

a high-angle/low-angle shot	based on a novel by	scene
close up	cast	screen
cross-cutting	climax	soundtrack
dolly shot	cut	special effect
fade	flashback	stunt
fast motion	lighting	to be dubbed
freeze frame	shot/made on location	to be set in
zoom shot	performance	to star

People:

actor/actress	casting director	editor	producer
art director	clapper-loader	gaffer	sound mixer
boom operator	dubbing editor	key grip	star

Task 4 Multiple Choice

Choose the correct answer.

1. *The Descendants* _____ George Clooney who gives one of his best performances in this film.

A fades	**B** casts	**C** stars

2. The entire first act of *Life of Pi* was _____ in the town of Puducherry in India.

A shot on location	**B** cut in place	**C** set on site

3. *Life of Pi* is _____ a Canadian fantasy adventure novel by Yann Martel.

A basic to	**B** basically	**C** based on

4. In a _____ the camera is below eye level, which makes the character appear more powerful.

A high-angle shot	**B** low-angle shot	**C** zoom shot

5. A _____ is also called a tracking shot because the camera is moving steadily on a track, following a person.

A dolly shot	**B** freeze frame	**C** zoom shot

6. You re-order a series of scenes to create a film that goes that goes forwards and backwards in time.

A fade	**B** fast motion	**C** cross-cutting

7. A scene in a film or novel set in a time earlier than the main story, which is introduced to enhance tension, is called a _____ .

A flashback	**B** lighting	**C** cut

8. The most decisive moment, the culmination, a moment of great intensity in a film or book is called _____ .

A summit	**B** climax	**C** stunt

9. *Transformers*, a robot science-fiction film, was immediately praised for its breathtaking _____ .

A cast	**B** soundtrack	**C** special effects

10. The chief electrician in charge of lighting on a movie set is a _____ .

A clapper loader	**B** gaffer	**C** key grip

11. The _____ belongs to the sound crew and extends the microphone over the actors but out of sight of the camera.

A boom operator	**B** sound mixer	**C** dubbing editor

12. The _____ creates scenes, supervises and unifies the vision, decides on visual elements used.

A producer	**B** art director	**C** casting director

Tickets:

admission
box/ticket/booking office
to book a ticket
sth is fully booked, booked up, sold out;
concessions for students or old people

LITERATURE

Written works in prose and verse (poems, plays and novels).

BOOKS

adventure story	detective story	guide (book)	romantic novel
anthology	dictionary	horror	science fiction novel
atlas	directory	love story	short story
autobiography	drama	manual	spy story
best seller	encyclopedia	memoirs	thriller
biography	essay	murder mystery	travel guide
children's book/literature	fairy tale	non-fiction	whodunit
classic	fantasy novel	novel	young adult fiction (YA)
cookery book (cookbook)	fiction	poetry book (poems)	
crime story	ghost story	reference book	

Parts of a book:

acknowledgements	climax	foreword	jacket
appendix	contents	glossary	preface
bibliography	cover	illustrations	title
blurb	footnote	index	volume (part)
chapter			

Task 5

Complete this table of words relating to the arts.

noun	person	verb
edition		
	novelist	—
play		
poetry/_____	poet	—
art		
criticism		

noun	person	verb
		act
		cast
composition		
—		conduct
		dance
	dramatist	
—		prompt

Adjectives to describe a book/film/play: Divide them into 3 categories: positive, negative, neutral.

absorbing	electric	horrific	overrated	suspenseful
appealing	enjoyable	humorous	phoney	tedious
believable	entertaining	imaginative	picaresque	thought-provoking
bland	exciting	impressive	popular	threatening
bloody	excruciating	innovative	powerful	thrilling
brilliant	exhilarating	insightful	predictable	tiresome
brutal	exquisite	intense	preposterous	tranquil
callous	extensive	intimate	pretentious	trivial
charismatic	fascinating	intricate	prying	unconvincing
charming	fast-moving/-paced	intriguing	readable	under-rated
cliché-ridden	feel-good	intrusive	riveting	unpretentious
comical	first-rate	juicy	romantic	violent
compelling	flawed	legendary	sentimental	vivid
critically-praised	funny	light-hearted	shocking	wacky
dazzling	gloomy	lively	slow	weak
disappointing	gory	low-budget	spine-chilling	witty
disgusting	gripping	moving	static	wooden
distasteful	gritty	non-linear	stunning	zany
dramatic	hilarious	ordinary	subtle	
dull	honest	original	surprising	

Task 6

Match the words on the left with the explanations on the right.

1. antagonist 2. dynamic characters 3. flat characters 4. main characters 5. minor characters 6. protagonist 7. static characters 8. stock characters	**A** _____ the hero, the main/principal character, the leading actor **B** _____ opposes the hero, an adversary, often the villain **C** _____ do not change throughout the story **D** _____ go through a change, they make the story come alive **E** _____ static characters with a limited number of qualities, have few and simple characteristics **F** _____ represent specific stereotypes, based on clichés, e.g. the mean stepmother, the dumb blond **G** _____ background characters, do not play a continuing role **H** _____ major characters, more important to the story

Useful phrases:

What's on at the cinema/theatre next month?

to go **to** the cinema/theatre,

to enjoy yourself, enjoy doing sth., have a good time (doing sth.), have fun (doing sth.), to amuse yourself

The book is about/on sth/sb., it deals with sth./sb., to cover sth.

I couln't put it down.

The film kept me at the edge of my seat.

The Odeon is **showing** "The Aviator".

to see a film in the cinema

I couldn't relate to any of the characters.

I could relate to the subject matter.

Talking about reading and reading habits:

Which kind(s) of books do you like? Which book(s) would you recommend? Do you prefer hardback or paperback?

What does reading mean to you? Give reasons for reading: e.g. for pleasure ...

What does a good book have to be/have? Do/Can you learn from books?

Do you have a favourite character? Do you like twists in the plot? Give examples. Describe them.

Should young people be encouraged to read more books? Give reasons.

Weigh the advantages and disadvantages of reading a printed book over computers or CDs.

Is reading a waste of time?

Talking about films:

Decide what the best film was you've ever seen and give reasons.

Which genre/type of film do your favourite films belong to? Describe the typical features.

Summarise the plot of a film you have been to lately. What did you (not) like?

Compare cinema and theatre and weigh the advantages and disadvantages.

MUSIC		FINE ARTS	
blues	opera	(self)portrait	landscapes
chamber music	orchestral music	20th century	painting
classical music	pop	abstract art	photography
country	rap	contemporary art	portrait
folk	reggae	drawing	sculptor
heavy metal	rock	fake	sculpture
jazz	soul	frame	sketch
modern music	techno	French impressionists	still life
		great masters	surrealist
Rock band:	drummer	original work of art	art reproduction
Lead singer	guitarist		
backing singers	keyboard player		
bass player			
album	Melody		
charts	number one		
cover version	track		
lyrics	tune		

Some phrases and ideas:

to have an ear for music   tc have a wide taste in music

Talking about music:

What kind of music do you listen to? What is it about music that you like? What effect does music have on you? What kind of music person are you? Can you play any musical instrument? Do you go to concerts? How does music make you feel? What makes a song popular? What would life without music be like? How does music influence your mood? (dark – light, calm – aggressive, energetic – relaxed, intense, cheerful, emotional, tranquil)

Ideas when talking about a work of art:

the subject matter: people, a face, buildings, objects ...
lines, shapes, colours, textures, organization of objects, emotional quality, mood, symbols, materials, style, time period, culture

Do we need the arts and artists? Why (not)?
What makes something art? What is anti-art?
Describe your favourite museum/gallery. What makes it attractive to you, to other people?

MEDIEN

NEWSPAPERS and MAGAZINES

types of printed material:	kinds:		
booklet	broadsheet (paper)	gutter press (infml)	provincial press
brochure	colour supplement	international press	quality paper/press
flyer	daily paper	local paper/press	quarterly
leaflet	evening paper	magazine	Sunday paper
manual	financial press	morning paper	tabloid (paper/press)
pamphlet	foreign press	national paper/press	today's paper
prospectus	glossy (magazine)	popular paper/press	weekly paper

Task 1

Match the words on the left with the explanations on the right. Write the correct number next to the explanation. There are more explanations than needed.

	A _____	an expensive magazine printed on shiny paper with a lot of colour pictures	
1. broadsheet	**B** _____	a reference book that gives you instructions how to operate something	
2. flyer	**C** _____	a magazine published four times a year	
3. glossy	**D** _____	a newspaper printed on a large size of paper, more serious than smaller newspapers	
4. gutter press	**E** _____	a newspaper of small format, with a lot of pictures, short articles, less serious	
5. pamphlet	**F** _____	a small sheet of paper that advertises a product/an event, distributed to a lot of people	
6. quarterly	**G** _____	a newspaper published 52 times a year	
7. supplement	**H** _____	a very thin book with a paper cover informing you about a particular subject	
8. tabloid	**I** _____	newspapers that print a lot of shocking stories about people's private lives	
	J _____	an extra separate section, in the form of a magazine, inserted into a newspaper	

What is inside a newspaper or magazine?

advertisement	current affairs	letters page (letter to the editor)
agony column	editorial/leader	news reports
article	feature	newsletter (bulletin)
caption	foreword	obituary
cartoon	front page	review
classified advertisements/ads	gossip column	scandal
column	headline	small ads
comic strip	horoscope	sports pages
cover	issue	supplement
crossword	leading article	weather forecast

censorship	libel/defamation of	subscriber	to seek publicity
coverage	character	subscription	to show
deadline	plagiarism	to edit	to surf
exclusive	press release	to hit the headlines	to write for/in
facsimile	readership	to increase circulation	unbiased account
journal	respect for privacy	to print	website
paparazzi	rumour	to publish	

People: correspondent   critic   editor   journalist   reporter

copy	of a particular day, e.g. *a copy of yesterday´s paper*
edition	printed at the same time: e.g. *a special / the evening / a paperback/hardback edition*
issue	all copies produced on a particular date, e.g. *12 issues a year*

Task 2

Scrambled words: Find the missing words.

1.	dishonest, immoral things that famous people are supposed to have done	A A C D L N S
2.	a picture, words, which are intended to persuade people to buy sth	A D E E E I M N R S T T V
3.	it gives the editor's opinion about something	A D E I I L O R T
4.	a game in which you write the answers in boxes	C D O O R R S S W
5.	words above or below a picture in a newspaper	A C I N O P T
6.	the title of a report	A D E E H I L N
7.	an article about someone who has just died	A B I O R T U Y
8.	newspapers printed at the same time	D E I I N O T
9.	it is about a special subject	A E E F R T U
10.	people who follow celebrities to sell photos to newspapers	A A A I P P R Z Z

Task 3

Match the words on the left with the explanations on the right. Write the correct number next to the explanation.
There are more words than needed.

1. agony aunt		
2. classified ad	A _____	untrue statements about somebody are printed
3. current affairs	B _____	a small advertisement for selling and buying things
4. censorship	C _____	the copies sold in a certain amount of time
5. facsimile	D _____	significant political events happening now
6. circulation	E _____	an exact copy of a piece of writing or a picture, a duplicate
7. libel	F _____	books are examined to remove anything that is thought offensive
8. rumour		

1. subscriber		
2. to edit	A _____	to produce copies of books, newspapers in a considerable number
3. to hit the headlines	B _____	all the people who read a newspaper every day
4. to print	C _____	to be reported widely in newspapers
5. to publish	D _____	the information is fair as the reporter is not influenced by others
6. unbiased account	E _____	to revise, to remove mistakes to prepare a newspaper for printing
7. ghost writer	F _____	to release a book, to bring it out
8. readership		

Answer the questions:

How do you choose your newspaper? A good sports section? Sharp political columnists? Amusing cartoons?
    A useful international section? Few ads? Price? Crosswords? Size? Pictures/photos?

Which newspapers do you read? Give reasons.

Why do people still read newspapers?

Would you like to be a journalist? Why (not)?

TELEVISION AND RADIO

Programmes:

broadcast	educational programme	reality TV
cartoon	feature film	report
chat show	food programme	rerun
children's programme	game show	sitcom
comedy	makeover (show)	soap (opera)
commercial	music programme (classical music)	sports programme
cookery programme	nature programme	talent shows
crime series	the news	talk show
current affairs programme	news bulletin	telethon
detective series/stories	news flash	travel programme
documentary	phone-in (call-in) programme	TV film
docusoap	play	weather forecast
(costume) drama	quiz (show)	

a **serial** = a story that continues from one episode to the next.

a **series** = the same characters, the same format but each programme is complete in itself.

Synonyms:

television (set)	TV	telly	the box	the tube

People:

announcer	crew	newscaster	reviewer	viewer
audience	journalist	newsreader	spokesperson	weatherman/weathergirl/
cameraman	news anchorman	(news) presenter	talking head	weather forecaster

a programme about/on	pay-TV	to broadcast
cable television	perform live	to catch up on news
channel	press conference	to come on
footage	remote control	to listen **to** the radio
hit	satellite dish	to miss it
in/on the programme	satellite TV	to rehearse
live (TV) coverage	special issue	to switch channels/stations
media attention	television channel	to switch/turn over to
media coverage	television network	to switch/turn/put it on/off
media frenzy	That's news to me.	to watch TV
news agency	The news gets out/gets about.	to watch/see a programme/a film
news breaks (become known).	to announce	TV aerial
news broadcast/newscast	to be on (TV)	What's on TV?
on TV, the radio	to break the news to sb. (gently)	What's the news?

The mass media: the means of communication that reach large numbers of people in a short time.

    broadcast media (TV, radio)   print media (newspapers, books, magazines),
    outdoor media (billboards)   digital media (the Internet, email, blogs)

"**the media**": collective term, refers to the communities and institutions, like *the press*.

can be followed by a singular or plural verb, some prefer the plural verb (media is a plural form).

"**media**" + singular refers to the means of communication. *The Internet is the best new media (or medium) for advertising. The media is not interested in the truth of this story.*

the press: 1. newspapers, etc., radio and TV news   2. journalists, news reporters, broadcasters etc "a bad/good press": comment/judgement in a newspaper. *All European institutions try to get a good press.*

Task 4

Complete each sentence with a word or words from the lists above.

1. Comedy series in which the same characters appear in different everyday situations and which are broadcast every week are called _ _ _ _ _ _ _ .

2. A TV serial which deals with the daily events in the lives of the same group of characters and their personal relationships is called a _ _ _ _ _ _ _ _ _ .

3. _ _ _ _ _ _ _ _ _ _ _ _ _ are programmes that present detailed information about a particular subject.

4. _ _ _ _ _ _ _ _ _ are long TV programs that try to raise money for a charity.

5. Mostly well-known people answer questions asked by a host or the audience and talk about themselves on a _ _ _ _ _ _ _ _ or a _ _ _ _ _ _ _ _ .

6. Only the most important information that has happened recently is reported, often suddenly in the middle of a programme. This programme is called a _ _ _ _ _ _ _ _ _ _ _ _ or a _ _ _ _ _ _ _ _ _ .

7. A _ _ _ _ _ _ _ _ _ _ is an advertisement broadcast on TV or radio.

8. The news was _ _ _ _ _ _ _ _ _ early this evening.

9. An _ _ _ _ _ _ _ _ _ _ or a _ _ _ _ _ _ _ _ _ _ reads news or information on TV or on the radio.

10. The host or _ _ _ _ _ _ _ _ _ introduces the different parts of a television or radio show.

11. "Thank you for joining _ _ _ _ _ _ _ _ _ _ _ _ of today's landing of Discovery. Commander Collins and her crew are finally climbing out of the shuttle ..."

12. A number of news media organizations captured _ _ _ _ _ _ _ of the riot.

13. A very successful reality TV show that helps its participants change their image or improve their lives is called a _ _ _ _ _ _ _ _ show.

14. Are you pregnant? Then you might ask yourself how you can prepare to _ _ _ _ _ _ _ _ _ _ _ _ _ _ your boss?

15. People who live according to the slogan "Time is Money" tune in briefly to _ _ _ _ _ _ _ _ _ _ _ _ _ and information.

Discuss these questions:

Describe your viewing habits: How much TV do you watch every day?

Is it a source of information and/or entertainment?

Do you discuss what you see on TV with your parents/siblings/friends?

What do you usually/often/sometimes/never watch? What are your favourite programmes?

Weigh the advantages and disadvantages of different media sources (TV, radio, Internet, newspapers).

Which ones do you use? What is the best way to find out about what is happening in the world?

Is it important to you to know what is happening in other countries?

Decide if you believe everything you see and hear on the news and give reasons.

Think of some news stories of the past days. What were they about? Compare the same news story in different newspapers. Are they presented in the same way?

Would you like to meet and spend a day with a celebrity? Who? Why?

Weigh the advantages and disadvantages of being a famous person.

Would you be happier if you were famous?

"Everyone has the right to freedom of opinion and expression." This is a fundamental human right. Why is freedom for the media a priority? Give reasons why independent and free media are essential to democracies.

Evaluate the limits of free speech. Can you have too much press freedom? Has the freedom of the press gone too far, does it break the boundaries of the right to privacy?

KOMMUNIKATION

Forms of communication:

verbal communication		non-verbal communication/messages
written: memos, letter, emails, reports	**oral:** face-to-face (interpersonal), through phone, voice chat, video conferencing	(hand) gesture, body language, facial expression, smile, physical appearance, clothes, actions, posture, eye contact, tone and pitch of voice
formal: lectures, conferences	**informal:** the grapevine, informal rumor mill	**visual:** signs, drawings, illustration, color, graphs, charts

Task 1   word-formation

Complete the following table.

verb	abstract noun	noun (person)	adjective
			challenged/challenging
chat, chatter	_____ , _____		
		communicator	
contact			—
			conversational MIND: converse (=opposite)
	expression	—	_____ , _____
		gossiper	_____ , _____
impress		—	_____ , _____ ,
	information (U)	_____ , _____	_____ , _____ (=relaxed, friendly)
interact		—	
	message		—
	perception	—	_____ , _____
receive		_____ , _____	_____ , _____
transmit	_____ , _____	—	—
	_____ , _____	—	verbal

MIND: contact (U): communication between people, no pl

contact (C): someone you know who can help you: to have a lot of useful contacts

Task 2

Match the verbs with the nouns to complete the collocations.

verb	noun
1. disclose	A _____ in touch
2. get by	B _____ a mobile phone
3. go	C _____ up a language
4. have a chat	D _____ in a language
5. have	E _____ a text message, an email
6. keep	F _____ on the Internet
7. make	G _____ conversation
8. pick	H _____ over a cup of coffee
9. read	I _____ confidential information
10. send	J _____ the Net
11. surf	K _____ a blog
12. use	L _____ no contact with

Some tips on how you can develop your communication skills:

Task 3

Match to complete the phrases.

1. listen	A _____ respect for sb
2. avoid	B _____ into a dialogue
3. be	C _____ close attention to
4. boost	D _____ your confidence
5. convey	E _____ stance
6. empathize	F _____ misunderstandings
7. maintain	G _____ focused
8. pay	H _____ a good listener
9. personalize	I _____ a positive attitude
10. relaxed open	J _____ a message
11. stay	K _____ actively
12. willing to enter	L _____ with others

Some more tips: Maintain good eye contact. Vary your vocabulary. Clarification, e.g. by asking questions, is important to check that the listener's understanding is correct. Respond to convey your interest. Sloppily written emails waste everybody's time and money. Don't ramble endlessly, or you'll come across as a poor communicator. Good manners make a big difference to how others feel about you.

Important collocations:

communicate	accurately, clearly, effectively, successfully, well, directly, easily, verbally, electronically
speak	appropriately, loudly, softly, clearly, slowly, calmly, sharply, at length, eloquently, encouragingly, coherently, intelligibly, meaningfully, freely, openly

effective, poor, direct, open, two-way, interpersonal to have, establish, facilitate, improve a breakdown in, a lack of, problems of modern means of	**communication**
get your ~ across, leave, take, convey, receive, pass on, carry, deliver, send, transmit	**a message**

Task 4

Match the words on the left with the explanations on the right. Write the correct number next to the explanation. There are more words than needed.

1. bilingual	**A** _____	information spreads quickly from one to another through conversation
2. conventions	**B** _____	rules for behaving properly in social situations
3. etiquette	**C** _____	a person who transmits a message, communicator
4. first impression	**D** _____	sth that is accepted as the normal and right way
5. intended meaning	**E** _____	the feeling we have when we meet another person for the first time
6. monolingual	**F** _____	a person who decodes the message, interpreter
7. multilingual	**G** _____	the things/ideas you get from another person's speech
8. on/through the grapevine	**H** _____	the speaker wants to convey this idea to the audience
9. perceived meaning	**I** _____	informal conversation about unimportant subjects
10. receiver	**J** _____	being able to speak two languages fluently
11. sender	**K** _____	being able to speak several different languages well
12. small talk	**L** _____	being able to speak one language, your mother tongue

Task 5

Try to guess the meaning of the following idioms in italics and paraphrase them.

1. Stop **beating about the bush**. Just tell me what's happened!
2. Something's upsetting you. Why don't you **get it off your chest**? Tell me what it is.
3. I'll **get straight to the point**. I'm afraid I'm going to have to make some budget cuts.
4. Okay, don't return her calls. She'll soon **get the message**, and leave you alone.
5. Could I **have a quick word with you**?
6. I **heard it on the grapevine** that they are getting married, but I don't know when.
7. **Just between you and me**, I think he made up the whole story about his work.
8. Working together with Carl is easy because he and I are **on the same wavelength**.
9. I hope she'll get the job. I'll **put in a good word for her**.
10. I know it's true! I heard it **straight from the horse's mouth**.
11. Her mother could **talk the hind legs off a donkey**.
12. He was so excited about going to the US, she was **talking nineteen to the dozen**.
13. Sometimes talking to her is like **talking to a brick wall**.
14. He **doesn't mince his words**.

NATUR UND UMWELT

The natural world

bank	cove → bay → gulf	grow crops
beach	dam	hedge
bottom	delta	hillock → hill → mountain
brook→ stream → river	desert	hilly
canal	estuary	ice fields
cape	falls	island, group of islands
cave	farmland	jungle
channel	field	landscape
cliff	foot	meadow
coast, coastline	footpath → lane → road	mountain (range)
conservation area	geysers	mouth
continent	glacier	national park
copse → wood → forest	gorge	nature
countryside	ground	oasis

ocean	reef	sugar/tea/coffee plantation
paddy field	ridge	summit
path	riverside	thermal springs
peak	rocks	top
peninsula	scenery	torrent
plain	sea	tributary
polar ice	seaside	valley
puddle → pond → lake	shore	vegetation
(tropical) rainforest	soil	volcano, pl. -es
rapids	source	waterfall

Task 1

Which of the following words collocate with one another? Match two words, one from each list. Words may be used more than once.

coniferous	national	area	plantation
conservation	paddy	desert	populated
deciduous	polar	eruption	range
densely (heavily)	sparsely (thinly)	field	region
equatorial	tea	fire	springs
forest	thermal	forest	wave
hot	tidal	park	
mountain	volcanic		

Task 2 word-formation

Complete the following table.

Verb	Noun (abstract)	Noun (person)	Adjective	Synonyms
		consumer		eat, drink, use (up)
contaminate		—		pollute, poison
			contributory	give, supply
	destruction			damage
dispose of		—		throw away
	emission		—	give off
—	environment			surroundings, habitat
—		—	extinct	die out, no longer exist
influence		—		affect
	pollution, pollutant		—	make sth dirty
recycle		—		use sth again
		reductionist		make sth smaller, lessen, diminish
		—	sustainable	support, maintain
		—	threatening	endanger, warn

ENVIRONMENTAL PROBLEMS

acid rain
animal rights
the atmosphere
captivity
carbon dioxide emissions
climate/climatic change
damage/harm/pollute the
    environment
damage to the environment
deforestation
desertification
destruction of the ozone layer
destruction of the rainforests
dramatic increase
dump nuclear/toxic waste
endangered species
exhaust fumes

factory
factory farming
floods/flooding
food chain
fossil fuels
genetically modified crops
global warming
greenhouse effect/gases
harmful (to the environment)
heavy industries
ice caps
in danger of/on the verge of
    extinction
intensive farming
misuse the world's natural resources
overfishing
overpopulation

ozone layer
pesticides
poaching
poisonous gases (CFC gases)
polluting/polluted/ (air, river, sea)
pollution of the environment
radiation
road traffic
sea level
smog
threat to biodiversity
uninhabitable
unleaded gas/petrol
waste disposal
the worst case scenarios

Task 3

Complete each sentence with a word or (part of a) phrase from the lists above. The first letter has been given.

1. Environmental p_____ is the release of dangerous environmental c_____.

   To be more specific, the nitrogen oxides produced by industry are often referred to as p_____

   as well, although the substances themselves are not h_____. In fact, it is the sunlight that

   transforms these compounds into s_____.

2. N_____ w_____ is radioactive for thousands of years.

3. Consequences of g_____ w_____ are c_____

   c_____ and the rise of s_____ due to the melting of the i_____

   c_____. This will cause f_____ in many low-lying areas of the world.

4. The o_____ l_____, which acts as a shield protecting the Earth from UV

   r_____ from the sun, is getting thinner, specially over Antarctica and over North Pole.

5. A_____ r_____ is caused by the burning of fossil fuels. It can kill marine life and vegetation.

6. Some gases in the atmosphere produce the "g_____ e_____", trapping the

   heat of Earth without allowing it to escape into space. The concentration of the most important greenhouse

   gas, c_____ d_____, has increased in the a_____ and is

   going to increase in the next future, because c_____ d_____, with water,

   is the final product of the burning of f_____ f_____ (oil and derivatives, coal,...) and of living and

   dead vegetation. Carbon dioxide is produced by road transport and by burning f_____ f_____ in

   power stations, factories and in the home. Another source of carbon dioxide is d_____ and the

   burning of the tropical r_____.

7. Exporting t_____ w_____ to developing countries has been common practice in the recent past:

   developed countries used to solve the industrial w_____ problem comfortably and cheaply.

8. What do you think is the Earth's biggest threat to b_____? D_____ threatens

ecosystems across the globe, in particular the tropical rainforests.

9. While you are doing this exercise, one of our species will become e_____. One in four of

the world's mammals are threatened with e_____ in the not-too-distant future. Tigers are

e_____. There are only about 3,000 wild tigers left.

10. Many people are not aware of the dangers of e_____ f_____ but they are responsible for

a lot of illnesses.

11. Why are national parks important? National parks p_____ habitats for native plants and

wildlife. They maintain b_____ and protect endangered species.

12. One of the first g_____ m_____ animals for consumption might be salmon.

Activists claim that food containing g_____ m_____ ingredients as well as

all f_____ f_____ animal products should be identified with a label.

ALTERNATIVE SOURCES

achieve/promote sustainable
  development
biodegradable material/packaging
bottle bank
curb/limit pollution
cut down on
conserve/preserve biodiversity
conservation/protection of the
  environment
eco-friendly products
ecological balance
environmentally friendly

locally grown food
natural habitats/resources
obtain electricity from renewable
  sources
organic farming
preserve/protect the environment
prevent damage to ecosystems
public transport
quality of life
recycle bottles/paper/plastic/waste
recycling point
reduce emissions

reduce your carbon footprint
renewable energy/resources research
save an endangered species
solar panels/power/energy
subsidised fares
switch to
tackle the threat of climate change
think more long-term
tidal energy
unleaded petrol
wind power

Task 4

Jumbled words: Rearrange the letters. The first letter of each word is in bold. The clues after each jumbled word will help you.

adil**t** **e**enryg	A renewable source of power produced by the regular rise and fall of ocean waters
ceyrcel	to extract things that have already been used so that they can be reused
eprinstoerva	keeping something in good condition or in its original state
el**u**ndade **p**lorte	gasoline which does not contain a certain environmentally harmful substance
lt**b**oet **b**nka	a container in a public place where you deposit empty glass containers so that they can be recycled
alwrebnee yrg**ee**n	unlike fossil fuels, which are exhaustible, these power sources regenerate and can be sustained indefinitely.
baleit**s**usna	using natural resources without causing damage to the environment and by avoiding depletion
tilmortn**e**nienavs	someone who is concerned about the natural environment and wants to protect it
artun**al** **h**ittbaa	the home or place where a particular plant or animal is normally found
sroal wor**pe**	using the sun's energy

| area | boundary | climatic regions | nation | region |
| border | capital (city) | county | province | |

country:	1. an area of land with its own people and government
	2. contrasted to towns and cities
the countryside:	refers to the natural features of the country (fields, rivers, flowers,...)
landscape, scenery:	refer to the way the natural features of the countryside are arranged
scenery:	emphasizes the attractiveness of the landscape

People involved in natural disasters:

casualties refugees survivors the dead the wounded victims

Task 5

Which verbs collocate with the following natural disasters? Use a (collocation) dictionary.

An earthquake ...	A (forest) fire ...
An avalanche ...	A flood ...
A blizzard ...	A hurricane ...
A drought ...	A storm/thunderstorm/snowstorm ...
An epidemic ...	A tornado /a typhoon/a cyclone ...
A famine ...	A volcano ...

MODERNE TECHNOLOGIEN

Task 1

Complete the phrases with the right words from the box.

| enter | surf | download | go | cut | sign | put | back |

to access your mails
to browse websites
to cyberbully somebody
to _____ online
to _____ something on the Web
to send attachments
to text somebody
to upgrade your computer

to _____ up your files
to click a button
to _____ podcasts
to navigate websites
to save a document
to _____ off a computer
to transmit information
to upload a file

to bookmark webpages
to _____ and paste something
to _____ a web address
to post information
to select a word
to _____ the Net
to update your online profile
to use your mobile phone

Task 2

Choose the right word.

1.	far on or ahead in development or progress	A	automated
		B	advanced
2.	a person who fears, dislikes, or avoids new technology	A	technophile
		B	technophobe
3.	a system that is easy to use or understand	A	state-of the-art
		B	user-friendly
4.	designed to reduce the amount of work needed to do something	A	labour-saving
		B	outdated

5. no longer produced or used		**A** obsolete	
		B high tech	
6. the latest or most advanced stage in the development of something		**A** cutting-edge	
		B computer literate	

Task 3

Here are the definitions for the remaining words from task 2. Can you match them?

1. a person who is enthusiastic about new technology _____

2. having sufficient knowledge and skill to be able to use computers; familiar
with the operation of computers _____

3. operated by largely automatic equipment _____

4. old and no longer suitable for modern purposes _____

5. the latest and most sophisticated or advanced stage of a technology, art, or science _____

6. using the most modern or advanced technology available _____

Study these words.

access	advance	appliance	application
automation	back-up	battery	binary system
broadband	camcorder	central processing unit, CPU	charger
component	computer addiction	computer age	computer buff
computer scientist	computer technology, ICT	connection	copyright law
cyberspace	data	developer	development
device	digital camera	digital divide	digital native
dishwasher	e-book	e-mail	engineer
equipment	features	file	firewall
flash drive	gadget	hairdryer	home page
improvement	information technology, IT	innovation	instruction manual
Internet security	internet service provider, ISP	invention	joint photographic experts group, JPEG
keyboard	land line	laptop	laser printer
local area network, LAN	machinery	maintenance	means of communication
microwave	mobile phone	modern media	monitor
network	operating system	plug	portable document format, PDF
printer	privacy	programmer	progress
recipient	remote control	research	revolution
satnav	scanner	screen	screensaver
search engine	server	subject line	technician
technological change	technology	touch screen	vacuum cleaner
video conference	virus	washing machine	wide area network, WAN
WiFi hotspot	wireless networks	word processing	world wide web, WWW

Task 4

Insert the correct word into the following sentences.

1. The _____ prevents people without authorization from accessing a system and potentially damaging it.

2. When the _____ goes down, we cannot access the Internet, save files, or communicate with other computers on the network.

3. In my computer class, I learned how to use several different graphic design _____.

4. I would like to work in the _____ department at a company because I like to work with computers and help people use them more effectively.

5. Before I left for my trip to London, I used a(n) _____ to search for information about the sights.

6. I like to _____ songs from the Internet so that I can listen to them on my computer.

7. I _____ (ed) my résumé from my computer to an online job board.

8. My brother is a real _____! I mean, he knows more about computers than anyone else!

9. "_____" refers to high-speed data transmission in which a single cable can carry a large amount of data at once.

10. The Audi A6 comes with _____ and climate control as standard.

11. The digital tools that are reshaping our economy make more sense to young _____ than to members of older generations.

12. The _____ feature on Android phones lets you use your mobile data on multiple computers or tablets at once.

13. Today, _____ do not serve the same purpose as they did in the past, when they actually saved your screen from what is called „image burn-in".

PERSÖNLICHE ZUKUNFT, PLÄNE

Different verb forms are used to talk about plans for the future, depending on what kind of plan it is.

will	for plans decided at the moment of speaking – **SPONTANEOUS DECISION** So there's no bread left? *Don't worry, I'll buy some on the way home.*
going to	for plans decided before the moment of speaking – **INTENTION** I know there's no bread. *I'm going to get some.* It's on my shopping list.
present continuous	for fixed plans with definite time and/or place – **ARRANGEMENT** *I'm starting university in October.*

Task 1

Fill in the gaps with these words and phrases.

a certificate	a degree	a diploma	a family	a job	a qualification	children
earn	enter	fail	go to	leave	make	married
pass	provide for	revise for	rich	start	start	take

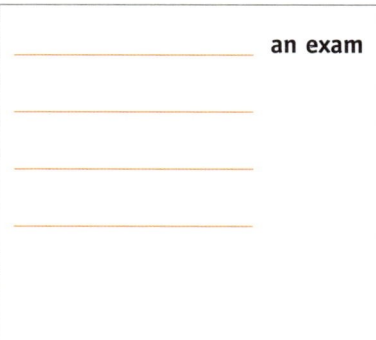

_____ school/
college/
university

_____

_____

_____ an exam

_____

_____

get _____

_____

_____

_____

_____

_____ a lot of money

_____

have _____

_____

_____ a family

_____

Task 2

Dreams – Match the expressions with their explanations.

1. a childhood dream | A a dream about sth that cannot happen
2. a daydream | B a dream that will take a long time to achieve
3. a distant dream | C a dream you had when you were little
4. a dream comes true | D a dream you have had all your life
5. a lifelong dream | E better than anything you ever imagined
6. an impossible dream | F I never expected that to happen!
7. beyond your wildest dreams | G ideal or perfect employment
8. dream job | H In your dreams!
9. Dream on! | I pleasant thoughts that make you forget what you are doing
10. It went like a dream. | J something happens after you have wanted it for a long time
11. Not in my wildest dreams! | K something went very well or successfully without any problems
12. the man/woman of your dreams | L the perfect man/woman for you
13. to achieve/fulfil/realize a dream | M to wish to achieve great things
14. to have great dreams | N to do or get what you want

Task 3

Ambitions – Do you have or have you had any of these ambitions?

to be a film star	to be a politician	to be an astronaut	to be happy	to get married
to go to university	to write a book	to have children	to learn Chinese	to live by the sea
to make a lot of money	to make an invention	to own a car	to travel the world	to work abroad

Task 4

Ambitions – What other ambitions and dreams do you have?

Make a list:

_____

_____

_____

Which of your ambitions are
- realistic?
- quite likely to be achieved?
- unlikely but possible to be realized?

Why?

- nearly impossible?
- completely unrealistic?

Task 5

Use these phrases to talk about your future.

I'd really like to study/find a job ...
What I would love to do is ...
My dream is to ...
I'm dreaming of becoming a ...
I've always wanted to work in/with/for ...
The most important thing for me is to ...
I want to dedicate my time and energy to ...
I'm very much interested in ...
I want to have/make a career.

I wish to broaden my horizon/expand my knowledge.
I really need to improve my language/people skills.
I intend to apply for a job as a ...
First I need to do my military/community service.
I definitely don't want to ...
I'm having trouble deciding.
I don't know what I want.
I have no idea.
I really don't know.

Task 6

Put he words below into the correct category.

stuck in a rut		part-time job	well paid job	stuck behind a desk	stressed
manual labour		joy	self employed	job satisfaction	money
healthy	independent	dissatisfied	loving family	knowledgeable	happiness
wise	contentment	confident	power	realize my dreams	estate car
content	start a family	love	famous	good team player	successful
voluntary work	run my own business	work full-time	work with my hands	good working conditions	my own boss

Things I want to have	Things I want to be	Things I want to feel	Things I want to do	Things I don't want to be

Mind the difference:

JOB	WORK (uncountable)	CAREER
regular activity you do and receive money for (= profession/occupation)	activities done to reach a goal	many different jobs over the years
a demanding/lucrative job a fulfilling/rewarding job a dead-end job an office/holiday job a steady job quit/lose a job	freelance/office work skilled/unskilled work out of work be at/get off work look for work her line of work	embark on/pursue a career a promising career career prospects switch your career ruin your career a promising career

INTERKULTURELLE ASPEKTE

Task 1

Match the following nouns with the definitions. Write the most appropriate noun next to the definition. The nouns must be used more than once.

melting pot	minority	multiculturalism

	a small group within a community or country that is different because of race, religion, language,…
	also known as "salad bowl theory": each ingredient keeps its flavour and integrity, while adding to a successful end product;
	antonym: majority, dominant group
	large numbers of people from different races, countries, cultures, ethnic groups, social classes come to live together and can assimilate;
	the belief that it is important and good to include people or ideas from many different countries, races or religions;
	also known as "assimilation"
	synonym: weaker group
	forces other peoples and immigrants to give up their native cultures in order to be absorbed into mainstream society;
	cultural mosaic in Canada;

Task 2

Match the adjectives on the left with the explanations on the right.

multicultural	people of several ethnic groups
multiracial	put in a powerless, unimportant position within a society/group
multiethnic	people or ideas from many different countries, races, religions, languages and traditions
marginalized	made up of different races

Related phrases:

mainstream culture

to incorporate immigrants into the mainstream

to abandon one's culture and traditions

to retain and practice one's cultural traditions

a minority of

to be a minority

to be in a/the minority

to be superior to diversity

to give rise to conflicts

to outnumber

to adopt new customs

racism (U)	the unfair treatment of people, or violence against them, because they belong to a different race from your own; the belief that different races of people have different characters and abilities, and that your own race is the best; the discrimination against and social marginalization of people based on their race;
race	people can be divided according to their external anatomical features, like skin colour, hair type ... or geographic origin (Irish ...); synonym: breed; e.g. Caucasian, Asian ...
ethnicity	a shared cultural heritage, e.g. Norwegian, Brazilian, Scottish, Jewish
racist (n, adj)	a person who believes that people of other races are not as good as people of their own race
racial segregation	people of different races are kept apart
tribe	families or communities in a traditional society that speak the same dialect and have the same customs, often led by a chief; tribal (adj); USAGE: only used in historical contexts; better: community, people

Collocations:

racial (adj., only before noun)	~ abuse	~ discrimination	~ harmony	~ riot/riots
	~ amalgamation	~ disparity	~ hatred	~ segregation
	~ attack	~ equality	~ mixture	~ superiority
	~ conflict	~ group	~ oppression	~ tension
	~ differences	~ harassment	~ prejudice	~ violence
	~ disadvantage			
racist (adj.)	~ belief	~ attitude	~ persecution	

a form of ~	the fight against ~		(the) human ~		~ relations
blatant ~	to be a victim of ~		mixed ~		~ equality
overt ~	to combat/fight (against) ~	**racism**	blond ~	**race**	~ discrimination
rampant ~	to experience ~		coloured ~		~ prejudice
			alien ~		~ riot

singular: a person (a man, woman or child), a member of the human race, a human, a human being

plural: people, all people: the human race (sg), humanity (U), man (sg, no article), mankind (U)

ethnic (adj)	1. a group of people having a common tradition, the same language, customs, history,... 2. a non-Western cultural tradition
ethnic	~ background ~ diversity ~ look ~ conflict ~ stock ~ cleansing ~ group ~ makeup of a population ~ minority ~ tensions

USAGE: In British English "black" is most generally accepted nowadays. In American English "African American" or "Afro-American" is preferred. "Colored" and "Negro" are both considered offensive. The terms "Indian" and "Red Indian" are old-fashioned, "American Indian" and "Native American" (official term) are well established.

Task 3

Choose the right word to go with each meaning. Write the number of that word next to its meaning.

1. descent 2. ethnic 3. ghetto 4. green belt 5. racism 6. reservation 7. twilight zone 8. neighbourhood	**A** _____ beliefs and institutions that discriminate against socially marginalized people because of their race **B** _____ a district of a town or the area you live in, vicinity **C** _____ a part of a city where a minority group lives, often crowded or slum areas **D** _____ ancestry, origin **E** _____ relating to a community having a common cultural tradition **F** _____ an area of land that is kept separate for occupation by North American Indians or Australian Aboriginals

AUSTRALIA

Task 4

Do you know the terms?

1.	the remote bush country of Australia	
2.	the country's informal nickname	
3.	an informal reference to a resident of Australia	
4.	the indigenous peoples of Australia	
5.	a social division in a traditional society	
6.	the stage of human social development which is considered most advanced	
7.	Aboriginals who were forcibly removed from their families as children by the Australian Government in the early 20th century	
8.	a journey undertaken through the outback by an Australian Aborigine for religious and cultural reasons	
9.	a ceremony performed at times when an individual changes his status	
10.	a situation that tests a person's endurance	

CANADA

Task 5

Match the words with their definitions.

1. ancestor 2. Arctic 3. Eskimo 4. heritage 5. Inuit 6. Inuk 7. Inuktitut 8. maple-leaf 9. Mountie	**A** _____ a member of an indigenous people inhabiting northern Canada; a term recently regarded as offensive **B** _____ a term used by the people inhabiting the Canadian Arctic to refer to themselves **C** _____ the language of the Inuit **D** _____ a person from whom one is descended **E** _____ the emblem of Canada **F** _____ the region around the North Pole **G** _____ a member of the Royal Canadian Mounted Police **H** _____ a member of the Inuit people **I** _____ traditions, beliefs that are part of the history of a group; sth that is passed down from preceding generations

Task 6

Match the words with their definitions or synonyms.

1. be culturally aware	**A** _____	involve oneself deeply in an activity
2. be culturally diverse	**B** _____	stay alive, continue to exist
3. be immersed	**C** _____	behave in a way that most people think is correct; adjust, adapt
4. conform	**D** _____	share
5. egalitarian	**E** _____	put up with sth painful; suffer; bear
6. endure	**F** _____	be different; a variety of ethnic groups exist within a society
7. have in common	**G** _____	see the positive and negative aspects of cultural differences
8. survive	**H** _____	believing in the principle that all people deserve equal rights

prejudice (C,U) – an unreasonable dislike, distrust of or preference for sb/sth
– a preconceived opinion that is not based on reason or experience;
– unfair and unfavourable feeling formed without thinking deeply or without knowledge, resulting from fear, distrust

Task 7

Complete the following table.

verb/adjective	noun
to be prejudiced against/in favour of sb/sth, to have a prejudice	prejudice against/in favour of
to prejudge sb/sth	—
to be disadvantaged, to be at a disadvantage, sth puts sb at a disadvantage	
	discrimination
to segregate sb from sth	
	desegregation
	marginalization
tolerant/intolerant	
	oppression
to be inferior or superior to others	
	inequality - equality
to deny sb sth	
—	civil rights movement, struggle for equal rights
—	non-violent protests, doctrine of non-violence

	collocation			Synonym
prejudice (n.)	a victim of ~	cultural ~	personal ~	bias
	arouse/feed/stir up ~	deep ~	pure ~	bigotry
	blatant ~	deep-rooted ~	racial ~	discrimination
	blind ~	eliminate ~	serious ~	injustice
	break down ~	encounter ~	strong ~	intolerance
	challenge ~	express ~	suffer ~	partiality
	class ~	irrational ~	to have/hold ~	predisposition
	colour ~	old ~	unfair ~	prejudgement
	come up against ~	overcome ~	without ~	unfairness
	confirm ~			

	collocations		synonyms		
Prejudiced (adj)	~ thinking ~ thoughts	biased bigoted discriminatory intolerant	one-sided partial predisposed	unfair unjust warped	
prejudice (v.)		bias dispose incline	influence predispose	sway warp	

Task 8

Match the words with the correct meaning. There are more words than meanings. Write the number next to the meaning.

1. unconscious bias
2. to discriminate against
3. discrimination
4. bigoted
5. prejudice
6. to segregate sb from sth
7. disadvantage
8. tolerance

A _____ prejudiced in their views, intolerant of the opinions of others
B _____ to separate one group of people from the rest
C _____ the ability or willingness to accept differences between people
D _____ inclination, prejudice in favour of a particular person/thing, bias against
E _____ irrational dislike of somebody holding ill-formed opinions;
F _____ to treat one group of people worse than others

Task 9

Fill in the blank spaces. One blank space represents one letter.

Let's have a look at human rights violations. It should be everybody's duty to prevent majority-minority tensions from developing into conflict. There i_ no secu_ _ _ _ without hu_ _ _ rights, a_ _ that, o_ course, incl_ _ _ _ minority rig_ _ , too. Integ_ _ _ _ _ _ _ involves responsi_ _ _ _ _ _ _ _ _ and rig_ _ _ on bo_ _ sides. Educ_ _ _ _ _ _ should pro_ _ _ _ children wi_ _ the nece_ _ _ _ _ _ skills t_ live i_ a multi-e_ _ _ _ _ society. Preju_ _ _ _ _ _ create stereo_ _ _ _ _ which a_ _ built o_ distorted ima_ _ _ of peo_ _ . At la_ _ I'll exp_ _ _ _ to y_ _ the Jim Crow l_ _ , which enfo_ _ _ _ racial segre_ _ _ _ _ _ by preve_ _ _ _ _ _ black peo_ _ _ from drin_ _ _ _ water fr_ _ the sa_ _ water foun_ _ _ _ _ as _ white per_ _ _ could.

Ther_ _ _ _ _ , blacks we_ _ denied t_ _ same rig_ _ _ as t_ _ whites.

Problems:	results:

cultural differences
large families
education: fewer education opportunities, difficulties
    with the language;
overcrowding: poor-quality housing, cheap rents,
    substandard dwellings/housing in undesirable areas;
long-term unemployment: lack of money, fewer skills,
    jobs are poorly paid, cannot afford good housing;
environment
high rate of crime: violence, drugs, muggings →
police harassment, lack of trust
	vicious spiral/circle
	riots
	fear
	rude, disrespectful treatment
	verbal abuse
	racial prejudices
	discrimination
	jealousy among rival communities
	segregation of ethnic groups in cities results from
	    differences in wealth, colour, religion

ERWACHSENWERDEN UND IDENTITÄTSFINDUNG

Make sure you understand all these words and phrases.

Growing up

to achieve one's goals
to aim high
to assert oneself
to be born into a rich family
to be born of/to poor parents
to be interested in sth
to consider one's options
to deny one's origins
to develop one's personality/interests
to find fulfilment
to find oneself
to find/realize one's dream (job)
to focus on sth
to get an education
to give sb a sheltered/strict/middle class upbringing
to grow up
to have a proper/privileged/conventional upbringing
to have a positive outlook on life
to have realistic goals
to have/show certain personality traits
to overcome problems
to pursue a dream
to realize your full potential
to seek happiness
to shape sb's personality
to share certain values with sb
to stick to one's principles
to work hard for sth

Strengths/Strong points

to be ambitious
to be an achiever
to be assertive
to be good/talented at sth
to be mature
to be self-assured
to be self-aware
to be self-confident
to be selfless
to believe in oneself
to feel accepted

Life stages

infancy
childhood
adolescence
adulthood
midlife
old age

Verbs

to conceive
to expect
to give birth to
to adopt
to bring up
to raise
to rear   a child
to pamper
to spoil
to cuddle
to encourage
to abandon
to punish
to abuse

Weaknesses/Shortcomings

to be a snob
to be confused about sth
to be nervous
to be self-conscious
to be uncertain
to fail in sth
to feel like an outsider
to feel rootless
to feel threatened by sth
to go through an identity crisis
to have an inferiority complex
to have self-doubt(s)
to lack self-confidence/self-respect
to be uncommunicative
to be withdrawn
to feel isolated
to feel misunderstood

Task 1

Complete the sentences with the words from the box.

bond with	close-knit family	family gatherings	lot in common
sibling rivalry	stable home environment	striking resemblance	

1. Having meals together is crucial to the building of a _____ .

2. Very often _____ starts even before the second child is born, and it continues as the kids grow and compete for attention.

3. _____ can be a chance for family members to reconnect and _____ each other.

4. Peter bears a _____ to his father – he's got the same hair, nose and eyes.

5. When a family has a _____ , children feel loved and protected.

6. Samuel and Frank have a _____ – I can see why they like each other.

Task 2

Match the words with their definitions.

1.	a delinquent		**A**	a child who has just learned how to walk
2.	a toddler		**B**	a grown-up
3.	a teenager		**C**	a person who does work without getting paid to do it
4.	a role model		**D**	a person who is famous
5.	a juvenile		**E**	a person who is admired and looked up to
6.	peers		**F**	a person whose behaviour is a good example for others to be imitated
7.	middle-agers		**G**	a term used when speaking angrily to a young person
8.	a hero		**H**	a young person between 13 and 19
9.	young lady/man		**I**	a young person in the process of developing from a child into an adult
10.	a volunteer		**J**	a young person who commits a minor criminal act
11.	an adult		**K**	a young person who is not yet old enough to be considered an adult
12.	a celebrity		**L**	brothers and sisters
13.	siblings		**M**	people between 45 and 65
14.	the elderly		**N**	people past middle age
15.	a pensioner		**O**	people who belong to the same age or social group as someone else
16.	a philanthropist		**P**	sb who has reached the age where they can no longer work
17.	an adolescent		**Q**	sb who makes an active effort to promote human welfare

Task 3

Scrambled words – Can you find the adjectives described here?

1. willing to comply with an order or request   **B D E E I N O T**
2. conducting oneself in an appropriate manner   **A B D E E E H L L V W -**
3. intelligent and quick-witted   **B G H I R T**
4. having exceptional talent or natural ability   **D E F G I T**
5. not doing what sb with authority tells you to do   **B D D E E I I N O S T**
6. causing or showing a fondness for causing trouble in a playful way   **C E H I I M O S S U V**
7. badly behaved   **A G H N T U Y**
8. bad-tempered, and resentful; refusing to be cooperative or cheerful   **K L S U Y**

9. showing a stubborn intention to do as one wants, regardless of the consequences   **F I L L U W**
10. often ill; in poor health   **C I K L S Y**
11. having been deserted or left   **A A B D D E N N O**
12. regularly or repeatedly treated with cruelty or violence   **A B D E S U**
13. suffering a lack of proper care   **C D E E E G L N T**
14. born of parents not lawfully married to each other.   **A E E G I I I L L M T T**

Task 4

Role Models – Editing: In most lines there is a word that should not be there. Write these words in the spaces provided. Make a ✔ in the space if the line is correct.

A role model is someone who demonstrates a particular behaviour, skill, or social	✔
role for another person to emulate. Role models might ~~have~~ emerge because of character	*have*
and conduct or because of particular skills and talents. Unlike pop stars, actors, sportsmen –	
they are all role models who can have a positive or a negative effect on children. Young	
people not only look up to them and hold them up in high esteem, they also copy their	
actions, mannerisms and behaviours. Positive role models are not important because they	
set examples for people to observe and follow on. When people increase positive	
behaviours, they also increase their feelings of self-worth. Patterning to behaviours from	
positive role models can also help people build positive values. Positive role models	
provide for a sense of hope and show that dreams and goals can be fulfilled. They feel a	
sense of a duty to work for the common good of the community. Not only are they	
compassionate, peaceful, and trustworthy, they also possess in high standards and	
values. They are committed to what they do and can work through challenges.	
Although they are be admired for their courage and strength, they remain humble and	
modest. However, if there are also negative role models. Every day newspapers feature	
reports about instances of much questionable behaviour from celebrities: from betting	
scandals to doping, from racist remarks to violent outbursts. Children also try copy the	
language and fashion of their role models and – in the case of negative idols – might	
end up with speaking or dressing inappropriately for their age.	

POLITIK UND INSTITUTIONEN DES ÖFFENTLICHEN LEBENS

Task 1

Study these terms and use them to fill the gaps in the sentences below.

politician	a person engaged in party politics or in conducting the business of a government
politics	the activities associated with the governance of a country
policy	a deliberate act of government that in some way influences the society or economy outside the government
political	relating to the government or public affairs of a country
apolitical	not interested or involved in politics; of no political relevance or importance
unpolitical	not concerned with politics, politically structured, oriented, or focused

1. After the scandal the Secretary of State dropped out of active _____.

2. All the important local _____ attended the meeting.

3. Although both of her parents are politicians, she's completely _____.

4. He abandoned _____ and went into business.

5. His manners are as wild as his _____ are extreme.

6. I have always followed _____ closely.

7. It is my _____ not to accept gifts from voters.

8. It was claimed that the President's upcoming trip was purely _____.

9. Large numbers of otherwise _____ people responded to the war.

10. Let's not talk _____ now.

11. The company operates a strict no-smoking _____.

12. The government followed a _____ of restraint in public spending.

13. The government's controversial economic _____ have raised a lot of concern.

14. The new party quickly gained influence in Italian _____.

15. This was a period of _____ and economic stability.

Task 2

Study these phrases and fill in any missing prepositions.

to accept a bribe	to address problems	to amend a bill
to appoint sb _____ a post	to be elected _____ a committee	to be eligible _____ vote
to be in a party	to be _____ shaky ground	to bring sth _____ control
to buy _____ a politician	to campaign _____ sb	to cast one's vote
to dissolve parliament	to draw _____ a bill	to form a government
to fuel corruption	to go _____ the polls	to have a say _____ sth
to have an overall majority	to have the backing _____ one's party	to have/win a landslide victory
to hold a general election	to lose sight _____ sth	to rebuild the economy
to run _____ office/president	to stand down	to stay _____ office
to take advantage _____ sb	to take power/office	to throw support _____ sth
to toe the party line	to veto a bill	to veto law

Task 3

Cross out the wrong word in each sentence.

The term *anarchy/oligarchy* refers to a form of power structure in which power effectively rests with a small number of people.

The form of government in which the head of state is a president is called a *monarchy/republic*.

A *candidate/governor* is a person seeking or nominated for election to a position of authority such as president, prime minister etc.

A democracy is a form of government in which all *eligible/legitimate* people have an equal say in the decisions that affect their lives.

A dictatorship refers to an *autographic/autocratic* form of government in which an individual rules the country.

The formal decision-making process by which a population chooses an individual to hold public office is known as *electing/voting*.

The opposition comprises the major political parties *opposed/opposing* to the party in office and prepared to replace it if elected.

An *election/elective* campaign is a series of coordinated activities, such as public speaking and demonstrating, designed to achieve a political goal.

The *executive/judicial* branch of government is the part of government that has sole authority and responsibility for the daily administration of the state bureaucracy.

Task 4

Match the words with their definitions.

1.	Head of State	A	the most senior minister of cabinet in the executive branch
2.	President	B	the chief public representative of a country who may also be the head of government
3.	Prime Minister	C	the person who heads a monarchy
4.	Queen/King	D	the head of state in a presidential system

Task 5

Try to guess the missing German and English words.

Act of Parliament	verabschiedetes _____
_____	Verwaltung, Organisierung
administrative _____	Verwaltungspersonal
adult _____	volljährige(r) Bürger(in)
ballot box	Wahl_____
ballot paper	Stimm_____
by-election	Nachwahl
chamber	Kammer
_____ servant	Staatsbeamter/-beamtin
Civil Service	Staatsdienst
constituency	Wahl_____
constituent	Wähler(in)
_____-making	Entscheidungsfindung
_____ policy	Innenpolitik

first-past-the-post system	_____wahlrecht
foreign _____	Außenpolitik
polling _____	Wahllokal
_____ representation	Verhältniswahlrecht
representative	Vertreter(in) im Parliament
tax	Steuer
_____	Besteuerung
universal _____	allgemeines Wahlrecht

Task 6

Match the words with their definitions.

1.	lame duck	☐	A	a journalist who seeks out the scandalous activities of public officials
2.	incumbent	☐	B	a political analyst, commentator, or columnist who usually works for a newspaper or magazine, or in broadcasting
3.	hawk			
4.	reformer	☐	C	a politician anxious to change society or a political system
5.	sceptic	☐	D	a president with little power left
6.	pundit	☐	E	a representative to a party's national convention chosen by local voters
7.	nominee	☐	F	a supporter of aggressive foreign policy
8.	delegate	☐	G	someone who doubts if a policy will work
9.	whip	☐	H	the candidate chosen by a political party to run for a particular office
10.	muckraker	☐	I	the party member who makes sure that all other members are present for crucial votes and that they vote in accordance with the party line
		☐	J	the person who currently holds a position

1.	right winger	☐	A	a leader whose impassioned rhetoric appeals to greed, fear, and hatred, and who often spreads lies
2.	moderate			
3.	hardliner	☐	B	a militant conservative
4.	left winger	☐	C	a politician who does not support extreme views
5.	reactionary	☐	D	a politician who strongly believes in a fixed set of ideas and refuses to change
6.	demagogue	☐	E	a politician with socialist beliefs
		☐	F	another word for a political conservative

Task 7

Choose the correct words to complete the sentences.

1. In a democratic country voting is done through a secret _____.	A	ballot box
	B	ballot
	C	election
2. I really believe they have some good _____.	A	policies
	B	politics
3. This was the first time he _____ president.	A	ran on
	B	ran off
	C	ran for
	D	ran up

4. There is little support for the new _____. It will never become a law.

   A billing
   B law
   C check
   D bill

5. This time voter _____ was at an all-time low.

   A turnaway
   B turnup
   C turnoff
   D turnout

6. How old do you need to be to _____ in an election?

   A elect
   B select
   C ballot
   D vote

Task 8

Complete the sentences with a suitable word.

electorate	floating	hung	polling station	ratings	register	swing	votes

Are you coming to vote? The _____ will be closing in an hour.

I'd like to _____ to vote. (= enter my name)

Who got the most _____ in the election?

If no party has an absolute majority then there is a _____ parliament.

A _____ is a change in favour of a particular political party.

_____ voters are people who haven't decided who to vote for yet.

Popularity _____ are the results of surveys of public opinion showing how popular politicians are.

Some important collocations

abandon	be active in	be engaged in	be interested in	dabble in	
discuss	dominate	engage in	enter	follow	**politics**
get immersed in	get involved in	go into	interfere in	participate in	
reshape	retire from	talk	understand		

adopt	carry out	develop	establish	frame	
formulate	implement	introduce	operate	pursue	**a policy**
		shape			

Task 9

Try to explain these words.

parliament	coalition	majority	minority	constitution	electorate
separation of powers	checks and balances	ideology	left-wing	lobby	nomination
political suicide	poll	primary	red tape	spin	

Some more useful expressions.

political turmoil
the local community
public comment on sth
smear campaigns
public appearances
lightning-fast change
the debate on sth
a tax haven

public spending
a non-profit organization
a one-sided view
scare tactics
criticism from the opposition
rising commodity prices
the debate surrounding sth
widespread skepticism

decision-making power
public opinion on sth
an ill-conceived plan
adrenaline-filled speeches
discussions should center on
falling commodity prices
international development

DIE GLOBALISIERTE WELT

Task 1

Match the following types of globalisation with the meanings. Write the most appropriate adjective next to the meaning. The adjectives can/must be used more than once.

economic	cultural	political	environmental	technological	criminal

type of globalisation	meaning
	growing global communications system (mobile phone, Internet)
	spreading of North American and European values, Americanisation
	free movement of trade and money
	the increasingly global effects of human activity on the environment
	wider acceptance of global political standards, human rights, democracy, the rights of workers, environmental standards
	reduce the digital divide between developed and developing countries
	human trafficking, migrant smuggling, illicit heroin and cocaine trades
	global climate change, energy security, pollution
	the connections among languages, ways of living, arts, advertising, food, sport and fears of global homogeneity
	global consumerism, the greater global connectedness through international trade, investment and transport
	International governance, the increased coordination of actions by governments and international agencies
	cybercrime, maritime piracy, trafficking in environmental resources and firearms, terrorism
	the increasingly significant roles of international investment and multinational corporations

Task 2

Choose the right word to go with each meaning. Write the number of that word next to its meaning.

1. accountability 2. inequality 3. exploitation 4. globalisation 5. global citizenship 6. global village 7. interdependence 8. outsourcing	**A** _____ people, goods, money, ideas are moving around the world faster, more easily, more cheaply than before **B** _____ sending out work to a different manufacturer in order to cut costs **C** _____ the world is seen as one community in which people are connected by mass media and all depend on each other **D** _____ making use of and benefiting from sth, e.g. resources **E** _____ disparity, a situation in which some groups have more opportunities, power than others **F** _____ individuals and organizations work towards a more equitable, socially just and ecologically sustainable world **G** _____ the state of being liable, taking responsibility for sth that you have done or you are going to do **H** _____ a relation of mutual influence at a global level

Task 3

Look at the following positive and negative aspects of globalisation. Decide which ones are positive (+) or negative (−).

	+/−		+/−
people can improve their standard of living		loss of individuality	
instant communication		global spread of information	
respect for cultural identities		migration to richer countries has increased	
gap between rich and poor countries grow		more efficient, less polluting technologies	
creativity and innovation are encouraged		brain drain of skilled workers	
indigenous and national culture and languages can disappear		freedom of trade, barriers between countries are removed	
greater chance of spreading diseases worldwide, e.g. AIDS, bird flu, Ebola		factories are built because environmental laws are not as strict as they are at home	
interests of the richest countries dominate world trade at the expense of developing countries		TNCs bring wealth and foreign currency to local economies when they buy local resources, products, services	
labour intensive industries take advantage of cheaper labour costs		profits of TNCs are sent back to mother countries	
people and goods can travel more quickly, costs have decreased		LEDCs provide the North with cheap labour and raw materials	

Do you know what these abbreviations stand for?

AI	NGO
IMF	TNC
LEDC	WTO

Complete each sentence with the help of the scrambled words.

1. Factories in which employees work under harsh and dangerous conditions for low pay are called (**1**) _____. These (**1**) _____ commit (**2**) _____ violations, e.g. the workers are locked in the buildings. A lot of people think that these violations happened in the past but some big-name (**3**) _____ still commit such violations nowadays. 2. A (**4**) _____ is produced for commercial value, it is grown to be sold rather than for the farmer's own use. 3. When children are deprived of their childhood and their dignity because the work they have to do is harmful to their physical and mental development, the term (**5**) _____ is used. 4. Unrestricted access to all economies without any tariffs and duties is called (**6**) _____. However, the main goal of (**7**) _____ is to improve the quality of marginalized people's lives. 5. Due to fast transportation and communication, distances have lost their relevance. The world is getting smaller in size, places are no longer as far apart as once thought. This development is called (**8**) _____. 6. TNCs are large companies which have their (**9**) _____ in rich countries but they produce in LEDCs because (**10**) _____ and taxes are low, environmental standards are poor and trade unions are weak. But TNCs also bring jobs and money to the host countries and the quality of life of poor people (**11**) _____ because of employment.	1. a e h o p s s s t w 2. a h m n u 　　g h i r s t 3. a b d n r s 4. a c h s　c o p r 5. c d h i l 　　a b l o r u 6. e e f r　a d e r t 7. a f i r　a d e r t 8. g h i i k n n r s 　　d l o r w 9. a a d e e h q r s t u 10. a e g s w 11. a c e e i n r s s

Talk about these questions:

How does globalisation bring people closer together?
Is globalisation about making connections? Think about the global links in your home (clothes, furniture ...) and your local community (restaurants, cars ...)
Is globalisation inevitable?

MENSCHENRECHTE

human rights	basic rights that everyone has to be treated fairly without cruelty, especially by their government.
civil rights/liberties (pl)	a person's legal right to freedom and equality, to be able to vote, work, etc. whatever their sex, race or beliefs.

Collocations:

basic ~	economic ~	fundamental ~	social ~	
civil ~	equal ~	legal ~	voting ~	**right**
cultural ~	human ~	political ~		

right to	life vote education express views freedom of thought conscience and religion	freedom of opinion and expression freedom of speech freedom of peaceful assembly fair and equal treatment justice	political freedom protection from abuses of power freedom from slavery freedom from hunger health an adequate standard of living

to abdicate	to claim	to give up	to respect	
to achieve	to defend	to have	to retain	
to acknowledge	to demand	to know	to secure	
to assert one's	to deny	to lose	to stand up for	**right/s**
to be entitled to	to enjoy	to promote	to undermine	
to campaign for	to gain	to protect	to uphold	
human	to get	to recognize	to violate	

equal (adj.)	equality (U)	inequality (U)
to integrate into/with sth	to integrate sb into/with sth	integration

human rights issues:

freedom	economic development	to apply against sanctions against sb
justice	social well-being	to protect life
peace	discrimination (colour, race, gender,	to be treated fairly and humanely
security	minority, disability)	to treat eb equally and fairly
dignity	right and responsibility	to maintain peace and security
environment	to express one's beliefs freely	to develop friendly relations
law	to act against injustice	to encourage respect for human
freedom of thought		rights

	hunger		
human rights abuses /	torture	to suppress	to torture (sb to death)
human rights violations:	starvation	to punish	to kidnap
	mass illiteracy	to intimidate	to be imprisoned, tortured, killed
	sexual harassment	to imprison	to be held in inhuman conditions
	severe pain and suffering		

Torture techniques:	assaults with fists, rods and whip beatings boiling burning (with cigarettes, etc) drowning electric/electrical shocks	intimidation mock executions rape sleep deprivation solitary confinement thumbscrew use of chemicals
	brutal/mental/physical/psychological	torture
	to inflict/suffer/die under	

Related words:

convention	enactment	protocol	rule of law
declaration	illiteracy	public freedoms	treaty
democracy	participation	ratification	
disadvantaged	peace-making	resolution	

Task 1

Complete the text by using the words from the box below. Use each item once only (banked cloze).

adopted	Human	out	race	treaties
assert	individual	people	rights	violations
drafted	origin	protected	speak	

The Universal Declaration of _____ Rights is the general statement of human

_____ principles and sets _____ a list of basic rights for

everybody whatever their _____, sex, colour, religion, language, opinion, property,

_____ and birth. It was _____ in 1948 and from then on the UN

_____ a lot of _____ and declarations. It is important that all

_____ are careful about the _____ of human rights. Human rights need

to be _____ by every _____. We must _____ our right to

_____ and to be heard.

Task 2

Match the words with the correct meaning. There are more words than meanings. Write the number next to the meaning.

1. conscience	
2. enactment	**A** _____ a person who has the same status or rights in society
3. equal	**B** _____ to frighten, to threaten sb
4. illiteracy	**C** _____ a proposal, a law has been made official
5. solitary confinement	**D** _____ to keep, to continue
6. to abdicate	**E** _____ it tells you whether your actions are morally right or wrong
7. to intimidate	**F** _____ to fail to fulfil, to refuse
8. to retain	

MIGRATION

Task 3

Complete the table:

verb	noun (abstract)	noun (person)
_____	migration	_____
_____	immigration	_____
_____	emigration	_____
to alienate	_____	_____
—	_____	foreigner
—	asylum	_____
—	_____	citizen
—	_____	refugee
to deport	_____	_____
_____	expulsion	—
to persecute	_____	_____
to flee	—	_____
_____	_____	escapee

to provide to apply for to ask for to seek to be granted to grant	**asylum**

to take to seek	**refuge**

voluntary forced	**migration**

Task 4

Match the words with the correct meaning. There are more words than meanings. Write the number next to the meaning.

1. aliens	A _____ the movement of large numbers of people or animals from one place to another
2. asylum seekers	B _____ foreigners
3. benefits	C _____ refugees trying to be accepted into a country
4. immigration restriction	D _____ wave of people escaping from another country
5. migration	E _____ anti-foreigner feelings
6. refugee camp	F _____ welfare, money provided by the government
7. refugee tide	
8. xenophobia	

1. to deport	A _____ move from one town, country, etc. to another
2. to grant asylum	B _____ embarrass or make someone feel ashamed
3. to humiliate	C _____ people who move to and work in another country
4. to migrate	D _____ force somebody to leave the country
5. to settle	E _____ people wanting to be given refugee status
6. migrants	F _____ give protection to
7. would-be refugees	
8. foreigners	

Task 5

Look at the following list of words and decide whether they are push factors or pull factors. Write each word in its appropriate box.

years of hardship
to stream into the promised land
racial discrimination
persecution
warforced labour, slavery

overpopulation
natural disasters
lack of food, famine
hope for a better life
opportunity for working

harshness of their lives
extreme poverty
better-paid jobs
being pushed out of a country

push factors affecting forced migration:	**pull factors:**

GESELLSCHAFTLICHE GRUPPIERUNGEN

Language related to people with disabilities: always refer to the person first, not the disability:

disabled

sb with a (physical) disability

sb has a disability

people with special needs

woman with cerebral palsy

the blind/deaf community

sb who cannot speak, who has a speech disability

wheelchair user/person who uses a wheelchair/in a wheelchair

person with a psychosocial/emotional/intellectual disability

sb uses a cane

deaf

hard of hearing

accessible toilet

Antonyms: non-disabled, person without disabilities, able-bodied

Don't use: disadvantaged, handicapped, defective, challenged retard, spastic, special, brave, cripple, psycho, handicapped, wheelchair-bound.

Marginalized groups include:

girls	individuals with disabilities	lesbian
women	nomadic populations	bisexual
youth	people affected by HIV and AIDS	transgender people
indigenous people	street children	refugees
ethnic minorities	child soldiers	asylum seekers
poor households	gay	migrant workers, ...

Task 1

Choose the right word to go with each meaning. Write the number of that word next to its meaning.

1. alienation 2. blame 3. deprivation 4. exclusion 5. low self-confidence 6. low self esteem 7. relegation 8. stigma	**A** _____ not having sth that people need, loss **B** _____ no confidence in yourself, no good opinion about yourself, feeling of being less deserving than others **C** _____ feeling of worthlessness and uncertainty, negative thoughts about yourself, you doubt your abilities **D** _____ emotional isolation, estrangement **E** _____ putting sb in a less important position **F** _____ expression of disapproval or reproach, responsibility for a problem **G** _____ negative and unfair beliefs that a society has, feeling that sth is wrong or embarrassing, a mark of disgrace or infamy **H** _____ a situation in which sb is deliberately prevented from being involved in sth,

Collocations:

large, significant, substantial, small, tiny, vociferous, ethnic, national, racial, religious, oppressed, persecuted	**minority**
minority	opinion, view, interest, position, community, group, government, party, problem, population, rights

Let's get talking (siehe auch Kapitel **Interkulturelle Aspekte**):

Think of reasons why the following groups might be marginalized: ethnic groups, families, individuals, youth, young girls, single mothers, certain religious sects, artists, the Roma, indigenous people, children with disabilities. What contributes to marginalization?

REGELN, VORSCHRIFTEN, GESETZE

Study the list and complete it.

Crime	Criminal	What does he do?	Explanation
abduction	_____	abducts people	seizing or taking a person away by force
_____	arsonist	puts sth on fire	setting buildings on fire
assault	_____	assaults people	hurting another person physically
attempted murder		tries to kill people	trying to kill someone (but failing)
blackmailing	blackmailer	blackmails people	threatening to tell secret information about sb unless they give you money
bribery	_____	bribes people	giving money in order to influence sb
burglary	burglar	_____ houses	entering a building and stealing sth
child abuse	abuser	abuses people	injuring a child on purpose
drug dealing drug _____	drug dealer drug trafficker	deals with drugs traffics in drugs	trading illegal drugs
drunk driving	drunk driver	drives under the influence	driving after having had too much alcohol
_____	forger	forges sth	copying a document, work of art, etc.
fraud	_____	deceives people	deceiving or cheating sb to get money
hacking	hacker	hacks computers	gaining unauthorized access to data in a computer
hijacking	hijacker	hijacks planes	using force to take control of a plane, ship, etc.
_____	hooligan		behaving violently or destructively
human trafficking	human _____	illegally moves people	illegally moving people for the purposes of forced labour or sexual exploitation
kidnapping	kidnapper	kidnaps people	taking a person to a secret location using force
_____	manslayer	kills people	killing sb by accident through a careless or dangerous act
money laundering	money _____	launders money	concealing the origins of illegally obtained money
mugging	mugger	_____ people	taking sth from sb by force in the street
murder/homicide	_____	murders people	taking someone's life through violence
_____	perjurer	perjures himself	wilfully telling an untruth under oath
pickpocketing	pickpocket	pickpockets sb	stealing from sb's pocket without them realizing
pimping	_____	pimps sb to sb	living off the proceeds of prostitution
rape	_____	rapes people	violently attacking a person sexually
robbery	robber	_____ people/places	taking property unlawfully by force
shoplifting	shoplifter	shoplifts	stealing things while pretending to shop
smuggling	smuggler	smuggles goods	bringing illegal goods into a country
speeding	_____	speeds	travelling at a speed greater than the legal limit
tax dodging	tax _____	dodges taxes	avoiding taxes
terrorism	terrorist	terrorizes people	using violence in the pursuit of political aims
_____	thief	steals things	stealing secretly and without violence
torture	_____	tortures people	inflicting severe pain on sb to force them to do sth
vandalism	vandal	_____ sth	damaging public or private property

Task 2

Choose the right words to complete the sentences.

acquitted	broken the law	charge	evidence	fine	guilty	innocent
jury	life sentences	parole	sentenced	statement	verdict	

1. A _____ of assault has been brought against this man accused of beating up a young woman.

2. He got a small _____ for speeding.

3. He has _____ several times and every time he got away with it. It's unbelievable!

4. He was found innocent but we believe he is _____.

5. He's currently serving two _____ for murder.

6. In his _____ to the police, the man said that he had left the party at 10 pm.

7. It is definitely better to risk sparing a guilty person than to condemn an _____ one.

8. One witness gave _____ at the trial which suggested the police had arrested the wrong person.

9. People are no longer _____ to death in the UK.

10. She was sentenced to 20 years, but with _____, she'll serve 15 years at the most.

11. The defendant was _____ because there was not enough evidence to convict him.

12. The jury returned a _____ of not guilty.

13. The _____ took 17 hours to find him not guilty.

Task 3

Cross out the wrong word or words in each sentence.

1. The murder **jury/trial** is getting a lot of news coverage all over the country.
2. The murder **weapon/victim** was a young mother of three.
3. The old man **testified/confessed** that on the night of the murder, he had heard the accused threatening to kill the victim.
4. The **plaintiff/complainer** stated that the defendant had deliberately destroyed his garage.
5. The police are appealing for **witnesses/suspects** to come forward.
6. The police are **interviewing/investigating** a series of disappearances.
7. The **defence/prosecution** had to drop their case when their only witness died.
8. They can't prosecute him on what the neighbours think – it's all **hearsay/heresy**.
9. This **convicted/convinced** drug dealer is also serving time for theft and assault.
10. This man won't get **bail/bale** because he is extremely violent.
11. Under **counter-examination/cross-examination**, his evidence showed some serious inconsistencies.
12. You are under arrest! We have established motive and found evidence – and you don't have an **alibi/evidence**.
13. She was arrested and taken into **custody/detention/prison**.
14. **Capital/death/execution** punishment has been abolished.
15. He was given a light sentence because it was his first **case/charge/offence**.
16. The case was dismissed for lack of **evidence/a jury/witnesses**.
17. Members of the jury, have you reached a(n) **answer/summary/verdict**?

Task 4

Put the words below into the correct category.

accused	appeal	arsonist	burglar
community service	corporal punishment	death penalty	defendant
defence	evidence	find sb innocent/guilty	fine
forger	house arrest	imprisonment	inquiry
jail time	judge	jury	juvenile offender
lawyer	license suspension	life in prison	offence
prison sentence	prosecution	put sb on probation	release on bail
suspended sentence	testimony	trial	verdict

Criminals	Law courts	Sentences & Punishments

Task 5

Match the expressions on the left with the explanations on the right.

1. detention
2. boot camp
3. child abuse
4. child neglect
5. youth gangs
6. detention hearing
7. juvenile delinquent
8. aging out
9. street/abandoned children
10. juvenile delinquency
11. truancy
12. misdemeanour
13. liable
14. law-abiding
15. deterrent
16. rehabilitate
17. curfew
18. felony
19 adolescent
20 sub-teen
21 legal age

A a child or teenager who commits a serious crime or repeatedly breaks the law

B a crime regarded as more serious than a misdemeanour

C a group of young people who are often considered a social problem by adults and law enforcement

D a minor wrongdoing

E a preadolescent child

F a regulation requiring people to remain indoors between specified hours, typically at night

G a short-term militaristic correctional facility in which inmates undergo intensive physical conditioning and discipline

H a term used to explain the fact that criminal activity declines with age

I a thing that discourages someone from doing something

J a young person in the process of developing from a child into an adult

K children who experience violence in their immediate social environment as observers or victims

L criminal acts performed by young people

M failure of caretakers to provide adequate emotional and physical care for a child

N juvenile hearing to determine whether to keep the juvenile in custody

O obedient to the laws of society

P responsible by law; legally answerable

Q temporary custody of a juvenile in a state facility

R the action of staying away from school without good reason; absenteeism

S the age at which a person enters into full adult legal rights and responsibilities

T the physical, emotional or sexual mistreatment of children

U to teach a criminal to live a normal and productive life

Task 6

Match to complete the phrases.

1.	to act	☐	**A**	a crime
2.	to be accustomed	☐	**B**	a privilege
3.	to be entitled to	☐	**C**	against government policies
4.	to commit	☐	**D**	civil responsibility
5.	to disobey	☐	**E**	consent
6.	to enjoy	☐	**F**	home
7.	to follow	☐	**G**	irresponsibly
8.	to have a sense of	☐	**H**	law
9.	to have the right	☐	**I**	life around
10.	to leave	☐	**J**	orders
11.	to mature into a	☐	**K**	parents
12.	to need parental	☐	**L**	receive help
13.	to obey your	☐	**M**	responsible adolescent
14.	to protest	☐	**N**	the rules
15.	to respect	☐	**O**	to criticism
16.	to turn your	☐	**P**	to vote
17.	to violate a	☐	**Q**	your elders

FUNCTIONS

AGREEING AND DISAGREEING

Agreement – neutral

I	absolutely completely entirely heartily strongly	agree ...

True enough.
That's just what I was thinking.
I can't help thinking the same.
I couldn't agree more.
I think we are in agreement on ...
I agree in principle, but ...
I would tend to agree with you on ...

Agreement – informal

Well, this is it.
Dead right.
I'm with you there.
I'd go along with you there.

Agreement – formal

I'm of exactly the same opinion.

That's	exactly precisely	my own	view. opinion.

I am in	total complete	agreement.

Disagreement – neutral

I	don't	agree with ... know (about) ... think ...

That's not the way I see it.
Actually,
In fact,

But isn't it more a	matter question	of ...?

Disagreement – informal

I can't go along with ...
I don't see why.
You must be joking.

You can't	mean that! be serious!

Disagreement – formal

I'm afraid I	entirely disagree (with) ... can't accept ...

I can't say that I share	your view of ... your assessment of ...

I see things rather differently myself.

I'm not	at all entirely	convinced	that ... by ...

ASKING FOR INFORMATION

Neutral

Can/Could you tell me ..., please?
Could you find out ...?
Can you help me?
Could/May I ask ...?
Excuse me, do you know if ...?

Sorry	to trouble you, to bother you,	but do you know ...?

Do you (happen to) know (anything) about ...?
I'd like to know ...

I'm	interested in ... looking for ...

Informal

Any clue ...?
Have you got any idea ...?
Heard about ...?

Formal

I wonder if you could tell me ...
I hope you don't mind my asking, but ...?
Would you mind telling me ..., please?
Could you give me any information about/on ...?

Could you	expand on that? give us some details on that?

BEING IMPRECISE

a large number of	about	approximately	the kind of	the sort of	the type of	up to

Examples

a large number of people
about 50 students
approximately 900 dollars
the kind of book children like
the sort of people I can't stand
the type of place he likes to visit
a growth of up to 30%

Phrases

I'm not really sure, but I think …
It's difficult to say, but I'd guess …

DEGREES OF CERTAINTY

Saying you are SURE – neutral

I have no doubt (about) …
I know …

I'm	quite absolutely fairly	sure certain	about …

He must be/have …

Saying you are SURE – informal

Yes (, really).
Absolutely certain/positive.
I'm a hundred per cent certain.
You can be sure (about) …

Saying you are SURE – formal

I don't think there can be any doubt	about that. as to …

It's quite certain …

There's	no very little	doubt in my mind	as to … about …

I'm (quite) convinced …

There can't be any doubt	as to … about …

That's my conviction.

Saying you are NOT SURE – neutral

I can't	make up my mind (whether) … decide …

I'm	not really sure (about) … in two minds (about) …

Saying you are NOT SURE – informal

I can't say for certain.
I'm not too sure …
I couldn't say, (really,) …
This is right off the top of my head, but …

Saying you are NOT SURE – formal

There's	some doubt an element of doubt	in my mind about … about/as to …

I'm not at all convinced (about) …
It's not at all certain …
One can't say with any certainty (about) …
I find it difficult to reach a conclusion (on) …

DEMANDING EXPLANATIONS

Can you explain why …?
Can you tell me why …?
Do you really expect me to believe …?
Does this mean …?

Do you mean to say that …?
How come …?
I don't understand why …
Why is it that …?

EXPRESSING LIKES AND DISLIKES

Likes – neutral

I have always	liked ... loved ...

I	quite	like ... love ... adore ... fancy ...

I'm very keen on -ing
I really enjoy -ing

...	is	wonderful very enjoyable great

...	is	a lovely way a marvellous way	to do sth. of doing sth.

There's nothing I	like enjoy	more than ...

...	fascinates attracts appeals to	me

I am	more tempted by ... also captivated by ... fascinated by ...

Likes – more informal

I really go for ...

I'm	absolutely	crazy mad nuts wild	about ...

You can't beat ...
I'm over the moon about ...
... is really terrific.

Likes – more formal

What I	particularly most greatly	enjoy is ...

I'm (really) very fond of -ing ...
... is one of my favourite ...

I have a	particular special	fondness for ...

Dislikes – neutral

I'm afraid	I don't like ... I've never liked ... I can't work up any enthusiasm for ...

I	really	loathe detest hate	-ing
I'm not	really	very keen on	-ing

I think ... is	pretty really	awful. unpleasant.

There's nothing I like less than ...

...	disgusts repels revolts	me

Dislikes – more informal

I can't	stick ... bear ... stand ...	-ing

Oh no!
Oh God!
Oh hell!
Oh, how awful!

... is	ghastly. rubbish.

I never could put up with ...

Dislikes – more formal

I	don't think ... is	particularly very	pleasant enjoyable

I can't say .... appeals to me very much.
I have to admit I rather dislike ...

I must say I'm not	too particularly	fond of ...

I especially dislike ...
I am not over-enthusiastic about ...

I have a particular	dislike of ... aversion to ...

EXPRESSING PLEASURE AND DISPLEASURE

Saying you are pleased – neutral

I'm	very	pleased	with ...
	really	delighted enthusiastic excited	about ...

How marvellous!

...	is	wonderful! marvellous! good/wonderful/splendid news. the best thing/news I've heard in years.

Saying you are pleased – informal

Great!
Terrific!
Fantastic!
Super!
Smashing!
I was (quite) thrilled .../by ...

Saying you are pleased – formal

I'm delighted to hear that/about ...
It gives me great pleasure/satisfaction ...
I can't say how pleased/delighted I am ...

Saying you are displeased – neutral

I'm	very really	annoyed worried uneasy	pleasant enjoyable
		afraid frightened terrified	of ...

...	really makes me	cross. angry.
	annoys irritates	me.

Saying you are displeased – informal

I'm	scared stiff of ...	
	worried sick	about ...
		by ...

I've had enough of ...
I can't stand -ing
I'm fed up with -ing
I'm sick and tired of -ing

...	really makes	me mad. me see red. my blood boil.

I'm (really) in a flap/(about) ...
... gives me the creeps/jitters.

Saying you are displeased – formal

I'm	very	concerned anxious apprehensive	that ... about ...

...	is	extremely most very	irritating. annoying. exasperating.

I'm	extremely very most	displeased unhappy angry	about ...

I must say I resent/object to ...

... gives some cause for	anxiety. concern. worry.

EXPRESSING OPINION

Expressing your opinion

I	personally	think believe feel find suppose reckon (*infml*)	that ...

I	honestly	feel	that ...
	strongly firmly	believe	
	really	think	

I	am	absolutely quite	certain sure convinced	that ...

In	my opinion ... my view ... my experience ...

To my mind ...
From my point of view ...
For my taste ...

As		I see it, ...
	far as	I am concerned ... I am able to judge ...
		for myself ...

I	would	say suggest like to point out	that ...

I	am	of the opinion under the impression	that ...
	take	the view	
	have	a feeling the impression	

If you ask me ...
Undoubtedly ...
Without a doubt ...
There is no doubt ...

It	seems to me must be admitted goes without saying	that ...

My view is that ...
I, for my part, ...
Speaking for myself, ...
The way I look at it is this, ...
The way I see it, ...

I	cannot help cannot resist	thinking feeling mentioning stating adding	that ...

Asking for an opinion

What's your	view? opinion of ...? position on ...?
What	do you think (of ...)?
	would you say to ...?
How	do you feel about ...?

Could I ask for your reaction to ...?

I'd	like to	hear	your views your opinion	on ...
		know	what you think	about ...

I was wondering where you stood on this question?
Where exactly do you stand on this issue?

What are your	views (on) ...? feelings about ...?

Do you have any	particular views on ...? opinion on ...?

EXPRESSING PERMISSION AND OBLIGATION

Asking permission

Is it alright if I		*informal*
Can I		*neutral*
May I	smoke in here?	*more formal*
Am I allowed to		
Am I permitted to		*formal*

Would/Do you mind if I ...?

I wonder if I	could ...
	might ...

Might I possibly ...?
Excuse me, do you think I could ...?
Would it be possible ...?

Giving permission

Of course, Certainly,	it is.
	you can.
	you may.
	you are.

By all means (do ...).
Sure./Fine./All right./Feel free ...

No,	I don't (mind).
	not at all.

You shall do exactly as you wish. *(formal)*

Refusing permission

No, I'm afraid	it is not.
Sorry, I'm afraid	you cannot.
	you may not.
	you are not.

You must not ...
I'm afraid not.
I'm sorry, that's not ...
I'm sorry I'm not supposed to ...

You	shouldn't ...
	oughtn't to ...
	had better not ...

Expressing obligation

	must ...	*speaker's authority*
	('ll) have to ...	*official authority*
	need to ...	*internal obligation*
You	ought to ...	*may not be fulfilled*
	should ...	
	had better ...	*strong recommendation*
	shall	*very formal*

You	've got to ...	*informal*
	are required to ...	*formal*

EXPRESSING REGRET

I'm sorry.
I beg your pardon.
I apologise for ...

That was my fault.
I didn't mean to ...
How stupid of me!

I promise you that that will never happen again.
Please let me pay for the damage I've done.
I owe you an apology.

GIVING ADVICE

Asking somebody's advice

What would you advise me to do?
I need to seek your advice.
Can you give me some advice on/about ...?
What would you do (in my position)?

Responding

Let me give you a piece of/some advice.
I would advise you (not) to do it.
I wouldn't advise it.
My advice would be to ...
I'd advise you against (doing) it.
Take my advice! Why don't you ...?

Modal verbs

You	should (not) ...
	ought (not) to ...

If-clause

If I were	you, in your position/shoes,	I'd ...

Accepting/rejecting advice

That's good advice. I'll take your advice
I didn't ask for your advice.
It's not advice I need.

GIVING DIRECTIONS

Asking the way

Excuse me, how do I get to ...?
What's the best way to ...?
Where is ...?
Which way is the hotel?
Can you tell me where the library is?
I don't know where the theatre is.
Can you tell me how to get to the airport?
I'm lost.

On foot

Go straight on (until you come to ...).
Turn back.
Go back/along ...
Turn left/right.
Walk down ...
Cross ...
Take the first/second road on the left.
You can't miss it.

By underground

Take the Green Line to Central Park.
Transfer to the Jubilee Line.
Get off at Green Park Station.

By car

Take the M5.
Go through the tunnel.
Go over Westminster Bridge.
Take the second turn off.
Go out exit number 2.

Prepositions

at	between	across	at the end (of)
on	behind	on the left	in front of
in	near	on the right	straight on
into	next to	opposite	
around the corner			on/at the corner

GIVING REASON

Kinds

the pros and cons
the merits and drawbacks
the advantages and disadvantages
the arguments for and against
the causes

Particular reasons

For what reason?
for reasons of ...

| for | health | reasons |
| on | | grounds |

good cause for (a) celebration

| I have no cause | to complain.
for complaint. |

Enumerating

Also, ...
And another thing, ...
And besides, ...
In addition, ...
Not only that, but, ...
Not to mention the fact that ...
Plus the fact that ...
What's more, ...

Having good reason

Because ...
Because of that ...
That's why ...
The reason why ...
That's the reason why ...

| For | that
this very
some | reason |

For the simple reason that ...
This is my reason for ...

| I have | good
every | reason to believe that ... |

There is (every) reason to believe that ...
With good reason.
For reasons best known to myself.
All the more reason to do it.

Having no reason

without any reason
for no reason at all
for no other reason than that ...

| for no | particular
apparent | reason |

GIVING WARNINGS

Imperative

Watch out!

Be more careful!

Don't do this, or you will ...!

Phrases

I warned you not to ...

You have been warned!

You had plenty of warning.

Be warned!

I'm giving you a warning.

Take warning from this.

Let this be a warning to you.

I'm warning you!

GUESSING

Adverb

Maybe Perhaps	he is right.

Modal verbs

He	might be could be	in the garden.

Phrases

I'd say ...

It looks like ...

It's difficult to say, but I'd guess ...

I'm not really sure, but I think ...

Could it be ...

My guess is that ...

INVITING

Questions

Would you like to meet on ...?

Are you free on ...?

Will you be able to make it on ...?

What How	about ...?

Which would you prefer?

Could we change the day of the meeting?

Would you mind if we changed the time of the meeting?

I'd very much like you to ...

We'd	be delighted to ... very much like to ...

That would be very nice.

That sounds (like) a (very) nice idea.

With pleasure.

Great!/Lovely!/Smashing!

I'm afraid I can't	meet	on ...
	make it	at ...

I'm sorry, but I'm busy on ...

I'm sorry,	I'll be ...	on ...
	I'm + -ing	

I have to	cancel	our meeting.
	postpone	

Answers

Let me have a look at my	schedule. calendar.

I'd love/like to (very much).

MAKING A COMPLAINT

I have a complaint about ...

I want to lodge a complaint against ...

I wouldn't have any complaints if ...

Don't get me wrong, but I think we should ...

There may have been a misunderstanding about ...

Excuse me if I'm out of line, but ...

Maybe you forgot to ...

I'm sorry to have to say this but ...

I'm sorry to bother you, but ...

I think you might have forgotten to ...

I have no cause for complaint.

I can't complain.

Stop complaining!

MAKING SUGGESTIONS

Neutral

My	proposal recommendation suggestion	is that ...

I	propose recommend suggest	that ...

May I suggest ...?
Shall we ...?
We might as well ...
Let's ...

Strong

I strongly recommend that ...
I suggest most strongly that ...
I advise you most strongly to ...
In my view, it is high time that we started ...

Tentative

I would	propose recommend suggest	that ...

Wouldn't it be a good idea to ...?

If I	may might	make a suggestion ...

Why don't you ...?
Why not ...?
Perhaps you could ...
You could always ...
Have you thought about ...?
I have an idea. Let's ...
One way would be to ...
Try -ing

What How	about	-ing?

I wonder if I might suggest ...
If I were you, I would ...

OFFERING HELP

Are you looking for something?
Can I help you?
Do you need some help?
May I help you?
If you like I could ...

What can I do for you today?
Would you like some help?
How can I help you?
I'd be very happy to ...
Is there anything I can do ...

PUTTING THE RECORD STRAIGHT

Pointing out a misunderstanding

We seem to be talking at cross purposes.
I think you've misunderstood me.
Perhaps I haven't made myself clear.
That isn't quite what I meant.
I'm probably not making myself clear.

Expressing indignation

I have no idea who told you that.
Where did you get that idea from?
With respect, that is not what I said at all.
I'm afraid that just isn't true.

Rephrasing

What I	mean is ... am saying is ... am trying to say is ...

Perhaps I should make that clearer by saying ...

Let me	put it in another way. rephrase what I just said.

Allow me to rephrase that.
To be more specific, ...
Put simply ...
The fact of the matter is ...
Let's get this straight, ...

SOCIALIZING

Welcoming someone

I am pleased to welcome you to ...
It's a pleasure to welcome you to ...
Welcome to ...

Greeting someone

How are you (doing)? *(informal)*
How do you do? *(formal)*
It's a pleasure (to meet you).
So good to meet/see you.
Very nice to meet/see you.

Introducing oneself/people

Have you met ...?
I'd like to introduce myself ...
I'd like to introduce you to ...
May I introduce myself: ...
Let me introduce myself ...
(Excuse me,) My name's ...
We haven't met yet. I'm ...

Small talk

Could I take your coat?
Did you have any trouble finding us?
How do you take your coffee?
How was your trip?
How's the hotel?
How's the weather in ...?
What do you think of our weather?
Would you care for something to drink?

Getting to know people

How did you get into this line of business?
How do you like living in ...?
How long have you been working for ...?
What do you do in your spare time?
What's your home town?

Holding conversations

By the way ...

Do you see what	I mean?
	I'm getting at?

I wanted to ask you about ...
I was wondering if ...
I'd like to mention ...
So are you saying ...?
That reminds me ...
While we're on the subject ...

Every day contacts

Could I ask a favour of you?
Could you do me a favour?
How are things?
How are you today?
I was wondering if ...
Would you mind if ...
It's (going) fine, thanks.
Nice to see you again.

Making arrangements

Could we arrange dinner for ...?
We'd like to invite you to ...

What How	about ..?

Would you be interested in ...?

Would ...	suit you?
	be convenient?

Would you like to come to ...?
Shall we say about 7.00 pm?
I look forward to seeing you then.
Let me just confirm that ...

That sounds	fine.
	great.

Having drinks

Cheers!
Could I propose a toast to ...?
Here's to ...
I'd like to get the next round of drinks.
I'm treating you.
The drinks are on me.

Saying goodbye

Goodbye/Bye/Take care/See you.

Have a good	flight.
	trip.

I look forward to ...
I really do need to wrap this up now.

I'll	give you a call.
	email you.

I'm afraid I really must be on my way.

It was	nice	to meet	you.
	a pleasure	to see	

Please get in touch soon. Safe journey back!

STATING PREFERENCES

Asking somebody's preferences

What are your preferences as regards ...?
What is your preference?
Which (of them) do you prefer?
Would you prefer me to ...?
Just state your preference.

Saying why you prefer

The main advantage of ... is that ...
... has an advantage over ... in that ...
... is preferable to ... because ...

Saying what you DO NOT prefer

I'm against ...
I'd rather not.
I would prefer not to.
I prefer not to say.
I have no preference.

Saying what you prefer

I favour ...
I prefer (to do) ...
I'd rather ... than ...
I'd prefer ... to ...
I'd sooner ...
I tend to favour ... as opposed to ...

| I would prefer | you to do it. |
| | that you did it. |

I find ... preferable.
I have a (strong) preference for ...
I'd give preference to ...
It would be preferable to ...
My preference is for ...
I prefer it that way.
I would choose ... in preference to ...
... appeals to me more than ...
Rather than ..., I'd really prefer to ...

TALKING ABOUT INTERESTS

ASKING if someone is – neutral

Are you interested in ...?
Does ... interest you?
What are you interested in?

ASKING if someone is INTERESTED – informal

Are you keen on ...?
Do you go for ...?
Does ... grab you?

ASKING if someone is INTERESTED – formal

Does ... appeal to you?
Do you have any interest in ...?

SAYING you are INTERESTED – neutral

I am interested in ...
I have some/a great interest in ...
My particular/main interest is ...
... interests me a lot/a great deal.

SAYING you are INTERESTED – informal

| I | am (very) keen on ... |
| | go for ... |

SAYING you are INTERESTED – formal

...	fascinates		me
	intrigues		
...	has always	fascinated	me.
		interested	
I'm	quite	fascinated	by ...
	extremely	intrigued	

SAYING you are NOT INTERESTED – neutral

I am not very interested in ...

| I | don't have | any | interest in ... |
| | | much | |

SAYING you are NOT INTERESTED – informal

I'm afraid	...	leaves me cold.
		just isn't my cup of tea.
I'm afraid		I couldn't care less about ...
		I don't give a damn about ...

SAYING you are NOT INTERESTED – formal

I must admit I don't take any great interest in ...
I can't say ... concerns me a great deal.

TELEPHONE CONVERSATIONS

Answering the phone
Hello ... speaking.

Introducing yourself
This is Ken.
Ken speaking.
My number is ...

Asking who is on the telephone
Excuse me, who is this?
Can I ask who is calling, please?

Asking for someone
I'd like to speak to someone about ...
May I talk to someone about ...?
Can I have extension 321?

Could Can May	I speak to ..., please?

Is Jack in?
Can you ask him to call me back?
Could you connect me?
Is there someone you could connect me to?
Do you have their number?

Explaining why you are calling
I'm calling to find out ...
I'm calling about ...
I'd like to ask ...
I'd like to know ...
Could you tell me ...
I need to know ...
Do you know what I have to do?
Who should I contact for this information?

Connecting someone
Who do you want to speak to?
Can you hold the line?
Can you hold on a moment?
Please wait a moment.
Hold on, please.
I'll put you through.

How to reply when someone is not available
Sorry, the line is busy right now.

I'm afraid Mr X is not	available in	at the moment.

Mr X is in the meeting room right now.

I'm afraid Mr X	is	in a meeting out busy	right now.

Please ring again in 10 minutes.
Please call again.

No, that's okay.
I'll call back later.
When do you expect them back?

What to say when you cannot help the caller
There is no one here with that name.
Sorry, I can't help you. Try ...
I'm sorry, we don't handle that, try ...
You'll have to try ...

Taking and leaving a message

Can Could May	I take a message? I tell him who is calling?

Would you like to leave a message?
Is there anything else?
Can I leave a message?

PRACTICE MAKES PERFECT

 Die folgenden Übungen sollen dir zeigen, wie man all die Phrasen, die im Kapitel „*Functions*" angeführt sind, üben kann. Du brauchst dazu allerdings ein paar Freunde, die mit dir gemeinsam diskutieren möchten. Wichtig dabei ist, dass ihr wirklich die Phrasen aus den entsprechenden Rubriken vor euch liegen habt und auch verwendet. Denn die Wahl der passenden Phrasen ist bei diesen Übungen wichtiger als der eigentliche Inhalt der Diskussion!

Task 1

Work in groups of three. Choose a topic from the list below and take turns giving your opinions. Use appropriate phrases for stating preferences (page 160), agreeing and disagreeing (page 150), expressing opinion (page 154), likes and dislikes (page 152).

List of topics

Beauty is in the eye of the beholder.
Books are better than films.
Cars should be banned from city centres.
Cats are better pets than dogs.
Computers are great time savers.
Money makes the world go round.
Smoking should be allowed in all public places and buildings.
Soft drugs should be made legal.
Young people today have no manners.

Task 2

Work in groups of three and choose a proposal from the list below. One of you starts by making a proposal and supporting it with convincing arguments. Use suitable phrases for making suggestions and giving reason (pages 158, 156). The others should challenge this opinion and demand explanations (page 151). The speaker then gets the chance to argue his point and put the record straight (page 158). Swap roles.

List of proposals

All space exploration programmes should be cancelled.
Capital punishment should be reintroduced.
Flexible working hours should be introduced.
Shops should be open on Sundays.
Teachers should get better paid.
The speed limit on motorways should be reduced to 80 km/h.
Tobacco advertising should be forbidden.
Violence on TV should be banned.

Task 3

Work in groups of two and go through the list of predictions below. Tell each other how certain or uncertain you think they are (page 151). Don't forget to justify your answer! Feel free to agree or disagree (page 150).

List of predictions

A cure for cancer will be found.
Cars will become obsolete.
Marriage will be a thing of the past.
People will be put out of work by computers.
People will live to be 150.
People will spend their holidays on other planets.
There will be one world language only – all other languages will die out.

GRAMMAR REVISION

Die folgenden Minitests zu den wichtigsten Kapiteln der englischen Grammatik sollen dir helfen, deine Schwächen zu erkennen, damit du dann gezielt weiterüben kannst. Jeder Test umfasst zehn Beispielsätze, die wichtige Aspekte des jeweiligen Kapitels abdecken.

 Wenn du bei einem Test mehr als zwei Fehler gemacht hast, dann solltest du diesen Teilbereich der Grammatik mit einem entsprechenden Übungsbuch genauer wiederholen und durcharbeiten.

ADJECTIVE – ADVERB

Find the **mistakes and correct** them. If there are no mistakes, put a ✓.

> *Example:* Tom is a <u>hardly</u> worker. – *hard*

1. Tom acted unbelievably stupid at Muriel's wedding. _____
2. The weather was excellent while we were on holiday. _____
3. He laughed loud at the joke. _____
4. Sophie stared direct back at him. _____
5. She has never felt so confident. _____
6. Wearing this black dress, she thought she looked really well. _____
7. The hotels in LA are extreme expensive but ours was reasonable cheap. _____
8. The customer became violent when the manager asked him to leave. _____
9. Sue waved her hands around lively. _____
10. Have you seen John late? _____

ARTICLES, DETERMINERS, PRONOUNS

Cross out the **wrong alternative** in the sentences below.

1. *Each/Every* of the children has a wonderful souvenir for their parents.
2. Sadly, there were *few/a few* people at the funeral.
3. Many people are afraid of *death/the death*.
4. *Both/Either* players were warned, but *none/neither* of them took it seriously.
5. *All of us didn't want/None of us* wanted to play.
6. *Most people/The most people* believe that *marriage/the marriage* and *family life/the family life* are the cornerstones of *society/the society*.
7. *Unemployment/The unemployment* is a serious problem nowadays.
8. Don't hesitate to call me *sometime/anytime* you like.
9. They were talking for a long time, but the problem was that they were not really listening to *each other/ themselves*.
10. This friend of *ours/us* has got *an own/his own* yacht.

COMPARATIVE ADJECTIVES AND ADVERBS

Fill the gaps with the **comparative or superlative form** of a word from the box. You may have to change an adjective into an adverb. There are two more words than you need. Where necessary add **"than"** or **"as ... as"**

> *If I ate* _____ *you, I would be terribly fat.*
> *If I ate* **as much as** *you, I would be terribly fat.*

bad	*depressed*	*early*	*far*	*fast*	*fat*	*fat*	*few*	*friendly*
high	*informal*	*late*	*little*	*low*	*much*	*old*	*slow*	*thin*

1. If you can't swim _____ that, you're going to lose.

2. The British are considered to be rather reserved, but I found them much _____ I had

  expected.

3. In the past people used to dress up for parties. Nowadays everybody dresses _____ .

4. Our parents are coming tomorrow, but I'll be working late. _____ I can come is nine o'clock.

5. His _____ film was his _____ successful – a total flop!

6. If Mary had _____ meals _____ Pam, she would be _____ .

7. His _____ sister keeps getting _____ and _____ . And _____

  she eats _____ she becomes.

8. Uncle Pete hasn't seen much of the world; _____ he has ever been is Italy.

9. Yesterday they had their maths test. Tim did badly but his friend did even _____ .

10. I'm sorry but I can't understand you – could you speak _____ , please!

CONDITIONALS AND WISH-SENTENCES

Choose the correct verb form **A, B, C,** or **D** to fill the spaces in the following sentences.

> She _____ passed the test if she had studied more.
>
> **A would have**   **B had**   **C will**   **D would**
>
> She **(A) would have** passed the test if she had studied more.

1. I _____ happy to help you if you had asked me.
  A had been   **B would have been**   **C would be**   **D will be**

2. If he _____ his A-levels, he will buy a car.
  A would pass   **B had passed**   **C will pass**   **D passes**

3. I wish I _____ more time.
  A had   **B will have**   **C have**   **D has**

4. If you heat snow, it _____ .
  A will melt   **B melt**   **C melts**   **D would melt**

5. I _____ here now if you hadn't called.
  A wouldn't be   **B wouldn't have been**   **C weren't**   **D won't be**

6. She would take up golf if she _____ more time.

    A would have **B had** **C has** **D had had**

7. We wish we _____ you then.

    A knew **B would have known** **C had known** **D have known**

8. I wish you _____ arguing.

    A will stop **B stop** **C stopped** **D would stop**

9. Unless you _____ now, you will not catch the train.

    A left **B will leave** **C would leave** **D leave**

10. If they had known about your party last week, they _____ .

    A had come **B might have come** **C would come** **D came**

GERUND – INFINITIVE

Complete the second sentence so that it is **as similar in meaning as possible** to the first one.
Use up to **five words** including the word in **bold print**. Do **not change** this word.

> She had no intention of hurting you. – *mean*
> She _____ you.
> She **didn't mean to hurt** you.

1. Are you sorry that you didn't finish your studies? – *regret*

    Do _____ your studies?

2. Susan has no objection to Mary coming as well. – *mind*

    Susan does _____ as well.

3. Tom thinks it would be a good idea to take the bus. – *suggests*

    Tom _____ .

4. I can't wait to see him again. – *forward*

    I _____ him again.

5. Mum is certain that she posted the letter I wrote. – *remembers*

    Mum _____ I wrote.

6. Jack said he had to catch the next train. – *insisted*

    Jack _____ the next train.

7. The singer arrived an hour late, but we were glad we waited for him. – *worth*

    The singer _____ .

8. It looks as if this door is locked. – *appears*

    This door _____ .

9. I wanted to speak to my brother so I put down the novel I was reading. – *stopped*

    I _____ my brother.

10. Phil couldn't hear what they said because of the noise. – *prevented*

    The _____ what they said.

MODALS

Fill the gaps with the appropriate forms of the **modal verbs** below and put the **verbs in brackets** into the **correct forms**. In some cases, more than one answer is possible.

 I'd love to come, but I _____ **(finish)** this report by tomorrow morning.
I'd love to come, but **I have to finish** this report by tomorrow morning.

can	have to	may	must	need	ought to	should

1. I am trying to work! _____ **(you/really/make)** so much noise?

2. If you want me to help, I _____ **(know)** more about the problem.

3. In Austria, school children _____ **(wear)** uniforms.

4. You _____ **(bring)** your umbrella – the sun has been shining ever since we got here!

5. _____ **(shout)** at her like that? After all, she was only trying to help.

6. Don't worry, he _____ **(see)** you. There were too many people.

7. Put some food in your bag – the journey _____ **(take)** hours.

8. We really _____ **(spend)** more time with her. She's all alone now that her husband is dead.

9. Come on, mum! All my friends _____ **(be)** there until ten. – I won't hear any more of

this! You _____ **(stay out)** after dark!

10. I believe he said his name was Tommy. But what with all the noise, I _____

_____ **(mishear)** the name.

NOUNS – COUNTABLE AND UNCOUNTABLE

Choose the correct form and **cross out** the wrong alternative.

1. Five **beer/beers** and two **coffee/coffees**, please.
2. Nowadays it is not easy to find a **work/job**.
3. The lady at the tourist information desk was very helpful. She gave us some very useful **advice/advices**.
4. The team **is/are** not going to win again. **It is/They are** useless.
5. The team **is/are** at the bottom of the second division.
6. Have you got a copy of the complete **work/works** of Shakespeare?
7. Would you like some **fruit/fruits** after dinner?
8. Fish and chips **is/are** not a very healthy meal.
9. The United States **has/have** a very violent history.
10. For further **information/informations** apply to the manager.

PASSIVE

Rewrite these sentences in the **passive**.

She has informed the police about the burglary.
The police **have been informed** *about the burglary (by her).*

1. The government is now building a lot of new roads.
2. The police have just arrested another terrorist.
3. Will they publish this article in the next issue?
4. They will have constructed the new bridge by the end of the month.
5. I hadn't cleaned the attic in years.
6. We couldn't use our car because the garage was servicing it.
7. They told him to finish his experiments by Monday.
8. The company is going to open a new branch in Rome.
9. We should have asked him first.
10. They were making every effort to come to an agreement.

PHRASAL VERBS

Rewrite each sentence **using a verb from the box** so that the meaning stays the same.
You may have to change the form.

Her fifth husband secretly left with a girl 20 years younger than him.
Her fifth husband **ran off with** *a girl 20 years younger than him.*

call on	*come across*	*come up with*	*get along with*
get away with	*keep up with*	*look down on*	*look forward to*
make up for	*put off*	*put up with*	*run out of*

1. I've neither eggs nor cheese left. I'm going to the supermarket for some.
2. When Karen was rummaging through the attic, she found her old school books by accident.
3. Jane and Julian already felt excited about their wedding, but then they had to postpone it because the bride's father was in the hospital.
4. Thieves did not get caught stealing Munch's *The Scream* and were never found.
5. Tommy doesn't have a good relationship with his brother; they have little in common.
6. They don't want to tolerate their neighbour's dirt any longer. They're going bananas.
7. While we were in New York, we visited the Raymonds for a short time.
8. Nobody should have a low opinion of mentally handicapped people just because they are different.
9. He bought her a Porsche to try to compensate for his infidelity.
10. Nowadays it's hard to stay up to date with all the latest breakthroughs in medicine, but as far as I know scientists have failed so far to think of an explanation for cancer.

PREPOSITIONS

Fill each space with a **suitable word**.

at	by	in	into	during	of	on	to	towards	until	while

1. We got there _____ time to see that the train arrived right _____ time.

2. It's a typical love story: _____ the end they fall in love and _____ the end of the last chapter they get married.

3. My uncle used to live _____ the city centre, but last year he bought a house _____ the outskirts because he likes to be _____ the open air and watch the birds _____ the sky.

4. They usually get up _____ eight o'clock _____ the morning, but _____ a fine sunny morning they always rise early to go _____ a trip _____ the country.

5. When she turned _____ Baker Street, she saw three policemen coming _____ her and immediately turned right _____ the next crossroads.

6. George normally travels _____ public transport. Today, however, he arrived _____ a taxi because there had been too many people _____ the bus.

7. Our son will be away _____ Monday, but his girlfriend should be back _____ Saturday.

8. _____ we were _____ Paris, we stayed _____ a wonderful hotel; but _____ our stay _____ a tiny Greek Island we camped _____ the beach.

9. Have a look: This is a picture _____ my family; _____ the picture you can see my brother, who went _____ America _____ the age of 14, sitting _____ the corner of our living room.

10. When Marcus travels he prefers to pay _____ credit card, but _____ home he always pays his bills _____ cash.

QUESTIONS, NEGATIONS, TAG QUESTIONS

Translate the following sentences into English.

1. Wie geht es deiner Schwester heute? Geht es ihr besser? Machen wir einen Spaziergang, oder?
2. Wie schaut deine jüngere Schwester aus? Sie sieht Kate Hudson ähnlich, nicht wahr?
3. Welche Schuhgröße tragen Sie? Haben Sie die Schuhe eine Nummer größer probiert?
4. Hast du nicht in New York studiert? Du bist nicht nach Hawaii geflogen, oder?
5. Mit wem wollen Sie sprechen? Haben Sie schon mit dem Personalchef gesprochen?
6. Wer bot dir einen Job an?
7. Hast du sie nicht im Fitnesscenter erwischt heute morgen?
8. Ich komme spät, nicht wahr?
9. Sie wollen doch gut aussehen, oder?
10. Er war noch nie in Australien, oder? Wann empfehlen Sie, ist die beste Zeit, dorthin zu fahren?

RELATIVE CLAUSES

Make one sentence from each group of sentences, using **relative pronouns (who, which, that, whose, where)**. If the relative pronoun can be **omitted**, put it in brackets. Use **commas** where necessary.

 The Banks have four small children. The children often misbehave. The Banks can't handle them.
The Banks can't handle their four children, who often misbehave.

1. Harry lived with the Dursleys. Harry's parents had died. He was brought up in a cupboard under the stairs. Harry did not feel very comfortable in the cupboard.
2. Matilda is the most extraordinary girl. I have read about her.
3. The Orient Express is a famous train. It runs between Vienna and Paris.
4. Rosemary wore a canary yellow cardigan. Tommy had bought the cardigan on their honeymoon in California. Rosemary's blond hair was all over her face.
5. The window was at the back of the huge house. Behind the house there was a golden field of wheat.
6. One thing made him sad. This one thing was saying goodbye to his children. *(The only thing ...)*
7. Ellie works in a shop. The shop sells handicrafts and self-made jewellery. Richie has always dreamt of Ellie.
8. Ned turned and walked away. This made her very angry.
9. The gift shop sells these gorgeous notebooks. I have already bought two of these notebooks.
10. An old man died last Sunday. Maggie looked after the old man for a year. Big fireworks took place last Sunday.

REPORTED SPEECH

Read the dialogue between **Jude** and **Rebecca**. Imagine that Rebecca meets Pat the next day and prepares her for this evening's meeting. **What does she tell Pat**?
For each sentence, use the most appropriate **reporting verb** from the box below.

 *Colin to Sue: I'll begin with your news before she asks. Do you want me to add anything?*
Colin promised Sue that he would begin with her news before she asked. He wanted to know if she wanted him to add anything.

admit	advise	agree	answer	ask
complain	encourage	invite	murmur	persuade
promise	reply	suggest	tell	want to know

1. **Jude:** I am so depressed. First of all, Cliff has still given me no hint as to what is going on between us.
2. **Rebecca:** Ask him. Talk to him. Don't sit around brooding.
3. **Jude:** Okay, I will. When he comes back from his business trip, I will clarify everything. Secondly, I have put on weight since Christmas and I can't fasten the buttons of my Levi's jeans any more.
4. **Rebecca:** Write down everything you've eaten and check if you stuck to the diet.
5. **Jude:** You know that I like picking and mixing different diets. And thirdly, on New Year's Eve I intended to stop smoking. Now I'm smoking 20 cigarettes a day. What shall I do?
6. **Rebecca:** You can't go on like this. Stop thinking about all that. Are you going out with me and Pat tomorrow night?
7. **Jude:** Good idea. What time are you meeting?
8. **Rebecca:** Seven thirty. Café Paris. Don't worry!
9. **Jude:** How was the candle-lit dinner with George yesterday? Did you enjoy yourselves?
10. **Rebecca:** It was fantastic! I was on cloud nine.

TENSES

Present Tense

Put each verb in brackets into the **correct tense form**.

	present simple	present progressive
i	third person -s	am/is/are + ing-form
	wiederholte, regelmäßige Handlung	temporäre Situation
	Tatsachen, Fakten, Zustände	Handlung findet im Moment des Sprechens statt

1. I can't talk now. I'm on my way to work. I _____ **(drive)**.

2. Charles _____ **(live)** with some friends until he _____ **(find)** a flat.

3. My parents _____ **(live)** in Manchester. They have lived there all their lives.

4. Rainfall _____ **(result)** from warm air, which _____ **(contain)** water vapour.

5. It _____ **(cost)** the Millers a fortune at the moment to send their son to the United

   States for one year.

6. It _____ **(cost)** a fortune to fly first class to Sydney.

7. Our neighbour's son _____ **(constantly/have)** parties until five in the morning.

8. Campbell _____ **(pass)** to Almunia who _____ **(shoot)** just over the bar. Arsenal

   _____ **(attack)** much more in the second half ...

9. Robert _____ **(think)** of moving to California.

10. Up to a million people _____ **(gather)** in Times Square every New Year's Eve.

The Future

Underline the most **suitable future form** in each sentence.

will-future:	will + base form	I will play
going-to-future:	am/is/are + going to + base form	I am going to play
future progressive:	will be + ing-form	I will be playing
future perfect:	will have + past participle	I will have played
present simple:	third person -s	I play
present progressive:	am/is/are + ing-form	I am playing

1. That's great news! Peter and Mary **will come/are coming** to stay with us for a week.
2. I've got a blister on my toe. – Have you? Wait here and I **will get/am going to get** you a plaster.
3. The game **is going to start/is starting** at 7.05 pm. See you there!
4. Don't phone me between 5 and 6. I **will be having/will have had** my gym lesson then.
5. The plane **leaves/is leaving** New York at 18.15 and **arrives/is arriving** in Vienna at 08.50 the next day.
6. I've decided that from now on, we **will recycle/are going to recycle** all the glass bottles.
7. "Mr Keller isn't in at the moment." "In that case, I **will phone/am going to phone** him later."
8. Don't worry! Before they get here, I **will finish/will have finished** painting the windows.
9. The lion **is going to become/will become** extinct in 20 years or so.
10. Frank, what **are you going to buy/will you buy** with the money you won in "Who wants to be a Millionaire"?

Past Tense and Present Perfect Tense

Choose the correct way to **complete the sentences** below.

past tense	present perfect tense
Handlung ist abgeschlossen, vorbei	Bezug zur Gegenwart
kein Bezug zur Gegenwart	Ergebnis ist sichtbar, spürbar, etc.
bestimmte Zeitangabe: two days ago, last week,	eher unbestimmte Zeitangabe: ever, never, lately,
yesterday, on May 15th, 3 hours ago, etc.	just, already, since, for, etc.

1.	I am writing in reply to the advertisement ...	a. ... which *appeared* on 2 November. b. ... which *has appeared* on 2 November.
2.	Your bike looks very clean.	a. ... *Did* you *wash* it? b. ... *Have* you *washed* it?
3.	Paul lives in Edinburgh. I think ...	a. ... he *lived* there all his life. b. ... he *has lived* there all his life.
4.	I'm not really sure but ...	a. ... I think I first *met* him nine years ago. b. ... I think I *have* first *met* him nine years ago.
5.	When Frank came home last night ...	a. ... his wife *was waiting* for him. b. ... his wife *has been waiting* for him.
6.	Now look at you! You're all covered in dirt!	a. ... Of course I am! I *was cleaning* the cellar! b. ... Of course I am! I *have been cleaning* the cellar!
7.	How is your brother? – I have no idea ...	a. ... I *didn't hear* from him for ages. b. ... I *haven't heard* from him for ages.
8.	I am starving because ...	a. ... I *didn't eat* anything today. b. ... I *haven't eaten* anything today.
9.	When and where ...	a. ... *were* you born? b. ... *have* you *been* born?
10.	You really should smoke less, ...	a. ... you *were smoking* too much recently. b. ... you *have been smoking* too much recently.

Past Tense and Past Perfect Tense

Complete this story by putting the words in brackets into the **correct tense forms**.

past simple:	base form + -ed	he read
past progressive:	was/were + ing-form	he was reading
past perfect simple:	had + past participle	he had read
past perfect progressive:	had been + ing-form	he had been reading

1. It _____ *(be)* about half past eight on a rainy November night and Mr and Mrs Brown _____

   (go) to bed early.

2. They _____ *(put out)* all the lights and _____

   (just/go) to sleep when Mrs Brown _____ *(hear)* a strange noise coming from downstairs.

3. Mr Brown _____ *(get up)* to investigate.

4. When he _____ **(reach)** the bottom of the stairs, he _____ **(notice)** that the noise

_____ **(come)** from the living room, and it _____ **(sound)** as if somebody

_____ **(try)** to open the window that _____ **(lead)** into the garden.

5. Mr Brown _____ **(be)** really scared, but he _____ **(gather up)** his courage,

_____ **(pick up)** an old walking stick and _____ **(tiptoe)** into the living room.

6. When he _____ **(get)** to the window, he _____ **(peer)** cautiously round the edge of the

curtain. He _____ **(be)** relieved to see that the noise _____ **(be)** nothing more than a

branch of a bush scraping against the window.

7. Meanwhile, however, the Brown's dog, who _____ **(sleep)** in the kitchen,

_____ **(also/wake up)** and _____ **(silently/**

follow) Mr Brown into the living room.

8. While Mr Brown _____ **(look out)** the window, the dog _____ **(creep up)**

behind him and _____ **(rub)** his nose against his master's ankle.

9. This _____ **(give)** Mr Brown such a surprise that he _____ **(lose)** his balance and _____

(fall) against the window, breaking the glass and cutting his hand.

10. He _____ **(swear)** at the dog and _____ **(kick)** it out of the room.

WORD ORDER

Most of these sentences contain **one or two mistakes. Find**, **mark** and **correct** them.
Tick any lines that are correct.

1. Regularly he could hear his father's deep voice reading to them on winter evenings. _____

2. The afraid people hid in the cellars until the attack was over. _____

3. On the one hand he can become absolutely furious and on the other hand he is
under the immensely strong influence of his wife. _____

4. He gave her a red round beautiful wooden big jewellery box for her birthday.
Opening the present, she stammered she had seen a such gorgeous box never
before. _____

5. When finally they parted she drove to her parents the 30 kilometres back. _____

6. Jenny was never any good at hiding her true feelings.
What is more, she hates being laughed at. _____

7. They waited for an hour silently in the station.
But the people where freezing outside to death. _____

8. We flew to New York in August. Daily Austrian Airlines fly there.
New York is an exciting place to live. _____

9. She wanted to move abroad, but her parents tried to talk her out of it. _____

10. Not only Jack won a million dollars, but he met also his future wife. _____

LINK WORDS AND PHRASES

Putting ideas in order

1

at first

first of all

to begin/start with

let me begin by saying that ...

the first thing I want to say is

2

the next thing is ...

meanwhile

after that/afterwards/since then

then (again)

the next point I want to make is ...

later (on)

first(ly), second(ly), third(ly)

in the first/second place

another thing is ...

for one thing ..., for another ...

3

last but not least

eventually

last (of all)

the final point is ...

I want to make one final point.

finally

in the end

Contrasting and balancing ideas

although

as opposed to

besides

but

despite

even if

however

in contrast (to)

in spite of

instead (of)

naturally

nevertheless

of course

on the contrary

on the one hand ... on the other hand

otherwise

still

though

whereas

while

yet

in general ... in particular

in this respect ... in all other respects

Let us carefully weigh the pros and cons (of the matter).

So much for the cons, let us now turn to the pros.

It is the other way round.

| That is the reverse side of the | coin. |
| | story. |

The drawbacks (by far) outweigh the advantages.

There is certainly something to be said for both sides.

If we draw up the balance (sheet), ...

After carefully weighing the pros and cons, ...

Adding ideas

above all

again

in addition (to ...)

also

and (then)

besides

equally

further(more)

in addition (to that)

moreover

on top of it

too

what is more

Comparing ideas

compared with

equally

in comparison with

in the same way

likewise

similarly

Stressing a point

Above all, ...

What is	more (important) ...
	better (still) ...
	(even) worse ...

In fact, what seems more important to me ...

| The most important | factor advantage reason point consequence | of all is the fact that ... |

I want to emphasize once again that ...

Expressing attitude

actually
in fact
basically
theoretically

It is	astonishing
	hardly surprising
	obvious
	ridiculous

evidently
apparently
obviously
essentially
fortunately
unfortunately
maybe
perhaps
possibly
probably
surely
certainly
undoubtedly

There is	no doubt
	no denying

I greatly doubt whether ...
I wonder whether ...

it still remains to be	seen
	proved

This is a mere assumption.
Let us assume (for a moment) that ...
There is no proof that ...

Making transitions

Let us now turn to ...
Talking of ... reminds me

As	to ...
	for ...
	regards ...

Regarding ...
As far as ... is concerned.

With	regard	to
	reference	
	respect	

incidentally
besides
furthermore
moreover
by the way

In the same way	it is important to mention that ...
Likewise	it deserves mentioning that ...

Equally important is the fact that ...

Stating reasons and results

accordingly
as

as a	consequence
	result

because (of)
consequently
due to
hence
if ... then
owing to
since
so
thus
to such an extent that

the consequence	of ... is
the result	

therefore
that is (the reason) why
for that reason

Generalising

all told
on the whole
in general
generally speaking
by and large
all in all
all things considered

Reformulating

in other words
(or) rather
that is to say
to put it more simply

Introducing examples

a case in point is ...
for example (e.g.)
for instance
in other words
let me give an example ...
let us take the case of ...
namely
such as
that is (i.e.)
thus

Indicating time sequences

after (a while)
afterwards
at the same time
before (that time)
for (a long time)
in the meantime
meanwhile
next
since then
so far
then
up to (then)

Drawing conclusions

in conclusion we can say
it seems that ...
one might conclude
that is to say
this implies that ...
to come to the conclusion that ...
to conclude
we are certainly justified in saying that ...
we can only conclude

we may	conclude infer say state	that ...

I have come to the conclusion that ...

Summarizing

all in all
all things considered
all told
be it as it may
briefly
by and large
in a nutshell
in brief
in conclusion
in short
one last word
on the whole

summing up to sum up	one can say ...

to cut a long matter short
to say it quite bluntly

Useful verbs for text productions

to acknowledge
to aim at
to analyse
to announce
to argue that
to assess
to base one's arguments on
to be certain
to be convinced
to be disposed
to be inclined to
to call for
to claim that
to clarify
to come out in favour of sth
to confirm
to defend one's own view
to demand
to deny that
to discuss
to doubt whether
to emphasize
to enumerate
to evaluate
to examine
to explain
to express
to give convincing reason for
to highlight
to hold the opinion that
to illustrate one's argument by
to insist
to interpret
to judge
to maintain
to persuade
to point out
to provide evidence
to raise an objection
to rate
to refer to an example
to refute the idea that
to reject
to require
to state that
to stress
to tend to
to underline

INDEX